The Strategic Leader

New Tactics for a Globalizing World

The Strategic Leader

New Tactics for a Globalizing World

by

John R. Pisapia
Florida Atlantic University

Information Age Publishing, Inc.
Charlotte, North Carolina • www.infoagepub.com

Library of Congress Cataloging-in-Publication Data

Pisapia, John.
 The strategic leader : new tactics for a globalizing world / by John Pisapia.
    p. cm.
 Includes bibliographical references and index.
  ISBN 978-1-60752-152-5 (pbk.) -- ISBN 978-1-60752-153-2 (hardcover) 1. Leadership. 2.
Strategic planning. 3. Organizational change. I. Title.
  HD57.7.P566 2009
  658.4'092--dc22

                                                                      2009019539

To Barbara

She is always with me; even when she is not.

CONTENTS

Preface ix

Acknowledgements xiii

1. **Strategic Leadership: A Fresh Look** 1
Leadership Challenges in the Post Modern Condition 2
The Need for New Leadership Habits 5
Strategic Leadership 7
The Leadership Wheel 14

2. **Habit 1. Artistry: The Mega Habit** 21
The Yin and Yang of Leadership 22
Power, Purpose and Morals 23
Strategic Leaders are Managers and Leaders 26
Artistry—The Mega Habit 28
The Need for Multifaceted Leader Actions 30
The Leader's Wheel 31
Frame-Breaking or Frame-Sustaining Change 36
The Artistic Nature of Strategic Leadership 40

3. **Habit 2. Agility: Developing The Strategic Mindset** 45
The Habit of Agility 46
The Strategic Mindset 47
Developing the Cognitive Capacity to Think Strategically 58

4. **Habit 3. Anticipating the Future** 73
Context Matters! 74
The Habit of Anticipating 75
Look Outside the Organization 80
Look Inside the Organization 83

5. Habit 4. Articulating Strategic Intent   99
   The Articulating Habit   100
   The Leader's Role in Articulating Intent   100
   Light the Way   104
   Run to Daylight   115

6. Habit 5. Aligning Colleagues With Intent   121
   Leaders, Followers, and Colleagues   124
   Bonding   132
   Bridging   141
   Reaching   144

7. Habit 6. Assuring Results   155
   The Habit of Assuring   156
   Performance Builders   156
   Institution Builders   161
   Assuring High Performance   166
   The Levers to Develop High Performing Organizations   170

8. The Epilogue—Frequently Asked Questions   183

Appendix A—Reflective Questions   193

Appendix B—The Strategic Thinking Questionnaire   199

Appendix C—The Strategic Leadership Questionnaire   205

References   211

About the Author   223

PREFACE

THE STRATEGIC LEADER

There are only two possible ways for creative tension to resolve itself: pull current reality toward the vision or pull the vision toward reality. Which occurs will depend on whether we hold steady to the vision.

Peter Senge—*The Fifth Discipline*

Two decades have elapsed since Senge offered his view on vision and reality. Despite some successful efforts, the dilemma still confronts leaders who choose to lead organizations, groups and people. Will reality crush our dreams, or will our dreams create a new reality?

The Strategic Leader reveals the art and science of resolving the vision-reality dilemma in an increasingly complex world. It exposes the habits, actions, and tactics that leaders use to invent or reinvent their organizations for high performance. This book is the distilled product of my 23 years of management practice and 22 years of listening to and teaching both aspiring and accomplished leaders who have successfully, and sometimes unsuccessfully, answered the following questions.

Do I need to think differently? What is the environment telling me? Where are we going and where do we need to go? How do I position myself and/or my organization, team, and individuals to take advantage of opportunities presented by the environment? How do I multiply myself though other people? How do I find and turn talent into performance? How do I ignite the soul of followers to achieve greatness beyond what anyone imagined possible? How do I know if we are succeeding? How do we continually adapt to change and maintain profitability and our competitive advantage?

The Strategic Leader answers those questions by framing leadership around six habits—*Artistry, Agility, Anticipating, Articulating, Aligning, and Assuring*—which enable the strategic leader to create direction, establish alignment and commitment, and produce results in dynamic and complex environments.

Who Should Read This Book

The Strategic Leader is not limited to those at the top of organizations—it is geared to a wider audience at all levels who want to create a high performance life, team, or organization. The book offers new insights that are applicable, with some nuances and/or emphases, to leaders in complex leadership settings. It is equally applicable to the principal and the academic leader, the corporate leader, the consultant, the human resource manager, community leaders.

For novice leaders, the book offers a prescription that can be employed early in their leadership journey. For middle managers, the book provides a set of strategies, actions and tactics that can further their rise up the organizational ladder. For accomplished managers, the book provides a new way to understand their role in the strategic functions of leadership beyond what they were taught in strategic management classes. For professors and consultants, the book provides a valuable introduction to the principles of strategic leadership for their own teaching (seminars and classes), and for researchers it provides new knowledge in the application of strategic leadership.

Overall Objectives of the Book

My years of practice led me to conclude that something important was missing from the bipolar models of leadership (e.g., transactional-transformational and/or task behavior—relationships) particularly at the management and executive levels. My years of teaching practitioner students from education, business, nursing, community organizations, university administration, and medicine helped me understand their need for practical guidance rather than generalizations.

The Strategic Leader fills the gap between the need for new theory and the need for practicality by providing a prescriptive set of six habits that readers can apply to the development of a high performing organization across a variety of contexts. *The Strategic Leader* marries management with leadership and politics with ethics in a model that focuses on personal mastery and a holistic learning approach to building a high performing organization.

Through *The Strategic Leader* I challenge both the novice and the master to discover new ways of seeing and responding to themselves, individuals, teams, and their organizations. The book offers the following major innovative contributions to leadership thinking: the habits of the "Leadership Wheel"; how to use artistic actions and agile thinking; the importance of viewing followers as colleagues; the value of a generative approach to developing strategic intent using minimum specifications; how to make planning flexible, the development of social capital to mobilize followers; and the importance of anchoring strategic intent by creating self managed teams of followers.

My tone in this book is conversational to encourage the reflection and wisdom necessary to lead in challenging environments. I use terminology that is broad enough to cover the many different situations in which leadership occurs including corporations, government agencies, schools, non profits, churches, and even country clubs. Vignettes and stories gathered from public, business, educational, community, political and historical leadership, are used to illustrate the concepts. The coverage is readable without sacrificing scholarly depth. I use endnotes to attribute seminal ideas and support important conclusions and/or themes.

Themes Found in the Book

Three central themes are highlighted in this book. First, leadership is almost always situated within an environmental context and leaders must be trained to understand and address strategic themes emanating from that context. Complex modern environments present leaders with the twin challenges of leading for stability and change, and for *what is possible* and *what is thought to be right*. While strategic leaders foster a mindset of change for themselves and their colleagues, they do so with a clear understanding of the necessity of maintaining a level of stability in order for change to be successful.

Second, strategic leaders employ a holistic individual, team and organizational learning process that I characterize as the Leadership Wheel to keep their organization positioned within its environment. They use the four habits of the Leadership Wheel: *anticipating, articulating, aligning, and assuring*. Strategic leaders use these habits to develop consensus on direction, build the capacity of the organization to accomplish the direction, and connect it to power sources in their internal and external environments.

Finally, strategic leaders are involved in a constant cycle of leading and managing, sometimes simultaneously. They also juggle the political realities required to mobilize support for the organization's strategic intent by following the values identified as important by themselves, their colleagues, and the organization. Their ability to use two foundational habits; *agility* of the mind, and an artistic palette of managing, transforming, political, and ethical actions, determine how successfully they will be able to turn the Leadership Wheel and guide the organization on its journey to high performance.

A Guide to Leading Strategically

Think of *The Strategic Leader* as a guide to refer to on your leadership journey. It is designed to describe the six habits strategic leaders use and it provides examples from leaders who have performed the habits in the real world settings.

The first chapter introduces you to my point of view about leadership in complex times. In this chapter I describe the need for strategic leadership and how it differs from strategic management. You will be introduced to the Leadership Wheel, and the six habits that lead to high performance.

In chapters 2 through 7 you will discover the six habits that enable you to turn the Leadership Wheel—acquiring an agile mindset, artistry, anticipating, articulating, aligning and assuring. In chapters 2 and 3 you will learn cognitive and behavioral actions to lay the foundation within you to lead strategically. As the remaining four chapters unfold you will see the Leadership Wheel come to life.

Guidance for future growth is offered through three tools. First, a set of Cliff Notes at the end of each chapter serve as a one page "tear-out" which is both a distillation of the content, and a diagnostic tool you can use to start a peer discussion on inventing or reinventing your organization. Second, a set of chapter questions is found in the appendices for reflection and furthering your understanding of the habits. Finally, your path to discovering new habits is aided by two original self assessment tools: The Strategic Thinking Questionnaire (STQ) and the Strategic Leadership Questionnaire (SLQ) which are described in the appendices where an electronic link is provided for your own self assessment.

John Pisapia,
Boca Raton, Florida, November 2009

ACKNOWLEDGMENTS

*If I have been able to see further, it was only because I stood on
the shoulders of giants.*

—Isaac Newton, 1676

This book is the result of loving, caring support provided by my wife Barbara Romano Pisapia. A skilled leader in her own right, I have had the benefit of our constant conversation about ways improving the performance of organizations and the people in them. Her spirit runs through my leadership journey and through this book. She read and critiqued each draft as it came off the computer. She knows how far this work has come since its beginning. It is not farfetched to say that if it weren't for her, there would be no book, and my life and career also would have been diminished. Thank you Barbara; you have always been able to light up my life.

I have had a long, enduring, and passionate relationship with the concepts of leader and leadership. I have observed, studied, and practiced leadership for over 40 years. During this time, I have been blessed to learn from the athletic field, the graduate classroom, and the field of practice and the podium of leadership classes taught at three universities. This book is a product of those experiences extracted from my roles as student, follower, leader and professor. I have had many intellectual mentors whose thoughts guided my journey.

In my early foray onto the practice field, I was armed with early observations and trials on the athletic field. My role models were Vince Lombardi, "Red" Auerbach, and John Wooden. Leaving the athletic field for the academic classroom, I was introduced to the ideas of new teachers;

Ludwig von Bertalanffy, Chester Barnard, Max Weber, Mary Parker Follett, Talcott Parsons, Robert Merton, James March, Kurt Lewin, Andrew Halpin, Rensis Likert, and Douglas McGregor to name but a few.

Thus armed, once again I entered the world of practice to apply these new lessons. However, this time as I practiced, I reflected upon my earlier lessons and continued to study the work of Karl Weick, Henry Mintzberg, James McGregor Burns, Peter Drucker, Warren Bennis and Bernard Bass and their ideas helped me reframe my thinking. While I continued to find the lessons of my youth useful, I found these new ideas helpful in explaining new pressures I felt in my practitioner roles.

I took these observations and new learning's back to the scholar's bench, once again a professor, where I continued my studies, and discovered the ideas of Paul DiMaggio, Michael Fullan, Thomas Sergiovanni, John Morgan, Lee Bolman and Terrence Deal, John and Henry Gardner, and Peter Senge, to name a few. I began to reflect on my past attempts to exercise leadership and create my own theoretical frameworks to guide aspiring leaders which are shared in this book. I thank all of my teachers including the ones not mentioned in these paragraphs.

Needless to say I have picked and chosen based on my experiences as a manager and leader. What is found in this book is what I believe works. Hence, while I on stand on the shoulders of giants, I exonerate them from any miscasting of their influence. My purpose is to be comprehensive. But my purpose is also to whittle down the complexities of leadership to its basic constructs in the hopes that it will add clarity.

Many students and colleagues have helped me in this quest for clarity with their insights and critical review. I have learned much from my conversations and work with Daniel Reyes-Guerra my student and now my colleague. He was particularly helpful presenting cases, stories, and examples to bring my ideas to life. Thank you Daniel! Malmuz Yasin, my Malaysian student, colleague, and professor was very helpful in pulling together the disparate pieces of the strategic leader theory in his dissertation. Thank you Muzz! A great big thanks to Pamela Brown also a former student and now a colleague. An Englishwomen, she was the voice that urged me to include eastern as well as western examples and in this way brought an international view to the material. She also was my developmental editor, the person I depended on to edit the words and make sure they were in readable sentences. Steve Urdegar and John Morris opened my eyes to the power of statistics for which I am grateful.

Finally, as my vision broadened I found allies throughout the world on my leadership journey. Thank you Clive, Sun-Kung, Ying, Tie, Jorge, Asha, Angeliki, Rahimah, Vitallis, and Sergji! I have learned that people around the world are more alike than different, yet we have a lot to learn from each other. But that is another story.

CHAPTER 1

STRATEGIC LEADERSHIP

A Fresh Look

Leaders are people who, singularly or with others, define and then move individuals, groups, and/or organizations from A to Z. "A" represents where the organization and its members are currently, "Z" represents what the organization and its members want to achieve. The problem is that in the twenty-first century the space from A to Z is constantly changing. We are losing our assuredness about how the world we live in works. In the past, things seemed certain. Today, they are uncertain.

The twenty-first century began with an interesting confluence of demands upon organizations and their leaders caused by the move towards globalization. The heritage of the previous century was a search for absolute truth and an attempt to fashion, in a Newtonian sense, a coherent global view and a focus on efficiency of results. Leadership theorists emphasized management skills based on an efficiency of means, top-down decision making, bureaucracy, and central control to bring about organizational success.

This Newtonian idea of order is now reaching its apex at the same time a fundamental shift in the environment in which organizations work is taking place. The modern age, with its emphasis on rationalization and stability, is transitioning to the hyper-rationalized chaos of the postmodern condition. The entropy is marked by an emphasis on information and its

The Strategic Leader: New Tactics for A Globalizing World, pp. 1–19

pretation, webbed relationships, contextual values, learning organizations, relativism, and an ever-increasing complexity.

In a sense, the world is becoming one interconnected place. Events do not happen in isolation. Changing economies in Asia create problems for low-wage earners in Australia and the United States. The polluted skies of industrialized and industrializing economies create ozone holes in the atmosphere over other parts of the world. On a global scale, organizations are faced with an evolving context. This shift from a modernity which responded to the industrial age creates demands for organizations to be responsive and agile in a landscape filled with uncertainty and change. These conditions are fueled by changing technology, the global economy, rapid international communication, an exponential increase in information, and an international or global environment. The symbols of this movement are the internet and the processing chip. Its mantra is connectivity.

LEADERSHIP CHALLENGES IN THE POSTMODERN CONDITION

Charles Handy's (1994) use of the sigmoid curve (the S curve) is a good way to describe the era we live in today. The S curve represents a growth profile over time, beginning with a period of slow growth, followed by a period of rapid expansion, and ending with a period of stagnation. Near the end of a life cycle, a new S curve begins that eventually becomes the new paradigm. However, even though the slope of the current curve may be positive at a particular time, the top of the current curve will be reached, after which growth will wane. Because of this phenomenon, an eventual move to the next S curve has to occur, as seen in Figure 1.1. The common lexicon for this occurrence is "jumping the curve," meaning that well before the end of a life cycle leaders must prepare their organizations to move to the next S curve.

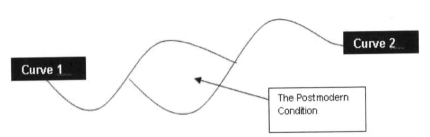

Figure 1.1. The postmodern condition within Sigmoid curves.

As Handy (1994) points out, the area of intersection of two S curves is a "time of great confusion as two, or more, groups of people or two sets of ideas are competing for the future" (p. 53). I refer to this juncture of curve 1 and curve 2 as the postmodern condition, which signals a shift to an unknown paradigm or new era replacing our modern one. As the term is used here, it is simply the condition that occurs when there is a movement from one S curve to the next. The ideas of chaos and a lack of order, multiple truths, and a rejection of the grand narrative, are typical of life in the postmodern condition. The illustration in Figure 1.1 signals the transformation from curve 1, (i.e., industrial capitalism) to curve 2 (i.e., a new globalized information age economy). Ernest Mandel, the Belgium Marxist, divided capitalism into three fundamental stages: original capitalism, followed by the monopoly (imperialism) stage, and the postindustrial, or more appropriately multinational capital stage.[1] The circumstances found in the postmodern condition mark the beginning of an economic system of capital based on globalization and multinational business. Best and Kellner (1997) explain that capitalism, the current Western model, is

> undergoing a global reorganization based on new technologies and a transnational corporate restructuring and that consequently our contemporary moment is between a disorganized and reorganized capitalism, a situation that requires intense focus both on political economy and on technology and culture. (p. 105)

Their description fits what I call the postmodern condition. A time when reality is neither yes nor no, but maybe, or it depends.

The globalization S curve represents our society's movement from capital to information as the source of wealth and exchange. Digitization of all information for accessibility and the consequent production of knowledge is becoming the new source of wealth that determines material gain and the achievement of power. Lyotard (1984) the French philosopher and literary theorist, recognized the preeminence of knowledge in the postmodern condition when he pointed out that:

> The relationship of the suppliers and users of knowledge to the knowledge they supply and use is now tending, and will increasingly tend, to assume the form already taken by the relationship of community producers and consumers to commodities they produce and consume - that is, the form of value. Knowledge is and will be produced in order to be sold; it is and will be consumed in order to be valorized in a new production: in both cases, the goal is exchange. Knowledge ceases to be an end in itself; it loses its use-value. (p. 125)

As predicted by the postmodern condition, change is inevitable as an organization or a society moves up the globalization S curve. Trying to steer clear of it is fruitless. Consider:

- Sudden and instant market changes, such as a rapid rise in oil prices, have caused demand for cars in the United States to shift from SUVs (sport utility vehicles) and gas guzzlers to sedans and hybrids, in the space of 1 year.
- E-mail and Blackberry's have reduced corporate communications turn-around from 15 business days to less than 15 minutes.
- Chinese families are spending one-third of their income on education.
- In China, India, and Thailand, whole villages are making the transfer from poverty to wealth in one generation.
- Countries such as the United States, the United Kingdom, and Australia now find themselves spending more money importing goods than they make exporting commodities.
- With a population of nearly 16.5 million and growing, New Delhi now adds 650 vehicles to its roads each day and the city issued more than 300,000 driver's licenses in 2007.

The above conditions do not reward leaders who continue to practice from rational and linear thinking models, or legacy and command and control models of leadership. The search for a definitive quantifiable solution to the future inherent in such management practices is no longer attainable.

In the global economy the spoils go to those who are creative and not to those who are only compliant. During this time of uncertainty new issues and changes create a web of demands that challenge organizational leaders. Their frame of reference shifts to issues of competition, technology, culture, and democratization. In this environment workers must be able to collaborate, socialize, and innovate.

The postmodern condition challenges leaders in every country and walk of life. They are faced with local constraints as they strive to meet the demands emanating from a globalized society. They have three options: (a) work to alter the environment, (b) change the organization to conform to the environmental demands, or (c) perish.

The leadership challenges in the postmodern condition are not easy and there is no clear path toward success. Where the conditions exist, the legacy model of leadership is not effective in creating necessary major and lasting change. A new theory of leadership that will bridge the gap between the fading modern S curve and the developing globalized S curve is needed.

Organizations confronted with the postmodern condition require leaders who can adaptively balance four counterweights of need; change, stability, ethical action, and political possibility. At the same time they must create and articulate common values and direction, establish cohesive structures and cultures, build the capacity of their organizations, and create learning communities that can manage themselves.

THE NEED FOR NEW LEADERSHIP HABITS

Today's leadership context is formed on quicksand. The trust we placed in our old maps has dissipated. As we plot our course it is almost impossible to predict long-term changes and influences. Answers and direction emerge without prior planning. Leaders need new maps to sail effectively through these uncharted waters.

Life in the postmodern condition is characterized by complexity, ambiguity, and messiness. The effects of these forces cause leaders to respond with such adaptations as; flattening of organizational structures, shortening life cycles of products, creating learning organizations, and building coalitions. The need to define change as nonlinear is at the heart of this new reality. Confronted with these modern challenges, leaders find themselves caught between the need for change and the need for stability. While the external environment requires change, forces in the internal environment such as the organization's need for productivity and the employees' need for some sense of order and security, push the organization toward stability. Leaders find themselves in a world tipping from modern to postmodern understandings where cause and effect are difficult to identify. They may fail in their leadership journey for a number of reasons:

- They were trained in and rely upon ways of thinking and a concept of change that are linear and do not work in situations characterized by ambiguity and complexity. Consequently, they fail to grasp the meaning of environmental changes and seldom arrive at their rationally planned destination; they are using an old road map.
- They are unable to identify critical societal and institutional forces affecting their environment. Consequently, they do not connect their organizations to the current major themes associated with success.
- They do not see their organization as dependent upon the actions and views of other organizations and individuals. Consequently,

connect with significant forces on their critical path to

connect the vital concepts of necessary organizational
ges to the minds and spirit of their followers. Consequently,
they are unable to benefit from empowered and self-managed followers that such connections encourage.

- They use a limited set of one-dimensional leadership actions to
influence followers to join in a common cause. Consequently, they
are effective only when environmental conditions match these
actions.

The problem facing today's leadership theorists and practitioners is
clear. Can a practical model of leadership be fashioned that will correct
the errors, redirect, and allow for ongoing change even when the road to
achieve that change is unclear? The design of such a theory rests on
developing new leadership habits.

Today, leaders must understand that their organization is in constant
development and position themselves to learn continuously from the
environment while seeking high performance marks. In doing so, leaders
must 'fit' the organization to its environment in order to survive. Fit organizations have the ability to perceive environmental themes and evolve
appropriately. However, because the environment is constantly changing,
leaders must continually rethink, revise, and restructure the organization
for it to stay connected. They must also establish a learning process to
ensure that the organization continues to develop.

In the postmodern condition, leaders must shift from an over-reliance
on the command and control (hierarchical) skills of the twentieth century,
to a greater reliance on the coordinative and collaborative (horizontal)
skills necessary to practice their craft in the twenty-first century. The command and control style is not completely obsolete but the leadership
emphasis must move toward the opposing end of the continuum. Leaders
must be flexible and able to adapt to different circumstances and conditions. At times they will exert their influence by using task and relationship behaviors. At other times they will use power, authority, persuasion,
bargaining, and incentives to influence followers.

In the postmodern condition leaders must practice as artists rather
than scientists if they are to prepare themselves and their organizations to
take advantage of opportunities associated with change. They will guide
the transformations with a profound appreciation of stability and a mantra of common values and adaptable ways and means. Through all their
artful behaviors leaders must maintain stability while challenging the status quo simultaneously.

STRATEGIC LEADERSHIP

I define strategic leadership as the ability (as well as the wisdom) to make consequential decisions about ends, actions and tactics in ambiguous environments. Strategic leadership marries management with leadership, politics with ethics, and strategic intent with tactics and actions. It is a strong model that bridges the new and the old. As such it shows great promise for overcoming the errors of leaders who practice from a legacy leadership perspective in an increasingly postmodern environment. Success in this strategic model of leadership is dependent on how proficiently the organization responds and readapts to its ever-evolving context and how effective the leader is in continually renewing the systems of learning within the organization.

This fresh look at strategic leadership should not be confused with strategic planning or strategic management. Strategic management provides overall direction to the enterprise. It focuses on strategy formulation through planning and decision making based on creating a mission statement, goals, subgoals, and action plans. Merely depending on the rationality and linearity of strategic management will not meet the requirements of the postmodern condition. Henry Mintzberg (1994a, 1994b) concludes that the search for the definitive quantifiable solution to the future is no longer attainable. In fact, it can stifle commitment, narrow vision and make change less likely.

According to the strategic leadership view, organizations exist in such unpredictable environments that precise, economics-based planning is not prudent. Mintzberg suggests that the difference is one of synthesis versus analysis. Strategic leadership depends on synthesis, whereas strategic management depends on analysis. Strategic leadership also focuses on strategy formulation (decision making and strategic intent) but couples it with the capabilities necessary for motivating organizational members to join in the pursuit of the organization's intent. It encourages implementation of that intent through open communication, cross-functional teams and a supportive culture. It is not a one-time search for a sustainable competitive advantage but a continuous monitoring of the environment with the object of making the right moves in a dynamically changing, competitive landscape.

Strategic leadership is not just within the purview of executives as traditionalists suggest. It must reach to the lowest levels of the organization. The notion offered here is that all leadership levels within an organization—supervisory, managerial, and executive—should be prepared to lead strategically. It should be recognized, however, that some tasks and actions will be more useful at the managerial and executive levels. The use of strategic leadership at all levels will be challenged by those in management or supervisory roles who believe they do not have enough discretion to fully make strategic choices. This perception is a relic of the legacy model of leadership. It is true that the greater the internal and external constraints - whether they stem from demography, ideology, or personality—the less discretion the leader enjoys.[2] However, today's emphasis on flatter organizations and leaders pushing the authority to act down the chain of command, results in more leaders possessing more discretion. These lower level leaders may not perceive that they have discretion or they may not want the responsibilities that come with the ability to make strategic choices. Whereas discretion increases the likelihood that leaders will seize opportunities and influence the direction of the organization, most leaders in lower echelon positions still have strategic choices to make regarding the ends they promote and the ways and means of implementation in their sphere of responsibility.

The leadership requirements in the postmodern condition do not match the styles of traditional heroic leaders. In the new reality leaders who have adopted habits that allow them to act and think strategically are rewarded. Such leaders are able to anticipate, blend, envision and maintain flexibility, maneuver and bond with colleagues. They are better able to see the path to the future, push the envelope of results, adapt to change quicker, attract talent, and they know how to turn talent into performance in pursuit of their goals. I refer to these high performers as strategic leaders who practice leadership by (a) using a holistic learning approach, (b) managing and leading simultaneously, (c) understanding the omnipresent nature of politics and ethics in organizational life, and (d) seeing as their main purpose as the development of a high performing organization.

We are all aware of leaders who are better at understanding, interpreting, and leading in these multi-polar messy environments. Such leaders understand that change is inevitable and that trying to avoid it is fruitless. They are able to live with and in an environment replete with vague roles, contradictions, and ambiguities. They view change as an opportunity and a challenge, and they are successful because they understand that their organization needs to be in constant development. They prepare themselves and their organizations to take advantage of opportunities associated with change. They guide the transformations with a profound appreciation of stability. Their mantras are common values and adaptable ways and means. Leaders I have just described are *acting strategically*. They work at understanding their environment, determining end results, creating a coherent organization, establishing relationships, and crafting a responsible learning organization. They scan the environment for themes and forces while building a set of common aspirations, values, and beliefs that fit the organization's direction with the environment. They continually adapt their strategies, actions and tactics to the changing internal and external environment as the organizational direction changes. A few examples might help your understanding of strategic leadership.

The Vignettes

Some strategic leaders are only partially successful. Consider the example of Henry Ford, who demonstrated the ability to make consequential decisions about strategies, actions, tactics and ends. First, he created a mass-produced car in an environment where mass production was not understood. Using the legacy model of leadership he created and dominated the new automobile market and made it conform to his point of view. Over time he became extraordinarily wealthy and a national icon. However, when Chevrolet CEO Alfred Sloan introduced annual styling changes, talked about planned obsolescence and began to make cars more inexpensively and in many colors, the environment changed. Unfortunately, Henry Ford refused to recognize that change because he believed that the black Model T, and later the Model A, were all that the market needed and should need. He lost his monopoly to new companies whose leaders understood that the consumers were no longer concerned only with price but also with fashion. His success was making correct strategic choices about the end result. In doing so he successfully altered the car-making business. Ford's failure was that once the environment changed, he refused to recognize the change and adapt, thus losing his company's dominant market share.

Carly Fiorina, the ex-CEO of Hewlett Packard, is another example of a leader who demonstrated the ability to make consequential decisions about the end result. At Hewlett Packard Ms. Fiorina championed the controversial purchase of Compaq Computer in an attempt to transform the printer-based company to one offering a full range of digital products and computer services to businesses and consumers alike. Evidently, the decision to acquire Compaq was one with which her board of directors was comfortable. However, when the company failed to gain market share in either the printer or personal computer business, Fiorina was released and the board sought a new executive who was able to execute the decision.

Fiorina's failure was in her limited ability to make consequential decisions concerning actions and tactics. Her charismatic top-down legacy leadership style, which made her a celebrity CEO, also made her the target of Wall Street. Shareholders accused her of neglecting the hands-on management needed to carry out her vision of expanding product line and services. Being right about the direction was not enough. She also needed to be right about the actions and tactics she employed to steward Hewlett-Packard in that direction. As Bolman and Deal (2003) note, "A vision without a strategy is an illusion" (p. 256). Yet Fiorina's vision was probably correct, especially considering the way the market rewarded Hewlett-Packard after her demise as CEO.

Other leaders are more successful. They develop a strategy and execute it. Consider Carlos Ghosn, born in Brazil, schooled in Lebanon by Jesuit priests, and graduated with a degree in Engineering from France's prestigious Ecole Polytechnique. In 1999, at the age of 46, he was sent to Japan to change the financial status of Nissan motors from $50 million in debt to profitability in 3 years.

Within months of his arrival Ghosn, employing a "listen first, then think, and then speak" philosophy and a generative inclusive style, made a consequential discovery that the company's profits were being hindered by too vague a vision and goals, internal problems and a *Keiretsu* (a group of several heavily interlocked businesses) that Nissan was locked into getting its supplies from. He also discovered that other cultural norms, such as the support of unprofitable businesses and a focus on worker rather than profitability and shareholder focused policies, stood in the way of company reform.

As Nissan's chief operating officer, his priorities soon became to; add 1 million in global vehicle sales; achieve an 8% operating margin; move to zero debt in 3 years; and introduce new models fast. His restructuring of the company put it solidly in the black in less than 18 months. Ghosn was promoted to President and CEO within a year.

Ghosn's success relied on his consequential decision to break with Japanese management traditions. His revival plan rejected Keiretsu and violated the other cultural norms of the company as well. Initially his plan called for cutting 20,000 jobs, shutting five plants, and divesting from 1,400 affiliated companies. He insisted on buying supplies wherever the price and quality were the highest. To solve his internal problems he mobilized the current management by instituting a cross-functional team concept where managers from different functional areas were assigned a common goal. Problems got solved quicker and he was able to connect the people who got things done with his overall plan. He tied the plan together by checking and appraising results based on facts.

Lou Gerstner, the former CEO of IBM, is also an example of a successful strategic leader. When IBM hired Gerstner plans were well underway to break IBM into smaller, more nimble businesses. Nevertheless, as Gerstner (2002) wrote in his best seller *Who Says Elephants Can't Dance*, customers no longer wanted to be locked into one supplier for their technology needs. They desired an integrator who can deliver a working solution to the customer. Gerstner felt that IBM, with its size and reach, was uniquely positioned to fill that role.

Gerstner (2002) called the decision to keep IBM together the most important decision he ever made; not just at IBM, but in his entire business career. Yet he also made it clear that it was the easy part of turning around IBM. He made a string of strategic decisions to help keep the company together. For example, he launched the successful strategy of offering solutions to customers that might well include hardware and software manufactured by IBM competitors. He committed IBM to open standards so that its products could be used by competitors and vice versa. He sent out a steady stream of e-mails to employees to keep them posted about what was going on. He changed the rules for promotions and the compensation system so that rewards were based on total corporate performance rather than division or unit performance. He demanded implementation and did not allow "push back." As a strategic leader he successfully scanned the environment for themes and forces, forcefully set common aspirations, and adapted IBM to its external environment while creating the appropriate internal environment to achieve those aspirations.

Rudy Crew, the former CEO of Miami-Dade (FL) and New York City schools, presents another image of a strategic leader. His former deputy in New York said he understands how to maneuver through the labyrinth of leadership. He is "a person who has a gardener's patience, a politician's oratory, and a jazzman's flair for improvisation."[3]

> He sees multiple angles, and he can anticipate what the angle is going to be…. He can size up a political situation and find the win-win here, the hill to die on, and the issue this guy's going to lose face on. If he cannot win by persuasion, he is perfectly happy to win by force.

Under his leadership a whole school district within New York City gained national recognition for innovation and increased academic success.

Dave Brubeck is one of the most well-known jazz pianists of all time; the first to make the cover of *Time Magazine*. His namesake quartet, formed in 1951, lasted for 17 years and became one of the most successful jazz groups in history. But the quartet's story is not their longevity or their popularity. After 3 years of struggling to find their sound the band began to click. In 1959 they produced the first ever million-selling jazz album—*Time Out*, toured the world many times, and introduced enormous numbers of people to the jazz sound. One song on the album (*Take Five*) became a synonym for jazz and a monument to cool. Why did this song stand out and have so much impact? Because most of the music in the album was written in what at the time were strange time-signatures. Time-signature is a term used to indicate how the rhythm of a song is constructed. It helps listeners count along with the number of beats to a measure and the note that takes a beat. Most songs are written in 4/4 time-signature; one measure has 4 beats, and the quarter note represents one beat. A listener can easily count along, thus adding to their pleasure.

Dave Brubeck felt that the usual 4/4 time and the occasional 3/4, or waltz time was too tame—there was more to jazz than that. With the album, "Time Out," he broke away from the usual time-signatures. The first track startles the listener immediately with a dazzling 9/8 rhythm, grouped as 2–2–2–3; a rhythm that Brubeck picked up in Istanbul from street musicians. Then there was a track in 6/4 time, followed by another track in which the time signature constantly vacillated between 3/4 and 4/4. These were followed by *Take Five*, a track in 5/4 time. There were 5 beats in one measure, and the quarter note represented 1 beat. With Brubeck on piano, and Eugene Wright on bass, they kept repeating the 5/4 time sound so the listener wouldn't lose count. Joe Morello picked it up on drums and the famous Paul Desmond improvised on liquid sax. The great achievement of this album was that Brubeck succeeded in creating coherent music out of a musical style that at the time was considered inaccessible and inappropriate for jazz. Until his retirement Brubeck could not play a concert without a rendering of *Take Five*. When asked how he would like to be remembered, Brubeck answered, "as someone who opened doors."[4]

The Lessons

These vignettes exemplify what strategic leaders make possible. The Ford vignette is illustrative of the way early strategic managers focused on end results. Ford's saga demonstrates the consequential decisions he made related to strategy and actions. It also underlines the importance of staying connected to the context. Ford lost market share to Chevrolet because he failed to do that. Ford might have maintained his company's primacy—if he understood that leadership is almost always situated in a context and the chosen strategy must continually adjust to fit that context.

The Fiorina vignette makes the point that strategic leaders must focus on developing the correct strategy and the details of executing it. Words alone don't transform reality. Strategic leaders assure that action follows words by connecting with people and measuring progress and results.

What we learn from Ghosn, Gerstner, and Crew is that we should not view strategic direction and implementation as separate entities. Ghosn articulated a new direction and executed it through people all ready in the organization. We learn from Ghosn that the biggest mistake leaders can make is not connecting with people and their situation, and not understanding their expectations. Strategic leaders explain very clearly what needs to be done, how we are going to accomplish the changes, and what the outcome will be if we are successful. They focus on delivering results quickly at the beginning of the execution of the strategy. Finally, they invest in some objective metrics rather than subjective views about good work.

What we learn from Gerstner is that sometimes the end sought is not the problem. Do you remember his claim "the last thing IBM needs is a vision?" He focused most efforts on execution and changing the culture through consequential decisions about the ways and means he employed. Like Rudy Crew, strategic leaders manage, lead, and then manage. They also juggle the political realities required to promote their ideas while following the values identified as important by the organization. Balancing leading with managing while considering politics and values are at the heart of strategic leadership.

Brubeck is listed as a strategic leader because he took the time to understand the context in which he worked. He honed his skills by traveling and listening to different rhythms around the world and then changed the jazz paradigm from 4/4 time to 5/4 time. In doing so he created a platform for his colleagues to work and improvise from, much like Bill Gates of Microsoft and Sergey Brin and Larry Page of Google fame. All of these leaders found innovations that successfully met an unrecognized need in the environment. The most successful strategic leaders do this over and over again.

The Empirical Research

The empirical research on strategic leadership is of three types. Most studies focus on the activities of upper echelon leadership such as making strategic decisions; creating and communicating a vision of the future; developing key competences and capabilities; developing organizational structures, processes, and controls; managing multiple constituencies; selecting and developing the next generation of leaders; sustaining an effective organizational culture; and infusing ethical value systems into an organization's culture.[5] Other studies[6] focus on the roles and capabilities needed by strategic leaders such as cognitive complexity, flexibility and social intelligence, ability to learn (absorptive capacity), ability to change (adaptive capacity), ability to perceive variation in the environment, and capacity to take the right action at the right time (managerial wisdom). A few studies argue that strategic leadership occurs in an environment embedded in ambiguity, complexity, and informational overload based on the argument that the environment surrounding organizations is becoming increasingly hyper-turbulent.[7] Virtually no studies report on extending strategic leadership throughout the organization.

THE LEADERSHIP WHEEL

My impression from the vignettes, empirical research and personal experience is that strategic leaders embrace six habits that are absolutely necessary and unavoidable in creating a high performance organization. Skilled application of these habits allow leaders to work at; understanding their environment, determining ends, creating a coherent organization, establishing relationships, and crafting a responsible learning organization.

Habit 1:   Artistically using a palette of managerial, transformational, political and ethical actions to create frame breaking or frame sustaining change.

Habit 2:   Agility of the mind; as well as actions.

Habit 3:   Anticipating changes, challenges, and opportunities in internal and external environments.

Habit 4:   Articulating a statement of strategic intent through a generative/minimum specifications approach.

Habit 5:   Aligning people and organizations by viewing followers as colleagues and developing the social capital necessary to mobilize them.

Habit 6:   Assuring results and learning by anchoring the learning in committed self managed teams.

My quick way of remembering the habits is by referring to them as *artistry, agility, anticipating, articulating, aligning, and assuring.* I graphically organized these habits in the form of a wheel to reinforce a holistic learning approach to leading which enables the leader to make consequential decisions about ends, actions and tactics in ambiguous environments.

The "Leader's Wheel" presents a multidimensional, multifaceted approach that embraces all the leadership elements used by the manager, the transformer, the political activist, and the judge. However, when used exclusively none of the habits are comprehensive enough to be sufficient in leading followers for long term success. The six habits composing the Leader's Wheel are depicted in Figure 1.2.

When the "Leadership Wheel" turns it means that learning is occurring, behaviors are changing, and individual, team and organizational performance is improving. The notion of turning the wheel stems from the

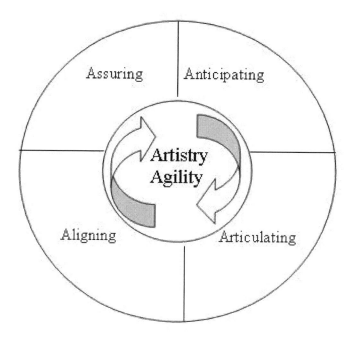

Figure 1.2. The Leader's Wheel.

Tibetan Buddhist practice of prayer wheels. When spun, the prayer wheel spreads spiritual blessings and well being from the Buddha Chenrezig, who vowed he would not rest until he had liberated all suffering. My use of the phrase *Turning the Wheel* is not as extraordinary but it is just as powerful.

The wheel provides a good symbol for situations faced by the leader. It represents the circular nature of leadership—there is no beginning or end. The first two habits—artistry and agility—found in the center of the Leader's Wheel, allow the leader to successfully employ the other four habits in an interlocking but iterative learning process.

Artistry is the megacompetence which enables the leader to effectively use habits 3, 4, 5 and 6 which compose the learning cycle of the wheel. It is the master ability and the key distinguisher between strategic leadership and traditional leadership. Traditionally leaders were encouraged to practice as scientists. They used a limited set of leader actions and employed a command and control, task and relationships, transformational or transactional style. Strategic leaders draw from a wide palette of leader actions to guide the organization toward achieving a strategic focus which reduces the complexity and ambiguity found in the postmodern condition. As artists, strategic leaders are flexible and able to adapt to different circumstances and conditions. Sometimes they exert influence by using command and control behaviors. At other times they use morality and virtue, or bargaining and incentives, to influence followers. At still other times they seek to emphasize and articulate common values, direction, and goal attainment.

The development of an *agile* strategic mindset is a precondition for successful use of the other five habits. It is a core competency that superior turners of the Leadership Wheel possess. The possession of basic attributes and skills is important to all managers and leaders. However, a strategic mindset separates strategic leaders from ordinary managers and leaders. The strategic mindset is developed by acquiring a growth mindset, a worldview based on the new science, and by practicing three important cognitive skills; reflection, reframing, and systems thinking. Through practice the strategic mindset develops and allows leaders to be successful in many different contexts and under conditions of ambiguity, complexity, and chaos.

The first two habits—*artistry* and *agility*—are in a sense analogous to the use of a mouse or touch pad on a computer. They enable the leader to maneuver and shape a learning process to help individuals, teams, and their organization find their way through the fog of change and thrive within it. Like using a mouse and cursor, artistic leaders go through screens of context—opening, closing, adjusting—using different windows, programs, icons, and subroutines that allows them to get optimum production and movement from the multifaceted operations they are trying to accomplish. Engaging their strategic mindset they search the internet for new and misplaced information, look for patterns, and synthesize new information. Strategic agility is fully achieved when leaders learn to think and act like artists.

The other four habits found around the outer rim of the Leader's Wheel are interdependent and interconnected through the leader's ability to maneuver and shape. Strategic leaders *anticipate* themes emanating from internal and external environments and power networks that can stifle or facilitate efforts to move organizations. Based on strategic anticipation, the best strategic leaders prepare their organizations for change by generating new organizational knowledge, learning about new opportunities, and foreseeing what organizational responses are available.

Strategic leaders articulate the acquired knowledge from the habit of *anticipating* through a statement of intent. They generatively create aspirations based upon shared values, flexible priorities, and articulated guiding principles. By *articulating* direction in this way, the organization's visions and values are fixed, and priorities and initiatives are flexible. These flexible priorities enable leaders to induce followers to join in a common purpose. By *articulating* direction through principles, not written policies and regulations, organizational members themselves are enabled and turn the Leader's Wheel by self managing their goals and priorities.

Strategic leaders create momentum by *aligning* strategic intent with individual, team, and organizational action. Alignment speaks to the frustration many leaders feel when they attempt to bridge the need of the human spirit for autonomy by using traditional management processes. These processes have a tendency to constrain behavior, induce passivity and create little real interest in achieving the goals of the organization. Strategic leaders understand the needs and desires of their followers so they employ enlightened communication tactics to help build social capital within the organization. By *aligning* in this manner, leaders help to mobilize and maintain forward momentum.

The habit of *assuring* refers to strategic leaders' ability to develop a deep understanding of the organization's strategic focus within followers, create communities of practice within the organization, read a dashboard of indicators, construct shared understanding of problems and opportunities and take appropriate action to facilitate or modify the organization's strategic intent. By *assuring* in this manner, leaders are enabled to embed the organization's strategic intent into the minds and spirit of the organization's members and cement lasting change in the organizational culture.

CLIFF NOTES

Strategic Leadership: A Fresh Look

This chapter described leading in the postmodern condition as the crucial dilemma facing leaders in the twenty-first century. This dilemma presents the leader with several consequential decisions. Do we stand pat and sustain the current way of doing things? Or, do we guide the organization to a new way of doing things by deciding what can be compromised and what cannot. As with most dilemmas there are no clear answers. What is known is that the postmodern condition does not yield to legacy models of leadership and continuing to practice from this model lends itself to error and failure.

The takeaway is that to become a strategic leader old habits need to be deemphasized and new habits need to be reemphasized. This transition from old to new habits is summarized in the table below. The remaining chapters in this book flesh out each of the new habits along with actions and tactics that make strategic leadership such a powerful way to develop a high performing organization.

Table 1.1.   Becoming A Strategic Leader

De-Emphasize Old Habits	Emphasize New Habits
Use a limited set of leadership actions	Employ multifaceted leadership actions
Think linearly rather than holistically Fail in context's filled with ambiguity and complexity	Develop an agile strategic mind Understand the new science and its tactics such as organizational fitness, chunking change, minimum specifications, flexible planning, edge of chaos, generative processes.
Fail to identify vital societal and institutional forces	Anticipate Gather environmental and social intelligence
Overuse measurement and plan rationally	Articulate Light the way and then run for daylight
Fail to connect the main ideas of necessary changes to the minds and hearts of followers	Align Create colleagues by relating—building trust, bonding; using story and active listening
Fail to see their organization as dependent on others	Align Create colleagues by reaching and bridging; using social influence and social power
Monitoring—inspecting	Assure Create high performance culture by performance and institution building—construct habits of inquiry, measurement and self-direction

NOTES

1. Cited in Jameson (1991, p. 195).
2. See Cannella and Monroe (1997), for a full discussion of this point.
3. Cited in Pinzur (2004, p. 1b).
4. Jazzblog (2006). *Dave Brubeck.* Retrieved June 1, 2008, from http://jack-sjazz.blogspot.com/2006/02/dave-brubeck.html; http://lcweb2.loc.gov/diglib/ihas/loc.natlib.ihas.200003794/lyricsFO.pdf; and www.davebrubeck.com
5. See Bourgeois and Brodwin (1984); Finkelstein, and Hambrick (1996); House and Aditya (1997); Hunt (1991); Ireland and Hitt (1999); Priem, Lyon, and Dess (1999); Selznick (1957/1984); and Zaccaro (1996).
6. For example, cognitive complexity (Hunt, 1991; Quinn, 1988), flexibility and social intelligence (Boal & Hooijberg, 2001; Hooijberg, Hunt, & Dodge, 1997; Zacarro, Gilbert, Thor, & Mumford, 1991), ability to learn, that is, absorptive capacity (Boal & Hooijberg, 2001; Cohen & Levinthal, 1990), ability to change that is, adaptive capacity (Black & Boal, 1994; Boal & Hooijberg, 2001; Hambrick, 1989), and ability to perceive varia-

tion in the environment and capacity to take the right action at the right time, that is, managerial wisdom (Boal & Hooijberg, 2001; Malan & Kriger, 1998).

7. See Eisenhardt (1989); Hambrick (1989).

CHAPTER 2

HABIT 1. ARTISTRY

The Mega Habit

Like a painter, the strategic leader must have an all-encompassing view of the beginning and the end, the whole and its parts as one instantaneous impression held retentively and untiringly in the mind of the leader.

—Sir Winston Churchill

The essence of this chapter is that the postmodern condition requires the finesse of the artist. Strategic leaders are essentially artists and since they work in a multifaceted reality they must apply a multifaceted set of leadership actions to turn the "Leader's Wheel." They lead, manage, and then lead again. In this chapter, I introduce the artist's palette of actions that strategic leaders use to manage continuity or change. I also illustrate the pyramids of frame breaking and frame sustaining change that cue actions.

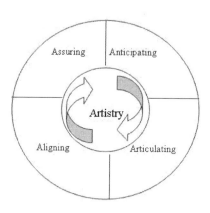

Figure 2.1.   The Leader's Wheel.

The Strategic Leader: New Tactics for A Globalizing World, pp. 21–43

THE YIN AND YANG OF LEADERSHIP

Stability and change has been the constant yin and yang of the manager-leader debate for decades. The consensus has been that in order to be successful during times of turbulence, organizations need leaders who can engage in, and balance, stability and change. During the past 4 decades there has been much scholarly debate about how to accomplish this seemingly unattainable goal. In the following paragraphs I describe the foundational underpinnings of strategic leadership and strategic leader actions. I begin by reviewing a short history of the leadership management debates.

In 1977, Abraham Zaleznik revolutionized management thought in his prize-winning article in the Harvard Business Review by raising the question, "managers and leaders: are they different?" He proceeded to describe the key differences between leaders and managers. Managers, he said, emphasize rationality, command, control, problem solving, and decision making. They focus on how to get things done while looking for compromises that shift the balance of power. Managers promote consistency to help organizational functioning on a day to day basis. Managers seek control, follow the rules, set objectives, plan, create priorities, budget, organize, problem solve, and get work done through others. They value stability and the use of legitimate power to do the regular work of the organization.

In contrast, Zaleznik (1977) saw leaders as proactive rather than reactive. According to him, leaders influence direction, action, and opinion. They shape ideas rather than respond to them. They take risks and strike out in new directions "using power to influence the thoughts and actions of other people" (p. 67). Leaders build a solid foundation and an agile workforce. Zaleznik argued that businesses needed both managers and leaders to survive and succeed. He believed organizations needed to hire different people to fulfill each role.

Other scholars (Bennis & Nanus, 1985; Collins, 2001; Drucker, 1999; Kotter, 1996; and Tichy & Devanna 1990) supported and extended Zaleznik's separation of manager and leader. According to Bennis and Nanus, managers handle the daily routine but never question it. They take a practical and instrumental approach by predetermining what their followers should do to improve processes and systems in order to achieve organizational goals. They explain, build confidence in, and support the status quo. John Kotter (1999) groups the main activities of managerial leadership into planning and budgeting, organizing and staffing, and controlling and problem solving. He describes leadership as a set of activities that produce change by defining "what the future should look like, aligns people with that vision, and inspires them to make it happen

Table 2.1.   The Differences in Management and Leadership

Management is about ...	*Leadership is about ...*
Planning and budgeting	Establishing direction and vision
Organizing and staffing	Aligning and empowering
Controlling and problem solving	Framing, reframing, reflecting, and systems thinking
Commanding	Building coalitions, self-managed teams, and supportive cultures
Accomplishing tasks	Transforming
Leading by procedures	Leading by principles
Emphasizing rationality	Accepting chaos
Maintaining order	Leading constructive change
Responding to ideas	Shaping ideas
Reacting to problems	Anticipating future problems
Limiting vision	Seeing an organization holistically
Coping with complexity	Coping with change
Setting goals out of necessity	Setting goals based on vision
Rewarding, compromising, and influencing	Educating, motivating, and inspiring
Seeking opportunities for stability	Seeking opportunity for change

despite the obstacles (p. 21)." Table 2.1 above further summarizes the distinguishing characteristics and differences between management and leadership.

POWER, PURPOSE AND MORALS

A year after Zaleznik's breakthrough idea, James McGregor Burns' (1978) seminal volume, *Leadership*, was published. In this highly cited work, Burns defined transforming and moral leadership as types of *transformational* leadership, which he contrasted with *transactional* leadership. In his definition:

> The *transforming* leader recognizes and exploits an existing need or demand of a potential follower. But, beyond that, the transforming leader looks for potential motives in followers, seeks to satisfy higher needs, and engages the full person of the follower. The result of transforming leadership is a relationship of mutual stimulation and elevation that converts followers into leaders and may convert leaders into moral agents. (p. 4)

By moral leadership, Burns (1978) meant that leaders take responsibility for their commitments. Followers have a responsibility to have adequate knowledge of alternatives, and the capacity to choose among those alternatives.

For Burns (1978), power and purpose remain key concepts of his theory of leadership. Like power, leadership is relational, collective, and purposeful. But the difference between simple power wielding and leadership lies in Burns' crucial variable of *purpose*. He differentiates between power wielders, who may treat people as things, and leaders who treat people as partners in the pursuit of a higher purpose.[1] He comments that:

> Some define leadership as leaders making followers do what followers would not otherwise do, or as leaders making followers do what the leaders want them to do. I define leadership as leaders inducing followers to act for certain goals that represent the values and the motivations—the wants and needs, the aspirations and expectations—of both leaders and followers. (p. 4)

The genius of Burns' view of leadership lies in the manner in which leaders see and act on their followers' values and motivations. Using the platform of power and purpose, Burns then lays out his conceptualization of leadership.

> The essence of the leader-follower relation is the interaction of persons with different levels of motivations and of power potential, including skill, in pursuit of a common or at least joint purpose. That interaction, however, takes two fundamentally different forms. The first I will call *transactional* leadership.... Such leadership occurs when one person takes the initiative in making contact with others for the purpose of an exchange of valued things. The exchange could be economic or political or psychological in nature.... The bargainers have no enduring purpose that holds them together; hence they may go their separate ways. (p. 4)

Burns (1978) considered this transactional exchange as a leadership act but not one that binds leaders and followers in a mutual and continuing pursuit of a higher purpose. Burns describes the second interaction as transforming leadership, which occurs when "one or more persons engage in such a way that leaders and followers raise one another to higher levels of motivation and morality." For Burns, transforming leadership ultimately "becomes *moral* in that it raises the level of human conduct and ethical aspiration of both leader and led, and thus it has a transforming effect on both" (p. 4)

With these words, Burns (1978) fathered a new leadership theory from which others began to build. In 1985, Bernard Bass interpreted Burns' work as having two axes, transactional and transformational. He even developed instruments to measure these dimensions. However, he modified Burns' concepts in significant ways. He proposed that "transformational leadership augments the effects of transactional leadership on the efforts, satisfaction, and effectiveness of subordinates, e.g., Lincoln, Roosevelt, and Kennedy ... were able to move the nation as well as play petty politics" (pp. 20–21) In his second modification, Bass removed the ethical and moral components which defined Burns' transforming leader. With these two modifications Bass created his *transformational* theory of leadership.

This change from Burns' (1978) transforming leadership to Bass' (1985) transformational leadership was very significant. In effect, Bass moved away from moral purpose as the criterion variable and replaced it with a more instrumental focus on the effort, satisfaction and effectiveness of subordinates. Rather than retaining Burns' dichotomy between transactional and transforming leadership, he described a variety of patterns through which degrees of leadership were layered. He limited his transformational leadership to the first two of the three tasks that Burns designated for the transforming leadership of executives: the capacity to change conditions and culture. He initially ignored Burns' third and final test of transforming leadership; leading for social change.

There have been several criticisms of the Bass (1985) modifications, particularly on the absence of moral purpose. Ciulla (1995), for example, suggested that Bass left himself open to rebuke. If his logic was followed, a great leader could be identified by the quality and quantity of changes implemented. Burns also weighed in on this debate by using Hitler as an example of a transformational but not a transforming leader because his purpose was immoral. Other leadership scholars—such as Heifetz in the field of public leadership and Fullan, Murphy, and Sergiovanni in the field of educational leadership - fought to retain moral purpose as the center of transformational leadership. Fifteen years later, these critiques were followed by Bass's (1998) revelation that true leaders seek "the greatest good for the greatest number without violating individual rights, and are concerned with doing what is right."[2]

Most organizational leadership scholars followed Bass' initial lead. Bennis and Nanus (1985), Tichy and Devanna (1990), Kouzes and Posner (2003), and Deal and Peterson (1994) took a more task-oriented view of implementing transformational leadership. Others offered servant and distributed leadership perspectives to augment transformational leadership. Senge (1990) and Howard Gardner (1995) championed a cognitive approach to describe transformational leaders. In all these approaches, the scholars retained the two-axis dimension suggested by Burns and

Bass. They made direction setting and vision the centerpiece of transformational leadership.

STRATEGIC LEADERS ARE MANAGERS AND LEADERS

There is a line from the Greek poet, Archilochus, which says, "the fox knows many things, but the hedgehog knows one big thing." This line has been used to describe two leadership *types*: hedgehogs and foxes. Hedgehog leaders know only one or two things that they persistently pursue. Fox leaders, on the other hand, know many things and pursue multiple goals. Zaleznik (1977) supported that analogy when he noted that managers and leaders are two different animals. Managers are risk-averse bureaucrats and leaders are inspirational visionaries. However, he saw hedgehogs as hedgehogs and foxes as foxes—the two never to be joined.

Scholars like Bennis, Kotter, and Burns, as well as practitioners like Andy Grove take exception with Zaleznik on this issue. In their view, although it may be challenging to balance strong leadership with strong management, this duality is necessary for the success of the organization. What organizations really need are both kinds of people—leaders who know how to manage, and managers who know how to lead.

A new breed of leader is required in the post modern condition where change and the need for stability are constants—leaders who are a cross between foxes and hedgehogs with both sets of qualities. Kotter (1988) illustrates this point by arguing that companies must embrace individuals who are both managers and leaders in order to thrive in times of increasing complexity. He notes that:

> In environments where competition is limited by regulation or a cozy oligopoly, leadership does not seem to make much of a difference one way or the other. Factors that economists and sociologists call structural are often the key to the issue. But in an intensely competitive environment, where the capacity to identify and implement intelligent change and to motivate superior performance is central to an organization's results, the capacity of management to provide leadership takes on new meaning. (p. 14)

Sashkin and Rosenbach (2001) attempted to resolve the leader manager paradox by proposing that effective transformational leaders use managerial processes to accomplish tasks, achieve goals, and empower and transform followers. Kotter (1988) also proposes that management and leadership are codependent in a complementary way when he says "managers promote stability while leaders press for change, and only organizations that embrace both sides of that contradiction can thrive in turbulent times" (p. 85). He estimates that producing change requires

80% leadership and 20% management. However, he argues that most change efforts fail because the percentages are reversed. Leaders try to manage change rather than lead it. He takes the proposal a bit further by suggesting that leadership must be dispersed throughout the organization and not just executed from the top.

Most revealing is Andy Grove's (past CEO Intel) practitioner perspective. He argues that implied judgment in this debate that leadership is better than management is flawed. In an e-mail to his biographer, Richard Tedlow (2006), he acknowledged that "you need both capabilities." He puts this view into perspective with an analogy to a tennis player: "A tennis player has both a forehand and a backhand. Not all tennis players are equally good at both, but we don't talk about backhand players and forehand players." In his practiced view, one should manage when management is needed and lead when leadership is needed.

The Two Tensions

The Zaleznik, Bennis, Kotter, Burns, Sashkin, and Rosenbach discussion illustrates the two dialectical tensions confronting leaders in the post modern condition (see Figure 2.2). What an organization *wants to be* is influenced by *what an organization is* and vice versa. What an organization *should do (what is right)* is influenced by what an organization is *actually able to do (what is possible)* and vice versa.

The first dialectical tension is between *what we are* and *what we should be*. The second is the tension between doing *what we should do* and *what we are able to do*. In order to address these tensions, a new conceptualization of leadership is necessary that includes the political and ethical dimension. The inclusion of these additional leadership behaviors establishes a mitigating yin and yang to the managerial and transforming duality. Political and ethical leadership actions move the lenses available to view leadership from a binocular viewpoint (leadership and management) to a

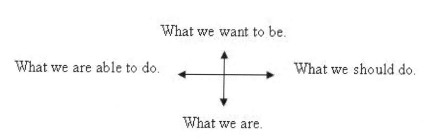

Figure 2.2. The leadership challenges presented by the postmodern condition.

kaleidoscopic[3] viewpoint (leadership, management, politics, and ethics). Understanding these tensions, and the four action-sets strategic leaders use to address them, is crucial to the ability to maneuver, particularly when organizations need to be improved at the same time they are being maintained.

Strategic leadership distinguishes the moral and political frames from within Burns' and Bass' transformational and transactional frames, and establishes them as important and critical leader actions. In order to transform and to sustain, leaders must be able to juggle the political realities while honoring the values identified as important by the organization and society. In other words, as they change or maintain focus on their leadership *ends,* they also need to engage in proper and powerful *means.* This flexibility is what makes the strategic leader unique.

It is important to note that leaders who are flexible can also have a moral anchor. Flexibility allows leaders to learn and adapt to realities around them. Strategic leaders accept the inevitability of change and the consequent need to reexamine their mental models, embrace the vital signals from their context and then rethink, revise, and reform their organizations as the situation dictates. Furthermore, even though *being right is not enough* for leaders, it does not necessarily mean that moral value is not important. In fact, the strategic leader must be a *moral steward* who interprets and understands the political realities of the organization and uses both managerial and transformational actions to maneuver the organization through its maze of complexities. I extend Andy Grove's suggestion that leaders should lead, when appropriate, and manage when appropriate by adding that leaders should compromise, when appropriate, and stand firm when appropriate.

ARTISTRY—THE MEGA HABIT

Max De Pree (1989) was on to something when he described leadership as an art. The stereotypical view of the worlds of artists and leaders can lead easily to the conclusion that they have little in common. They differ in motivations, responsibility, and interaction with people. However, both leaders and artists are comparable in their need for agility and creativity, cultural and environmental sensitivity, and the potential to make something happen or bring something into being.

As an art, leadership is not something to be learned and then executed. Rather, it is something to be lived, and built upon every day, much like white water canoeing. In that sport the first step is to learn to paddle efficiently on calm Level 1 rapids. However, from then on, every advance to a more difficult category of rapids requires adapting knowledge and skills to the situations that the canoe, the river, and the rocks present. So too, leadership is a constant learning experience that is wholly individualized and calls for adapting one's knowledge and skill to the current situation. Almost anyone can lead when there is moving water with few riffles, small waves, and few or no obstructions. However, it takes experience and courage to lead when the river is extremely difficult and long, with violent rapids. It is the difference between practicing leadership like a scientist, and practicing it as an artist.

The artist-scientist dichotomy is described in Table 2.2. The scientist approaches problems systematically, relies on objective observation, and extracts laws that prescribe their action. Scientists are masters of measurement. They are successful in rational stable environments. Artists, on the other hand, pay close attention to what is happening, focus on understanding patterns in events and flows of information, and act on that understanding. They are masters of creation and agility and can be successful even in turbulent, messy and chaotic environments.

Artistry can only be successful when the leader has the capacity to use multiple leadership actions. In stable environments, one set of actions is sometimes enough. In ambiguous, complex, and chaotic environments the

Table 2.2. Paradigms of Management Practice

	The Scientist	*The Artist*
Focus	Focus is on building theory.	Focus is on understanding events and acting upon their understandings.
Search	Seek theories that can produce laws that prescribe action.	Seek general explanations (theories) that guide actions.
	Approach problems systematically perform controlled, empirical, and critical investigations of hypothetical propositions about the presumed relations among natural phenomena.	Approach problems holistically, make intuitive assumptions, seek patterns, and draw conclusions.
Approach	Rely on objective observation, objective description, objectively determined explanations, and prediction.	Pay attention to what is happening, impose order on actions, and correct performance when it strays from accepted standards.
Decision Making	Use analytic, rational, sequential, convergent, logical, objective, and linear approaches to decision making.	Use intuitive, holistic, pattern-recognizing, adroit, subjective, and nonlinear approaches to decision making.
Role	Scientist Masters of measurement.	Artist Masters of creation

leader must stay firm and be flexible, balancing and initiating simultaneously. This ability to maneuver is a key distinguisher between strategic and traditional forms of leadership. Therefore, strategic leaders are individuals who are able to develop, understand and apply ethical moral foundations and interpret and understand political realities while they are leading and managing.

THE NEED FOR MULTIFACETED LEADER ACTIONS

One of the common errors leaders make is to use a limited set of leadership actions when influencing followers to join in a common cause. Such leaders are effective only when conditions match their one-dimensional set of actions. During the Renaissance, when Italian architects and artists confronted the question of how to draw three-dimensional objects on flat surfaces, they made the same error. They thought of a painting as an open window through which the viewer could see the world. Their goal was to paint that world realistically so they developed a system of mathematical rules known as linear perspective. They saw perspective as nothing more than seeing a place or set of objects behind a pane of transparent glass upon which they were to draw.

Leonardo Da Vinci learned these rules as a young man. He practiced using the window as a device for drawing perspective correctly while he was an apprentice in Verrochio's studio.[4] As his experience grew, his studies of perspective yielded an important distinction. Leonardo noted that a measured relation between object and image is only possible if the object is visible. As a result, artists in his day could only trace objects through the glass that were visible to them. Invisible objects could not be traced.

Leonardo's unique interpretation of perspective led him on a quest to find invisible objects in a scene and make them visible. In advancement of that goal he advised his fellow artists to leave the painting and relax every now and then, because he believed constant focus on the work caused a loss of judgment. "When you come back," he counseled, "your work and your judgment will be surer." He also recommended that artists look at their paintings from some distance away because then the work appears smaller and more of it can be taken in at a glance. At a distance the lack of harmony or proportion is more readily seen. He believed the artist could find hidden images or obscure information by gaining what he called aerial (distance) rather than linear perspective.

The first way strategic leaders can apply Leonardo's advice to search for the unfamiliar in the familiar, and the familiar in the unfamiliar, by pausing, feeling, and getting into the moment. Like the artists, they should distance themselves from the work for short periods of time.

Second, they should look for the invisible and find the things that are not in the present picture but may belong there. One way of doing this is by asking short powerful open ended questions such as: *what is missing? What is interesting, unique, or unusual about this situation?* Then, they should listen to and learn from the answers to discover new possibilities and paths in what is fast becoming a map-less terrain.

As important as Leonardo's viewpoint on perspective is for strategic leaders, it is not his most significant advice. Leonardo extended his lessons in perspective and became skilled in the use of other techniques such as his work in chiaroscuro (the light-dark technique of painting in which the figures portrayed have no clear outlines) and *sfumato* (the technique of coating objects in a picture with layers of very thin paint to soften edges and/or blur shadows). By extending his skill in the use of chiaroscuro, figures could be shown emerging into the light from shadows in a dreamlike effect of atmospheric mist or haze. Leonardo was the most skilled practitioner of perspective, *chiaroscuro*, and *sfumato* in the Renaissance. These techniques can be seen in his paintings *The Virgin of the Rocks* and *The Mona Lisa*.

THE LEADER'S WHEEL

As we have seen, the spokes of past leader wheels—leadership and management -present a limiting set of leader actions in postmodern times. If leaders only have a hammer, they tend to see every problem as a nail. In the limited tools scenario, leaders are only effective when conditions match their one-dimensional set of leader actions.

Artistry is the key distinguisher between strategic leadership and traditional or legacy models of leadership. Like Leonardo, today's leaders need a multifaceted set of actions that embraces all the leadership elements used by the manager, the transformer, the networker, and the judge, to lead in a multifaceted world. Following the axiom that, when a theory loses its power to account for a phenomenon a new theory is needed, I have added the two spokes of political and ethical leadership to the Strategic Leader's Wheel so that operates efficiently in the post modern condition.

The strategic leader is one who is able to use the actions available in each of the *Wheel*'s spokes—managing, transforming, political, and ethical—to adapt his or her approach to the circumstances of a given situation. The managing and transforming actions focus respectively on the need for order and stability and the need for change. The stabilizing aspect of leadership is found in the managing action-set of the Strategic

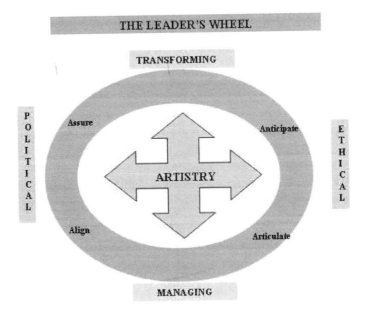

Figure 2.3.   The Strategic Leader's action sets.

Leader's Wheel. The adaptive or change orientation lies in the transforming action-set.

The other two spokes of the *Wheel*—political and ethical—act as opposing forces. They can enable, suppress, or hinder the organization's purpose and direction-setting actions. Political and ethical considerations constantly pull and push against each other compelling the strategic leader to adapt and refocus actions to maintain order or change.

The addition of these actions helps strategic leaders turn the *Wheel*. To illustrate these actions I have selected 10 sample items in each of the four action-sets from the Strategic Leadership Questionnaire (SLQ) (Pisapia & Reyes-Guerra, 2008) to demonstrate specific actions strategic leaders have at their disposal. (See Table 2.3)

The ability to transform is the frame-breaking aspect of leadership. Transformers are change and development oriented. They focus on the organization's intent and the *fitness* of the organization with its environment. They see themselves as leaders of leaders and their followers as colleagues who share the same values and commitment and can be depended on to be self managed. They use vision and persuasive stories to motivate their colleagues. Table 2.3 presents 10 specific actions strategic leaders operating from the transforming spoke of the Leader's Wheel can use to alter behaviors and execute a vision.

Table 2.3.   Samples of Specific Strategic Leaders' Transforming, Managerial, Political, and Ethical Actions

Transforming Actions

1   Challenge the mental models of all members of the organization.
2   Create a "readiness" for change among the staff.
3   Construct a statement of intent that provides direction and enable self-management with colleagues.
4   Communicate a compelling vision which significantly affects the behaviors of followers
5   Communicate through persuasive stories which significantly affect the feelings of followers.
6   Present an optimistic and reachable view of the future.
7   Interpret events and shapes meaning for followers.
8   Excite followers' emotional acceptance of challenges and changes.
9   Create a sense of joint ownership of values, vision, and priorities.
10 Encourage self management based on an agreed upon vision, values and priorities.

Managerial Actions

1   Plan, organize, direct, control, and motivate staff to accomplish the organization's goals
2   Specify the goals followers need to accomplish
3   Clearly describe the values, behavior, and standards necessary to be successful to followers.
4   Establish and emphasize formal and informal policies, routines, or priorities of execution
5   Clarify the specific meaning of our mission in terms of its practical implications for our work
6   Provide the resources necessary so a project can be properly implemented
7   Determine how things are to be done.
8   Emphasize a clear chain of command
9   Hold followers accountable for results
10 Take quick corrective action when mistakes are made.

Ethical Actions

1   Use knowledge about best practice as the basis for decision-making and action
2   Prudently listen, observe, and consider carefully before acting.
3   Create trust and understanding by being honest.
4   Demonstrate the will to put decisions into action.
5   Hold the line in a tough moral dilemma.
6   Ensure organizational actions are based on agreed upon core values
7   Act temperately – balance the emotional with the intellectual.
8   Display high regard for the common good.

Table continued on next page.

Table 2.3.   Continued

Ethical Actions

9   Value the rights of individuals.

10 Insert agreed upon values and knowledge into discussions and deliberations.

Political Actions

1   Maximize the balance of power in all organizational relationships.

2   Decide which issues are truly important and what can be compromised.

3   Develop external alliances to build a strong base of support

4   Generate support from people with influence and power

5   Come up with reasonable compromises for everybody's interest.

6   Identify the sources of power of individuals in a situation

7   Barter and exchange valued things to develop support for ideas, plans, and projects.

8   Attract and bond with followers through charm, consideration and personality.

9   Make friends with followers and supporters by doing personal favors.

10 Provide favored followers with inside information.

Source: Pisapia and Reyes-Guerra (2008). *The Strategic Leadership Questionnaire.*

The ability to manage is the stabilizing aspect of leadership. Managers are normally focused on maintaining a smooth running organization that achieves its goals. They tend to see followers as subordinates who can be developed into good workers. They make changes in the current way of operating to meet demands for improved products or processes and to remain both efficient and effective. They use actions related to planning, organizing, allocating and monitoring to accomplish these objectives. Table 2.3 presents 10 specific actions strategic leaders operating from the managing spoke of the *Wheel* can use to focus on the efficiency and effectiveness of current organizational operations.

Ethical leaders are normally focused on connecting changes with beliefs. This ability to uphold self-chosen principles and virtues, work for the common good, and value the rights of others in any situation is a balancing aspect of leadership. Ethical leaders make judgments about what is right and what is wrong then support their own view of what is right. They see followers as disciples and prioritize developing them into soul mates through moral appeal, spirituality and equity. They act virtuously, use best practice, and infuse their decisions with values and the common good to accomplish these objectives. Table 2.3 presents 10 specific actions strategic leaders operating from the ethical spoke of the *Wheel* can use to focus on doing the right things right.

Political leaders are normally focused on attaining and allocating resources to increase or maintain their power and facilitate organizational achievements. This ability to develop transactional relationships to support individuals and organizational goals is a balancing aspect of leadership. Political leaders see followers as competitors and focus on developing relationships with them by negotiating and accommodating their needs. They are pragmatic and emphasize doing what is possible in order to keep as many people satisfied as possible. They use actions relating to coalition building, negotiations, building networks and promoting consensus to accomplish these objectives. Table 2.3 presents 10 specific actions strategic leaders operating from the political action-set can use to focus on developing relations with followers and supporters.

Applying the Leader's Wheel

Effective leadership requires balance, knowing where to go, and the intuition to recognize which set of actions will be the most successful in any given situation. Analogous to Leonardo's use of perspective, chiaroscuro, and sfumato, strategic leaders coordinate a multifaceted set of actions to achieve an end creating a modern day potter's wheel of leader actions. The Strategic Leader's Wheel is rotated by skills and strategic thinking capabilities rather than feet. Instead of kicking the flywheel to keep the *Wheel* turning, strategic leaders use the paintbrush of the artist to mix and blend a palette of actions. They possess the same magical qualities that potters demonstrate when they shape the clay on their wheel. The habits around the outside of the *Wheel* are interdependent. They are connected when the strategic leader blends four types of leadership actions: managing, transforming, political and ethical.

The strategic leader applies artistic strokes for maneuverability, blending, and coordination to connect and turn the Leader's Wheel. When the hub-spoke-rim wheel relationship is properly tensioned the wheel acts as one unit. Force is transmitted between spokes at the rim, at the hub, and at the crossings between spokes.

Ed Tutland,[5] the CEO of a small medical supply firm added a directional interpretation to the Strategic Leader's Wheel.

> I viewed this strategic leadership model as a compass, with the transforming facet being *true north* and the managerial facet viewed as *south*. The *east and west* directions of this *compass* are the political and ethical aspects of leadership. Political forces which cause the organization to veer or vacillate off course require tradeoffs, and bargaining for power, to answer the question, "What is the best solution for the system?" The ethical facet forces the organization to vacillate in the direction that is best described as doing *the right thing right* or "what is the best solution for the organization?" The ethical

facet is intriguing because it includes acting from best practice as well as from a moral base.

A leader must know and understand the vacillating facets of leadership to *rechart* the organization toward goal attainment. The leader does this by focusing on leading for stability some time, and change at other times. The foundation of leadership lies in the managerial aspect. In times of stability it is the leader's job to maintain the pattern of work in the organization and modify or eliminate inputs or behaviors that are not standard to the organization. However, the more stability organizations enjoy, the more difficult it is to make changes when change is called for. From this perspective, the future of the organization lies in the transforming spoke of the Leader's Wheel.

The transforming leader continually positions the organization within its environment. When the need for change presents itself, organizational structures must be revamped to meet changing conditions and allow for better goal attainment. As the leader balances back and forth between management and transformation, the organization is in motion but does not stop innovating. The strategic leader is able to anticipate change and establish new relationships by linking internal and external environments. In this way, they chart the course for the never-ending dance of stability and change.

While the majority of the time leaders must stand for what is right, strategic leaders also realize that being right might not be enough. Further they understand what is right to one person or group may not be right to another, so they learn to compromise in order to bring about the changes needed. However, the ability to lead through purely ethical actions is almost always balanced by the reality of political needs. The strategic leader uses political actions to balance ways and means while being guided by ethics. Successful strategic leaders are comfortable in both arenas and are constantly able to balance political and ethical forces. The best of both worlds occurs when the leader is totally enabled politically and totally right ethically.

FRAME-BREAKING OR FRAME-SUSTAINING CHANGE

Another common error leaders make is to act before understanding situations. In the past organizational change has often been characterized as an anomaly—an unusual one-time-only encapsulated process that is set in motion by a change in executive leadership or an organizational crisis. However, organizations now operate in an environment characterized by constant change. Leading change in postmodern times is less about groundbreaking change processes kicked off deliberately as a reactionary measure, and more about balancing the constant shifting. This movement is sometimes in reaction to environmental forces, other times in anticipation and preparation; sometimes systemic, other times departmental; sometimes led by executive leadership at the top of the organization, other times led by the leaders at lower levels within the organization.

Strategic leaders must differentiate between two distinct types of change, frame-breaking and frame-sustaining, to act with confidence. Frame-sustaining change is change that enables the organization to adapt and work more efficiently on the things it is already doing. Frame-breaking change is change focusing on shifts in direction, procedures, and culture that enable organizations to work more effectively. In times of parenthesis, leaders do not need to learn how to lead change so that they can practice it at that one golden hour when frame-breaking change is needed. Rather, they need to learn to lead change as a way of life.

The first of several consequential decisions strategic leader must make is whether frame-breaking or frame-sustaining changes need to occur. Leaders like Ford and Gerstner made at least two consequential decisions crucial to their success.

Many leaders try to bring solutions that have worked in other contexts to the task at hand. Henry Ford misread the need for frame-breaking change and sustained his way of doing business. Lou Gerstner tried to find out what needed to happen in the organization and then built a change agenda. The first consequential decision facing new strategic leaders is between sustaining and changing organizational direction. Like Gerstner, they should ask, "What needs to happen here?" When the leader determines a need to sustain the current frame, managing actions are emphasized to make the machine run faster, more efficiently, and more productively. When there is a need to reexamine a fissure between external needs and internal beliefs, frame-breaking change is required and transforming actions are emphasized to provide long-term stability to their organization.

As leaders move to either sustain or break the frame, they are confronted with a second consequential decision. Should the leader stand firm and do the right thing, or be flexible and do what is possible?

The Pyramids of Strategic Change

While it is possible, theoretically, to lead through any of the four sets of leader action-sets, the strategic leader most often chooses between managing and transforming while negotiating the tension between the ethical and political aspects of the situation. The leader's managing actions focus on the stabilizing aspect, while the significant change orientation lies in the transforming aspect. No matter which action set is chosen, managing or transforming, these actions are balanced by political and ethical considerations.

We can envision the action sets as two pyramids. One pyramid is focused on stability and is balanced by political and ethical actions. When the leader is pursuing a managerial goal, the constant pull and push of political and ethical issues are present and must be dealt with. Conversely, when the leader is focused on transforming, the constant pull and push of political and ethical issues are also present and must be dealt with. The clash of the politics and values of the context are always present and must be considered when applying the strategic actions.

The pyramids of strategic change, illustrated in Figure 2.4, trigger leader actions. For example, is there a "fit" between the organization and its environment? If the answer is yes, the leader uses frame-sustaining actions. In frame-sustaining change, the organization adapts and learns to work more efficiently on the things it's already doing. If the decision is to sustain the current frame, then the leader applies managerial, political, and ethical actions.

Using the notion of the pyramids, strategic leaders choose one of the two approaches:

- Frame-breaking leaders focus on the triangular relationship between the political, ethical, and transforming actions to bring about the change desired.
- Frame-sustaining leaders focus on the triangular relationship between the political, ethical, and managing actions to maintain continuity and order.

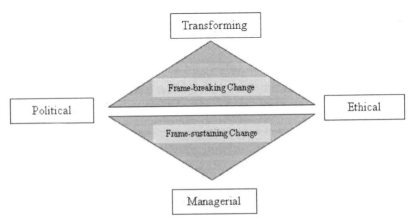

Figure 2.4.   The pyramids of strategic change.

Of these four action-sets, the managerial and transforming sets are directional. They are used to move the organization toward stability (management) or change (transformation). Leaders who are seeking to sustain and reinforce the stability of their organizations, like Henry Ford, engage in managing actions. This is described as "frame-sustaining" (managerial) leadership. On the other hand, leaders who seek to move the organization to meet the demands of the external and internal environments, like Dave Brubeck, engage in transforming, or "frame-breaking" leadership.

The directional leader actions (transforming and managerial) are each coupled with supportive ethical and political action sets. For example, when a leader is engaged in transforming leadership, the leader uses these supporting action sets to determine what is right (ethical) and what is possible (political). These action sets differ in that they are used in conjunction—as supporting actions—with directional transforming and management actions. They are therefore necessary components of a strategic leader's actions. While all four actions can be used individually, they are more useful when used in combination, depending whether there is a need for frame-breaking or frame-sustaining change. The major advantage of this approach is that management, leadership, politics, and ethics can be brought together to create one overall effect in much the same way that Leonardo used the tools of perspective, *chiaroscuro* (contrasting light and dark), and *sfumato* (subtle transition from light to dark) to produce his paintings.

In today's world, the more successful leaders use a wider range of influential actions to mobilize more people to accomplish the organization's objectives. Some leaders demand, others encourage; some guide, others compel or direct a course of chosen action. Some pull followers toward goals, others push followers toward goals. No matter how they apply their *artistry*, all leaders try to influence followers to achieve desirable outcomes.

Strategic leaders understand that a multifaceted reality requires a multifaceted set of leadership actions. However, it is not a matter of simply determining the situation or the context and applying the appropriate set of leader actions. There must be convergence! Artists adapt their knowledge and skills to the context and the various situations presented. Like Brubeck, they do not employ established systems and formulas that are restrictive and closed. Like Leonardo, they mix a palette of actions to maintain stability and challenge the status quo simultaneously.

At a time when organizations are struggling to find the right balance between the classic top-down hierarchy and the modern ideal of a leaner, flatter, and more participatory culture, leaders face a critical question: "Is it possible to loosen my grip on power, while actually enhancing my ability to get things done through others?" My answer is *yes*, provided leaders understand *what has to happen* and possess the ability to use multifaceted leadership actions. In stable environments one way of leading is sometimes enough. However, in ambiguous, complex, and chaotic environments the leader must stay firm and be flexible at the same time.

THE ARTISTIC NATURE OF STRATEGIC LEADERSHIP

I have grappled with metaphors to assist in understanding the artistic nature of strategic leadership. One metaphor that I have found particularly useful is that of moving through a labyrinth with its complex system of paths or tunnels in which it is easy to get lost. A popular childhood game may help illustrate the concept (See Figure 2.5).

The point of the game was to move a solid stainless steel ball from one corner of the top of a box to the opposite corner through a maze. It was a wooden box, the top of which was a board that had holes bored through it. Crisscrossing the top were little inlaid wooden barriers just high enough that the steel ball could not jump over them as it rolled around the surface. There were two knobs, one on each side. They controlled the pitch of the box top. Turning one knob tilted the top of the box front to back or vice versa, and the other knob inclined or dropped the top side to side. Yet the top of the box was always stable upon its very center. By moving the knobs, the steel ball rolled around. It took skilled and practiced hands to orchestrate the movements in such a way that the ball was always under control and moving, forward and back and side to side, avoiding the holes and using the little wooden curbs so that eventually, after much patience, the ball would arrive at the other end and the player became a winner.

Figure 2.5. The labyrinth of leadership.

The similarities between the artistry of the strategic leader and the skill used to play the game portrayed in Figure 2.5 are obvious. To be successful strategic leaders and game players must be able to make consequential decisions and maneuver. The steel ball represents the organization. The strategic leader applies pressure to the knobs to move the organization through transformation while maintaining stability as he or she goes through the labyrinth. Twisting the knob at each decision-making point, tilting between a managerial or transformational decision, the leader forges a path through the maze. Rarely can he or she do this by the use of just one knob. Therefore, simultaneously the leader turns the knob that governs the need for political or ethical decision making. Failure to negotiate successfully through the labyrinth means that the steel ball falls through a hole and the leader must begin again or move on to another game.

The difference between the game and the reality facing strategic leaders is that the game allows the leader to see a clear path to follow in order to achieve success. When leading today's organization through times of change, such a clear, linear, and stable path may not be visible. As in the game, two knobs are needed to move the steel ball along its path. In reality, leaders must be armed with a strategic mindset that uses the managerial—transforming and the political—ethical strategic action sets.

For strategic leaders, the labyrinth is exhilarating, and highly instructive. The journey itself is the message. Often the most important life lessons come when the road is going nowhere, or actually backward. This is the way it has been on my leadership journey. When my path turned away from the center, I felt I was "wandering through the Gobi desert," without signposts and without an oasis. Other times I felt like I was beating my head against a stone wall. It was not a lot of fun. In retrospect, though, these were crucial learning experiences.

CLIFF NOTES

Habit 1: Artistry: The Mega Habit

This chapter began by specifying and comparing the differences between leadership and management. Within these confines leaders make the common error of using a limited set of actions to influence followers to join in a common cause. A multifaceted set of leader actions which marries leadership with management, and politics with ethics, was provided to improve the flexibility and maneuverability needed to turn the Leader's Wheel. A second common error is often made when leaders act before they understand the situation and/or what kind of change is required? The pyramids of frame-breaking and frame-sustaining change were introduced to overcome this error and guide leader actions in mastering change. The takeaways are:

- Strategic leaders understand that when one works in a multifaceted reality one must apply a multifaceted set of leadership actions.
- *Artistry* is the key distinguisher between strategic leadership and traditional leadership.
- The leadership habits around the outer rim of the Leader's Wheel are interconnected by the leader's artistic use of the four sets of leader actions: managing, transforming, political, and ethical.
- The stabilizing aspect of leadership is found in the managerial spoke of the Leader's Wheel. The adaptive or change orientation lies in the transforming spoke.
- The focus of the political and ethical actions represented through the spokes can enable, suppress, or hinder the organization's purpose and direction-setting actions.
- The ability to transform is the frame-breaking aspect of leadership. The ability to manage is the stabilizing aspect of leadership. Ethical leaders are normally focused on connecting changes with beliefs. Political leaders are normally focused on attaining and allocating resources to increase or maintain their power and facilitate organizational achievements
- The first consequential decision facing new strategic leaders is between sustaining and changing organizational direction. They should ask, "What needs to happen here?"
- As leaders move to either sustain or break the frame, they are confronted with a second consequential decision. Should the leader stand committed and do what is right, or be flexible and do what is possible?
- The pyramids of strategic change guide the strategic leader in making choices among the four action-sets which act as triggers for leader actions.
- Strategic leaders manage when management is needed and lead when leadership is needed.

NOTES

1. For a good discussion of Burn's contributions see Ciulla (1995)
2. The concept of utilitarian leadership was placed in the literature by Jeremy Bentham (1988) who said it in the nineteenth century and described it as Utilitarianism.
3. Kaleidoscopes contain designs of many colors, shapes, and patterns. The designs are ever changing intricate and simple patterns.
4. See Bramly and Reynolds (1991).
5. Name changed to protect privacy.

CHAPTER 3

HABIT 2. AGILITY

Developing the Strategic Mindset

Mindset drives every aspect of our lives, from work to sports, from relationships to parenting.

—Dweck (2006)

This chapter demonstrates the need for an agile mindset, offers *old and new science* ways strategic leaders can interpret signals from the environment, and illuminates cognitive skills necessary to develop a strategic mindset. Differences between the old and new science of management are outlined along with seven new tactics strategic leaders can use as they turn the "Leadership Wheel" to negotiate their environment. The chapter ends by introducing the mental skills of systems thinking, reflection, and reframing, and how they can be used to develop a more agile mindset.

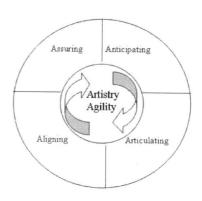

Figure 3.1.   The Leader's Wheel.

The Strategic Leader: New Tactics for A Globalizing World, pp. 45–72
Copyright © 2009 by Information Age Publishing

As a young professor I was assigned each year to teach a course at one of our campuses that was 3 hours of high and rocky terrain from home. The distance wasn't the most difficult part of the assignment; it was being alert for deer coming onto the road on my drive home at night. As I saw it, I was in control. All I needed was enough time to react and maneuver the car. So I would plow straight ahead, flashing the high-beams, honking the horn, veering and hoping that I would either miss the deer or that they would move off the road. After many near misses I decided to change my mindset and put the deer in control. Since deer freeze when bright lights shine in their eyes, I decided to turn off my lights briefly. It worked; the deer saw my car, did not freeze and ran off, avoiding me rather than me avoiding it. My personal take away from this experience was that the mindset you adopt profoundly affects the way you act.

THE HABIT OF AGILITY

Agility is the capability to rapidly and cost efficiently adapt mentally to changes in your environment. It is the key to shifting your perspective so intuition, analysis, or fixed paradigms are improved. At its optimum, it enables leaders to understand the ambiguity in postmodern complexities, and then identify levers that will initiate maximum change with the least effort in dynamic and turbulent environments.

Mental agility is a key core competence of strategic leaders. It is achieved by developing a strategic and flexible mindset. Mindset is the way you think about things. It refers to a set of beliefs and assumptions held by you, a group of people or an entire organization which creates an outlook and causes one to act in a certain way, as I first did with the deer in my headlights. Mindsets also frame the way you interpret day to day events. They can hinder decision making, and leader development and effectiveness.

Understanding the notion of mindset is important. It has the power to transform yourself and your organization. Mindsets stop people as well as enabling them to achieve their dreams. Carole Dweck (2006) the Lewis and Virginia Eaton Professor of Psychology at Stanford University, says simply that the world is divided between people who are open to learning and those who are closed to it, and this trait affects everything from your worldview to your interpersonal relationships. An easy way to understand the difference is to consider the way you think about talent or personality. In your view are these qualities fixed—meaning that they cannot be nurtured? Or, do you believe that talent and personality can be developed through commitment and effort?

People with fixed mindsets assume that ability is a fixed quantity. They tend to be judgmental of self and others. They are also inclined to see new endeavors as threatening, give up more quickly when frustrated, avoid activities they don't think they're good at, and insulate themselves from negative evaluation. Leaders with this mindset use less empowering behaviors, and function less well in teams and groups. They spend considerable time documenting instead of developing themselves or their organization.

In contrast, those with a growth mindset assume that people can improve just about anything through learning and purposeful practice (Sternberg, 2005). They are inclined to be open to and learning from feedback, willing to risk, get enjoyment from challenge, accepting of one's strengths and weaknesses, appreciating others' competence, resilient in the face of frustration/failure, and improving in new domains. Leaders with growth mindsets work well in teams and organizations, have more constructive problem-solving approaches, and foster change and collaboration.

Strategic leaders possess a growth mindset. Of course, fixed mindset versus growth mindset is not an either or situation. You can and probably do possess a growth mindset in certain areas, and a fixed mindset in other areas of your life. You might have one type at work, but maybe a different type when it comes to social interactions. They may also be different depending on your phase of life, situation, and age.

THE STRATEGIC MINDSET

The strategic mindset is flexible and committed to continuously raising performance. It looks for opportunities, conducts mental experiments, and decides quickly to adopt or abandon the opportunity. The strategic mindset is analytic, creative, evaluative, or pragmatic as the situation demands. What is missing in many managers and leaders is the ability to; see into the future, understand the roots of the past, grasp the big picture, and then invent a new future.

Strategic leaders keep in close touch with the leading edge movers and shakers of their industry. This enables them to understand how the landscape is changing. They also need to understand how their business works. On the one hand, strategic leaders need to establish direction and priorities. On the other hand, they must see that the desired result is achieved and not just talked about.

The strategic mindset requires an agile mind that can switch from "why and what" to "how" in an iterative process. In a sense, strategic leaders must incorporate tactical thinking in their repertoire of skills. Tactical thinking refers to performing each implementation task with quality and efficiency until the strategic goals are met or abandoned.

It takes both left and right lobes of the brain to develop the strategic mindset. Left brain thinkers are rational; they think linearly, logically, and analytically. They take things apart and arrange them in some sort of hierarchical order. The left lobe is good for tactical thinking when one needs to make things work. Right brain thinkers are inclined to think conceptually, holistically, and visually in a non linear generative fashion. They see things in light of their function and relationships, identify patterns and arrange them in some sort of connective order. In the strategic mind, they are not opposites but work together, back and forth between analytical and judgmental to growth and opportunistic thinking to extract as much information from the situation as possible so they can see the forest and the trees—simultaneously. Strategic leaders develop these capacities by adopting a "new science" worldview and using a more complex set of cognitive skills.

Worldviews

There is a growing acceptance that the possibilities for predicting the future are limited because of rapid environmental changes. Leaders are forced to take action that was not planned in advance. Under conditions of complexity and ambiguity leaders need space with fewer rules to find strategies that are uniquely good for outcomes they aspire to achieve.

The emerging notions of chaos, complexity and ambiguity alert strategic leaders to the need to change the way they practice management and leadership. Yet, many of today's leaders remain committed to the old leadership habits of control and prediction. Their worldview relies on the machine metaphor which results in a constant out-pouring of innovative strategies that some observers might call fads. This machine worldview also suggests leaders need to predict, direct, manage, and control change in their organizations. The major flaw in this thinking is that it does not allow for the increasing pace of change.

Though still dominant, the machine world view doesn't stand unrivalled. In the last decade it has been challenged by the complexity worldview which holds that the world we inhabit results from the interactions of a web of relationships impacting the environment of the organization. The complexity worldview places its faith in interdependent nonlinear relationships. The whole is different from the sum of the parts. Since events are not independent, they cannot be studied in isolation. Therefore the variables must be studied as part of one system. In short, the machine world view favors exclusion while the complexity world view favors inclusion.

The machine worldview takes its cues from Isaac Newton's discovery of simple laws which governed the motions of planets and apples. His legacy was formed by reducing complexity to simple laws of linearity, order, certainty, status, and control. One by one these simple laws fell to the theory of electromagnetism in physics, the theory of atomicity in chemistry and the theory of cells in biology.

At the heart of the machine worldview is the emphasis on linearity. Linearity is a comforting concept. It reassures us that when we change one side of an equation the other side changes at a constant rate. Changes in inputs yield stable changes in outputs. It also reassures us that the whole is the sum of its parts. Since variables are additive we can separate them and study them in isolation, then add them back to get a complete picture. Stable organizations can function in relative isolation from their environment because the patterns are predictable. They are closed systems.

Based on assumptions of linearity and independence, advocates of the *old* science proposed organizational designs which had clear singular purposes. They used command and control structures to create predictability of results. Organizational theorists, like Frederic Taylor and Max Weber,[1] ground the old science into theories of scientific management, rational systems, and bureaucracy. These theories formed the foundation of management and leadership training for decades. As the old science was embedded into the fabric of organizations, decision-making power was concentrated in the hands of those occupying positions of authority. These authority figures were expected to make correct judgments, determine how to structure and adjust the work, and therefore be worthy of higher pay.

Biologists and environmental scientists were among the first to defect from the tenets of the old science. In their view complexity is irreducible. The systems they experienced were so closely intertwined that they could not be studied sensibly through their simpler components. Complex systems like ecosystems do not respond to simple linear solutions.

The machine worldview nimbly pushed past these early defectors but others soon appeared. Complexity theorists claimed that creating organizations under the principles of the old science caused fragmentation of work tasks and reduction in the decision-making capacity of the individuals who were at the point of contact with customers, clients, or students. As opposed to the adherents of the old science, who assumed that fact can be divided from value, they suggested that decisions represent more than facts. Decisions also represent values and, for some decision makers, commitment and beliefs. The new theorists further pointed out that many systems do not operate under the simple linear dynamics espoused by the *old* science. Take weather forecasting as an example. The weather is governed by relatively simple physical laws and the variables to be considered are great. Hence, many times predictions were not dependable. To understand systems like the weather a *new* science was necessary.

In the 1950s systems thinkers shifted their focus to the effects of environmental feedback on organizations. They found that order and chaos are two extremes of structure found in systems. Orderly systems have little interaction and flexibility among their elements. They tend to be rigid and conforming. Chaotic systems are characterized by disarray and disorder. Systems thinkers proposed that productive organizations interact with their environment continuously and adjust themselves based on the feedback they receive. These findings shifted the focus of systems scholars to concepts such as interdependence and adaptation. They also influenced leadership practice. Instead of looking at organizations as isolated from their environment, leaders were encouraged to see the organization within an environment for which it had to accommodate, adapt or conform.

The new science is grounded in the principle of complexity. Complex systems are not graceful. They do not yield easily to predictability. Some pundits would say they are messy. Under conditions of complexity, there is rarely a simple cause and effect relationship between elements. A small stimulus may cause a large effect or no effect at all.

The complexity worldview relies on an organic metaphor to guide its actions. In the complexity worldview control is an outcome of change and occurs irrespective of efforts to manage it. In addition to the weather, examples of complex systems include: colonies of ants, bees, and termites, the stock market, families, and any organization that relies on the work of humans such as business organizations, hospitals, universities, public schools, and legislative bodies. In complex systems such as these, human beings have the freedom to act in ways that are not always totally predictable.

Thus, complex systems are more than the sum of their parts. They don't evolve, they co-evolve. Co-evolution is a process in which two or more related actions or processes support each other in ways that cannot be foreseen prior to their interaction. Systems that do not interact and share ideas cannot co-evolve. For co-evolution to occur, diverse ideas must be present, communicated, and dialogued. Without these conditions, any diversity of ideas becomes divisive and counterproductive.

Complexity is that state between order and chaos where complex systems seem to operate best. Complexity theorists point out that this space is looser, more fluid, and constantly shifting. Some call the space between these two extremes *the edge of chaos*. Malcolm Gladwell (2000) refers to it as the *tipping point*. This space is a critical point where a small change can push the system into chaotic, rapid, and radical change behavior, or lock it into a fixed, slow, and incremental change behavior. In fact, complex systems gravitate to the edge of chaos when given the chance to do so, never locking entirely into place or dissolving into turbulence. Therefore, when strategic leaders operate under conditions of complexity, their goal should be to manage at the edge of chaos.

Have you experienced the edge of chaos? Most of us have. It's that time when a plan has not yet come together, when we feel we are on to something huge but we are not even sure how close we are to a breakthrough. It's a time when there is not enough agreement and certainty to make a choice of the next step. But there is neither enough disagreement nor enough uncertainty to throw the plan into complete disorder.

While uncertainty is profuse in the region between order and chaos, it is not the paralyzing uncertainty of chaos, nor the stultifying certainty of order. Old science theorists would suggest trying to reduce the ambiguity by breaking the issues apart to find answers. New science theorists would suggest letting things simmer for a while longer to see what happens.

Under the rules of the new science, leaders act as artists in residence and constructors of knowledge. In complex systems the world is in a state of becoming where change must be led, not managed. Leaders holding the complexity worldview accept the paradox that both order and chaos must be embraced, since they exist naturally. In this new age, leaders must swim with the flow of events rather than trying to control them, while maintaining a constancy of purpose as they try to turn whatever happens to their advantage.

Organizational theorists like Chris Argyris, Peter Drucker, Peter Senge, and Jim Collins are grinding the new science into the theories of organizational learning and learning organizations. They hope it will form the foundation of the training of managers and leaders for decades to come. Strategic leaders just need to be careful not to overestimate their ability to predict what will happen when managing at the edge of chaos. It may only be practical to make general statements about the future rather than try to predict it as old science advocates would have them do. For example, while we cannot predict the exact closing Dow Jones Industrial Average, we can describe the overall market trend as bullish or bearish and take appropriate investment action.

Old Science—New Science

As you may have grasped from the above paragraphs, our existing principles of leadership and management are largely based on metaphors from a science that is hundreds of years old. It is time to face the fact that science itself has largely replaced these metaphors with more accurate descriptions of what is really happening in the world. The new science is replacing the old metaphors, not so much because they were wrong, but because they only described simplistic situations. Similarly, organizations today are not the simple machines that they were envisioned to be in the Industrial Revolution. People are no longer the compliant cogs in the machine that they were once thought to be.

We have intuitively known these deficiencies of the old science for many years. Herbert Simon (1947, 1955) and Charles Lindblom (1959, 1979) knew of these deficiencies when they introduced their tactics of *satisficing* and *muddling through* to work around rational decision-making structures proposed by old worldview managers. In the last 2 decades, management philosophies such as learning organizations, total quality management, empowerment, and so on, were introduced to overcome the increasingly visible failures of the simple organization-as-machine metaphor. Still, as I have pointed out, the machine metaphor remains strong and cannot be dismissed from consideration.

So what are the implications for leadership from the *old* and the *new* science? Contrast canoeing on Golden Pond with white water rafting in the Grand Canyon. You should now begin to understand the difference between the old science and the new science. To further your understanding, review the descriptions found on Table 3.1 which summarizes key concepts found in the preceding paragraphs describing the old and new science.

Complex systems work better with a general sense of direction that includes having *minimum specifications* in place. This concept can be illustrated through an analogy to a flock of geese. Why do geese fly in a "V" formation? Science tells us that as each bird flaps its wings, it creates uplift for the bird immediately following. By flying in "V" formation, the whole flock adds at least 71% greater flying range than if each bird flew on its own.

This explanation is deceptively simple. In 1987 Craig Reynolds developed a computer simulation of the flocking behavior of autonomous agents which he called the Boids and placed them in a simulated environment with obstacles. He programmed the Boids to follow three simple rules: (a) separation—try to maintain a minimum distance from all other Boids and obstacles and steer to avoid crowding local flockmates, (b) alignment—try to match speed with adjacent Boids and steer toward the average heading of local flockmates, and (c) cohesion—try to move toward the center of mass of the Boids in your vicinity and steer toward the average position of local flockmates.

When the simulation was run, the Boids flocked and flew around the obstacles on the computer screen even though there was no rule explicitly

Table 3.1. A Comparison of the Old and the New Science

The Old Science *Machines*	The New *Science Flow*
Traditional organizational thought takes its cues from the Newtonian notion that environments are linear, orderly, certain, static, and controllable.	Modern organizational thought takes its cues from the notion that environments are non linear, interdependent, and emergent.
Newtonian thinking resulted in systems built on predictability. The role of the scientist is to discover the inner workings of the machine to produce principles and laws.	Complexity results in systems built on unpredictability. The role of the scientist is to discover the order hidden in the creative tensions through self-reflection and reflective intuition.
Classical physicists believed that if they can improve their measurements and calculate with infinite precision, then they could gain absolute understanding of phenomena	Modern physicists believe that there is a limit to the accuracy of any instrument or measurement. Initial measurements, no matter how precise, lead to vastly different results.
Based on linearity. Big influences have big effects and little influences have little effects.	Based on non linearity. Little influences can have big effects.
Assumes that organization's function in relative isolation from environmental.	Assumes that organizations are organic entities that interact with their environment.
Focus is on clarity of purpose, command structures, and control processes.	Focus is on by becoming more adaptable in order to survive.
All problems are amenable to a solution and organizations could be made more predictable through planned structures.	Problems are seen as dilemmas and some are not amenable in current form. Reality must be constructed
Managers develop and follow detailed maps.	Strategic leaders discover the route and the destination through a journey.

telling them to do so. Reynolds' experiment demonstrated that simple rules can lead to complex behaviors formed by the interaction of the agents—in this case the Boids.

New Science Tactics for Strategic Leaders

Several important lessons for strategic leaders can be extracted from the Boids experiment and the new science point of view. The first lesson is that if the context is complex, leaders need to shift from an over reliance on the hierarchical skills of the twentieth century to a greater respect for the coordination skills necessary in the twenty-first century. The management behaviors of command and control still have a role to play in leading

leadership actions can be useful when organizations
ı to the edge of chaos, or when they find themselves
:actics of coordination and collaboration are more
ain the organization at the edge of chaos. Strategic
ıphasis on the new science tactics while using old tac-
s John Gardner (1989) so eruditely observed, leaders
who hold high rank in organized systems have power to further their purposes. "They may be persuasive but they do not lead by persuasion alone—
rather by persuasion interwoven with the exercise of power" (p. 56). Both
old and new science tactics have a place in the strategic leader's repertoire
as he or she navigates organizational life. The trick is to know which tactics
are germane to the context in which one practices leadership.

The second lesson the new science worldview suggests is that strategic
leaders should elevate the status of their purpose, aspirations, values, and
guiding principles to steer organizational activity. The organizational purpose and aspiration drive decision-making and must be shared by all. In
addition, the values and guiding principles must be compelling enough
to seep deeply into the organizational fiber so followers can become self-
managed participants in their organizations.

A third lesson is that leaders, following old science tenets, tend to over
specify when they create visions and plans to guide organizational work.
They believe they need to think of everything because the machine cannot think for itself. New science principles suggest that strategic leaders
use *minimum specifications* to guide their work with individuals, teams and
the organization because this allows them to swim with the flow of events
and gives followers opportunities to self manage. When strategic leaders
operate under minimum specifications, they create a simple tablet which
describes the general direction to pursue and a few basic principles to
guide how to get there. Under the concept of minimum specifications the
strategic plan should be able to fit on one page, front and back.

The U.S. Marines' interpretation of the rule of minimum specifications
—*keep moving, use surprise, take high ground wherever possible*—is a real world
example of this idea at work. Another is Karen Tumulty's 2008 description of how Barack Obama wrested the Democratic presidential nomination from Hillary Clinton. Obama laid down five ruling principles for his
chief operating officer: Run the campaign with respect; build it from the
bottom; no drama; the customer is king; and technology is our running
mate. Clinton, on the other hand, ran a top down organization where
decision making was held by a small group at the top. This resulted in
many mixed signals and decisions that came too late to execute at the
grass roots level. Obama's minimum specifications empowered his followers at the grassroots and in many states they organized the ground level
meetings for him for free.

Minimum specifications are also at work in the Police Department of Boca Raton Florida, where two words: *Protect and Serve* guide police officers' judgment in any situation. The Phoenix Fire Department uses "protect, prevent harm, survive and be nice" as their minimum specifications. It is amazing how many complex behaviors and adaptations these simple rules produce.

Obviously the use of minimum specifications does not apply to all situations. There are times when over specification is important such as in the operating room, or when creating a programming language for computer software. However, in less specialized environments over specification leads to unnecessary behaviors. For example, those of you that have been involved in detailed strategic plans with goals, objectives and subobjectives, can understand the frustration when external and/or internal environmental changes nullify your work and force you to enter yet another round of planning; an ongoing reality for those who work in state departments of once the legislature adjourns for the year.

The fourth lesson comes from a phenomenon known as The Butterfly Effect. It seems that the old adage "where you start—the initial conditions —makes a major difference to where you end up" is true. Complexity studies, beginning with the seminal work of meteorologist Edward Lorenz[2] in the 1960s, have shown that very small occurrences can produce unpredictable and sometimes drastic results by triggering a series of events. One conclusion drawn from his studies is that behavior in complex systems is non-proportional to the strength of a force's initial input— its nonlinear. Changing initial conditions change everything. Lorenz's metaphorical classification of this phenomenon was The Butterfly Effect.

Physicist Troy Shinbrot (1995) from Rutgers University, ran experiments with a fork to demonstrate The Butterfly Effect. When a fork is placed flat on a table, it stays there. When a fork is balanced on its points it becomes unstable and falls, no matter how carefully it is balanced, because any tiny fluctuation of air in one direction or another is enough to make it tip to the left or the right. The question becomes whether a fork balanced perfectly on its end can be made to fall to the left or the right? The answer is yes. The tiniest puff of air at the right time can make it fall in the chosen direction. The butterfly in Lorenz's butterfly effect represents the tiny puff of air that tips chaotic weather patterns from one outcome to another.

The metaphor has a pervasive effect on our understanding of the effect of initial conditions on results. It has even been turned into a 2004 movie aptly titled *The Butterfly Effect* (Bress & Gruber Mackye, 2004). The premise of the movie is that the lead actor plays a man who has found a way to travel back in time to his youth. Each time he returns to his childhood he makes minuscule changes that radically alter his life in the present, inevitably leading to different results.

The Butterfly Effect has obvious major implications for strategy implementation yet it is consistently ignored by organizations. The lesson for strategic leaders is that planning must be a learning activity where results and processes are annually reviewed, unintended consequences are identified, and new strategies are developed. It reinforces the need for continuous environmental scanning and scenario building to help the organization raise awareness, increase connectivity with the outside world, and reduce the permeability of its boundary. It also reinforces the use of multiple adaptive strategic leader actions—managerial, transforming, political, and ethical—as necessary to maintain stability while the organization is changing.

The fifth lesson from the new science comes from the principles of chaos and change theories. Under these principles, strategic leaders should encourage their organizations to get stuck *at the edge of chaos*, since most observers believe that is where creativity and innovation occur. Complexity researchers Ralph Stacey and others[3] have provided new tactics strategic leaders can use to move their organizations into the chasm.

Strategic leaders can move stable systems to the edge of chaos by using tactics such as; persuading their members to become better connected; increasing diversity either in the members themselves or in the nature of the relationships between them; increasing the amount of information transferred; and reducing the level of anxiety felt by organizational members. Conversely, if leaders find themselves in a chaotic system with too much uncertainty, they should reduce the use of these tactics because too much instability coupled with tightly drawn power differentials and weak control systems hinder the possibilities for change or creativity. There will be a tendency for either powerful resistance or *headless chicken* behaviors.

There is no formula to determine how much of the four tactics strategic leaders should use to move the system to the edge of chaos. Leaders have to see, experience, learn, and test to gain the wisdom to get it right. A suitable analogy is when the doctor says, "take 2 aspirins and call me in the morning." If the pain remains in the morning, he makes another diagnosis and prescribes a larger dosage or different medication. This is what doctors do as they practice medicine. They get test results, order the least invasive prescription possible, then retest, diagnose and prescribe in an iterative way. Over time, they gain the wisdom to increase the accuracy of their prescriptions. That is what strategic leaders need to do to move their organizations to the edge of chaos.

The sixth lesson is that in times of uncertainty, coherence can be encouraged through the application of *generative processes* in which strategies, tactics and actions emerge from dynamic interactive relationships inside and outside of organizations. Generative processes can reduce the negative effects produced by power differentials, high anxiety, low information flow, and lack of diversity.

In times of uncertainty strategic leaders foster generative processes and learn from the results by creating compelling visions which raise awareness and create anxiety. They connect important and diverse actors and ideas through dialogue, putting information into the system and expanding it beyond senior managers, reducing power differentials and allowing communities of practice to develop and self management to occur. Consequently strategic leaders who want to introduce change should reduce anxiety and power differentials, install sturdy control systems, and increase the rate of information flow.

The new science offers a seventh lesson for strategic leaders. For well over 5 decades, thoughtful students of management have shared the quest for more effective change models. Prevalent change models built on old science principles assume the system is linear and behavior and outcomes are predictable. Because outcomes are predictable, extensive advanced planning is required. Once a solution is chosen and the change program mapped out, it is communicated and rolled out through the ranks to engender participation and buy-in. When resistance rears its head it is overcome with power, persistence, and perseverance.

The problem is that old science organizations may operate successfully for many years by just improving on what they already know how to do. They perfect a winning formula. By *sustaining the frame*, they make the machine run faster, more efficiently and more productively. Eventually an unforeseen challenge disrupts this environment such as the introduction of vouchers as a way of introducing competition into public education or the use of a body scan to conduct a colonoscopy. At this point, when order and stability are challenged, "more-of-the-same" is not a successful strategy. It's time to *break the frame*!

Under new science tenets, change can be abrupt, radical, and as we have seen, unpredictable. Fit organizations are more successful at environmental change than those that are unfit. *Organizational fitness* is a term given to organizations that are more in tune with themes emanating from the environment. The degree of fitness can be expected to change as the environment changes. Therefore, continual rethinking, revising, and restructuring of the organization are necessary to stay connected to the environment.

The way to make a complex system work is to begin with a small working system, have multiple goals, strive to make good enough choices, and grow by *chunking*. Chunking simply means to start small when building a complex system. The UNIX computer operating system is a good example of an ever-evolving complex system that was built from chunks. The basic premise behind the UNIX system is that software functions should be small, simple, stand-alone bits of code that do only one thing well. These chunks are then embedded in an environment where they can easily pass their output to another *chunk*.

Another form of chunking takes its cue from organizational mutations that occur in nature. Once the mutation (chunk) is created it serves as the building block for future chunks. McDonalds' understands this form of chunking and continues to roll out new products built from the success of previous products; think McBurger, McChicken, McPizza. Steve Jobs of Apple also employed this tactic in the roll out of iTunes, iPod, and then iPhone. In postmodern times, a new product is built on the framework of a successful one—one chunk at a time.

The literature is saturated with old science linear change models that expect leaders to (a) create a vision of the future, (b) assess the current situation, (c) compare the present to the desired future and identify the gaps, (d) set goals and objectives to move from the present to the future and (e) move straight forward toward that future. The problem with this approach is that it has severe limits when environmental conditions become complex and chaotic. Strategic leaders understand these limits and place their faith and energy in Leadership Wheel actions guided by the new science principles and tactics summarized in Table 3.2.

DEVELOPING THE COGNITIVE CAPACITY TO THINK STRATEGICALLY

Strategy involves understanding the big picture, recognizing patterns and trends, excavating and prioritizing the primary issues, developing and predicting alternative scenarios, and establishing plan B and even C and D. "The essence of strategy is tradeoffs—making choices about what you won't do, in order to do other things uniquely well."[4] The strategic mindset understands tradeoff and is willing to turn down current opportunities for growth if those opportunities are not wholly consistent with the long-term strategy.

Developing a strategic mindset requires a different approach and a different kind of thinking. One thing is certain; linear thinking cannot effectively solve the problems we face in postmodern times. Most observers agree that the need for strategic thinking is more important now than at any previous time in history. The ability to think strategically enables leaders to cut through the fog, gain conceptual control and make sense of a vast array of forces, situations, ideas, and problems. However, there is confusion on what strategic thinking actually means. It is usually presented as a dichotomy between creative and analytical thinking. My per-

Table 3.2.   The Principles and Tactics Suggested by the New Science

Principles Suggested by the New Science	*Tactics Suggested by the New Science*
• Uncertainty	• Organizational fitness
• Ambiguity	• Minimum specification
• Complexity	• Flexible planning
• Nonlinearity	• Edge of chaos
• Interdependence	• Self organization
• Unpredictability	• Butterfly effect
• Environmental scanning	• Information flow
• Co-evolution	• Degree of diversity
• Emergence	• Contained anxiety
• Sensemaking	• Power differentials
• Reality is constructed	• Generative processes
• Adaptive work	• Chunking change

spective is that strategic leaders must be able to use both, while reflecting on their primary responsibilities of (a) asking the right questions rather than providing the right answers, (b) remaining open to emerging opportunities, and (c) selecting the appropriate ends, actions and tactics to further their goals. Furthermore, in today's complex environments strategic thinking is not just the purview of leaders at the top but leaders throughout the organization.

A few years ago, I invited Ralph Wilson, the Superintendent of Morganwood School District,[5] to talk to my leadership class about the role leadership theory played in his work. Wilson was recognized as the dean of superintendents in the state, not only because he had served in three school districts over the last 15 years, but also because his colleagues valued his thoughts and observations about their difficulties. His phone rang constantly as colleagues used him to check a perception or determine the significance of a situation. When I invited Ralph to be a speaker I had no idea what he would say, but I knew it would be interesting. Here's what he said:

> I really don't know why the professor invited me to share my thoughts about leadership theory with you tonight. I am sure he didn't confer with Professor Jacobson, who taught the theory class when I was taking my doctorate here, several years ago.
>
> In preparing for this class, I reviewed some of my old leadership textbooks. After reading for a while, I put them aside. They really didn't describe any-

thing I thought was relevant to my practice so I decided to structure my remarks around how I developed principles to guide my practice.

I don't know exactly when the light of understanding began to shine, but over the years I began to notice similarities in different events and activities. I guess the theorists call them phenomena. I gave these similarities code names, and I began to refer to them as my principles. My principles haven't been formed hastily. They help me understand individual and organizational behavior, and they do guide my actions. All of them are products of events that happen in the school district, in the world, reported in the newspaper and on TV, or in articles and books I have read on how to be a better leader and a better person. All of my principles have been gained the hard way. I earned them, and I have the battle scars to prove it. In the words of the scientists, they have been validated by my experiences—they work for me.

Even before I got my first job, I had a curiosity about why things happen and in particular, why they seem to happen in certain ways. With this basic curiosity, and by observing similar activities many times in three different school districts over the last 15 years, I noticed that when something unanticipated happened I would say to myself "Well there is number one at work, or there is number four at work." I was forming assumptions about why things were happening in a certain way. Every time I saw a similar activity, I was testing those assumptions with new information. Over the years I began to see how certain actions were related to other actions and actors. I'd generalize about situations from other situations I experienced. Although I didn't know it I was forming and mentally testing hypotheses.

After 15 years of seeing, experiencing, understanding, and acting, I've experienced most of what being a superintendent is all about and I have a pretty good sense of how my school district and the educational system works.

So I have set the stage for sharing my principles of operation with you. They are not in any special order. When I observe something that fits, I use the most likely candidate to understand the behavior I am seeing. If it doesn't work, I try another one. They help me understand events and they guide my actions. I am going to list them on the board and we'll see if they call up any images of understanding in your minds. Then I'll give you my interpretations.

Superintendent Wilson wrote the following four phrases on the blackboard and sat down.

- Don't die on every hill.
- Being right is not enough.
- Run for daylight.
- Deal with situations the way they are, not the way you want them to be.

The class entered a prolonged discussion of the principles. Students provided examples from their own experiences that they believed validated the principles. They even shared some of their own hard won principles.

Strategic leaders are grounded in reality. They think like artists most of the time and scientists some of the time. They try to figure out how things really work, not how they theoretically work, by seeing, experiencing, learning and acting. In a less practiced way, strategic leaders act much like crafty old Eleazer Hull, a New England sea captain whose services were much sought after, even though he had no formal training in navigation. When Hull was asked how he steered his ships with such a sure hand through the hazards and unknowns of the seas, he replied, "I go up on deck, listen to the wind in the rigging, get a drift of the sea, gaze at a star, and set my course."[6]

One year the state commissioner for navigation discovered that Hull was unlicensed and untrained in the science of navigation and told him he would have to get an education and upgrade his skills. Hull consented, graduated at the top of his class, received a certificate of achievement, and was told he was now licensed to return to sea. He did so. When he returned from his first 2-year-long voyage, his friends asked him how it felt to sail by the new scientific principles he had learned from books. Hull replied,

> Whenever I needed to chart my course I pulled out my maps, followed the equations, and calculated my location with mathematical precision. Then, I went up on the deck, listened to the wind in the rigging, got the drift of the sea, gazed at a star and corrected my computations.

Hull was crafty. He was able to marry analytic, creative, and reflecting thinking. He thought out the end and then the means. Maybe that is the answer to effective strategic leadership. Most researchers believe, however, that effective leaders demonstrate more complex mental processes than ineffective leaders. They point to the importance of leaders developing conceptual skills in order to; see the organization as a whole and understand how various parts of the organization relate to and affect each other; and to discern meaning in and establish relationships between events and bits of information that, at first glance, would appear to be discrete and unrelated.

Interpretation and meaning making are as much hallmarks of strategic leaders as they were with Captain Hull. The research is less clear on how they do it. Most interpretations begin with the leader's personal mastery[7] and his or her ability to think flexibly and strategically.[8] The mental processes necessary to work in ambiguous, complex, and problematic situations have been described as; analytical-logical or emotional-intuitive, conceptual, strategic thinking, holistic thinking, sensemaking; ecological thinking, practical thinking, contextual thinking, process thinking, creative thinking, critical thinking, and opportunity or obstacle thinking.[9]

In postmodern times, observation, interpretation, and synthesis are critical to success. Thinking is a mental activity that uses facts to work toward an end; seeks meaning or an explanation. It is self-reflective and uses reason to question claims and make judgments. Cognition is the way thinking is done. Mental or cognitive processes enable us to acquire knowledge by manipulating ideas and processing new information and beliefs in our minds. Memory, reasoning, the application of schemas and biases, making attributions, and thinking through a problem, are all examples of cognitive processes. Many important processes have been identified in the literature such as; chunking, cognitive reduction, cognitive heuristics, cognitive maps/schemas, mental imagery, creativity, mental models and schemas, critical thinking, pattern recognition, reframing, reflection, and systems thinking.[10] Perkins (1995) argues that there may be too many processes for the decision maker to remember, consider, and apply. Yet, regardless of the architecture presumed to underlie human cognition, knowledge must be retrieved, activated, and/or recreated to influence actions and perceptions.

Strategic thinkers work from a mental model of the complete system. This strategic mindset incorporates an understanding of both the external and internal context of the organization. Henry Mintzberg (1994) sees strategic thinking as a synthesizing process using intuition and creativity. The outcome is "an integrated perspective of the enterprise." From this integrated perspective, strategic thinking challenges existing assumptions and action alternatives, potentially leading to new and more correct ones.

Strategic thinking is creative, critical, and analytical although accomplishing all types of thinking simultaneously is difficult, because it requires the suspension of critical judgment. When applied correctly, strategic thinking enables the leader to recognize interdependencies, interrelationships and patterns, and make consequential decisions using both powers of analysis and intuition. Chilcoat (1995) and Pisapia, Reyes-Guerra, and Coukos (2005), suggest that effective leaders demonstrate more complex mental skills than ineffective leaders. Leithwood and Steinbach (1992) believe that efforts to improve the effectiveness of education may be more productive if more consideration was given to improving the quality of thinking and problem solving abilities of administrative staff and teachers rather than simply focusing on actions or behaviors.

Cognition is the way thinking occurs. Mental or cognitive skills enable the acquisition of knowledge by manipulating ideas and processing new information and beliefs in our minds. Information, memory, reasoning, application of schemas and biases, making attributions and thinking-through a problem are examples of cognitive skills. Some people take mental shortcuts, acting on what they expect to see.

My colleagues and I reviewed the literature on strategic thinking and identified three seemingly important cognitive processes thought to enable leaders to be successful in times of complexity; *systems thinking*, *reframing* and *reflection*. These processes allow the leader to make sense of complexities facing the organization and predict, respond and adapt to non-linear change opportunities and challenges. It is apparent that the three cognitive processes described in Table 3.3 complement each other. For example, the role of context, mental models, and framing is evident in each process.

Strategic leaders use information gathered during the process of reflection through systems thinking and reframing to make sense out of situations. These processes assist leaders to (a) reframe situations so they become clearer and understandable, (b) reflect then develop theories of practice which guide actions, and (c) think in more holistic ways. They also aid leaders in seeing events and problems in terms of concepts that are useful ways of thinking effectively about problems.

Andy Grove (1996) provides a good example of the use of strategic thinking, reframing and reflection in his story of the way leaders at Intel responded to a loss of $173 million dollars in 1986. The loss was attributed to Japan's emergence as the market leader in the memory chips business which was once the foundation of Intel's market preeminence. In 1985, the Japanese overtook Intel's lead in market share. Intel's initial response was to employ frame sustaining actions such as challenging the facts and then rationalizing them to fit their current conception of the company. Grove describes how eventually the facts had to be dealt with:

> We had meetings and more meetings, bickering and arguments, resulting in nothing but conflicting proposals. There were those who proposed what they called a "go for it" strategy. They rationalized, "let's build a gigantic factory dedicated to producing memories and nothing but memories, and take on the Japanese." Others proposed that we should get really clever and use an avant-garde technology; "go for it," but in a technological rather than a manufacturing sense and build something the Japanese produces couldn't build. Others were still clinging to the idea that we could come up with special-purpose memories. (Tedlow, 2006 p. 206)

Grove describes this period at Intel as *wandering in the valley of death*. After a year of aimless wandering Grove asked Intel founder and chairman Gordon Moore (of the famed Moore's Law) "if we got kicked out and the board brought in a new CEO, what do you think he would do?"

Table 3.3.   The Cognitive Skills Strategic Leaders Use
to Master Strategic Thinking

Reflecting: The skill used to process information, create knowledge from it, and apply it through practice.

Definition	*There are 5 abilities used in Reflecting:*
Reflection is the ability to use perceptions, experience and information to make judgments as to what has happened in the past and is happening in the present to help guide your future actions.	Ability to: • Recognize why certain choices work and others do not. • Question your assumptions and test whether your behaviors actually result in desired outcomes. • Use perceptions, experiences and knowledge to inform action and understand situations and how to think about them. • Use your own and other people's current and past perceptions, experience and knowledge to create an understanding of the present and the future.

Reframing: The skill used to collect and organize and reorganize information to define situational possibilities.

Definition	*There are 4 abilities used in Reframing*
Reframing is the ability to look at your reality using multiple perspectives, differing frameworks, different mental models, and different paradigms in order to generate new insights and options for actions.	Ability to: • Suspend judgment while you gather appropriate information. • Identify and understand • different mental models, paradigms and frameworks that you can use to think about situations, issues, or problems. • Use these identified frameworks to then understand a specific situation. • Review and reform your own and others' representational understanding of situations

Systems Thinking: The skill used to collect and think through and beyond information through an understanding of systems dynamics.

Definition	*There are 3 abilities used in Systems Thinking:*
Systems Thinking is the ability to see systems holistically by understanding the properties, forces, patterns and interrelationships that shape how a system works and provide you with options for action.	Ability to • Think holistically. • Recognize patterns and interrelationships. • Recognize and act upon the basic, underlying properties and patterns of a system's behavior.

Moore replied, "He would get us out of memories." In a moment of inspiration, Grove asked, "Why shouldn't you and I walk out the door, come back, and do it ourselves."[11] The rest is history. Intel got out of the memory chips business and into the microprocessor business and in 1987 saw its profits rise to $248 million. The Intel story is instructive for strategic leaders and strategic thinkers. Once a new frame was applied to the facts it became easier to understand both the predicament and the solution.

As we have seen, strategic thinking in all its forms is aided by the three important cognitive skills of systems thinking, reframing, and reflection. Each situation presents different motives, problems, and preferred outcomes that result in different choices of actions. The job of the leader is to use the skills and the information they gather to fit the circumstances they encounter.

Systems Thinking

Systems thinking refers to the leader's ability to see systems holistically by understanding the properties, forces, patterns, and interrelationships that shape the behaviors of the systems and decide which provide options for actions. This definition requires that leaders think holistically, defining the entire problem by extracting patterns in the information before breaking the problem into parts. This capability enables leaders to understand how facts relate to each other. It also enables them to understand what causes the demand for products or services that their organization produces before taking action to meet the demand and seek feedback to help individuals and the organization self correct.

Systems thinking helps the leader see patterns and interrelationships. It requires that the leader understands that he or she is part of a feedback process, not standing apart from one. This understanding represents a profound shift in awareness about the connectivity between members of organizations that influences the way a system works. The perspective gained from looking at feedback in this way suggests that everyone shares responsibility for problems generated by a system. This feedback perspective becomes especially significant when leading organizations. Organizations are always involved in skills that determine their output and direction. Peter Senge (1990, pp. 78–87) recommends that in order to understand the balancing feedback process the systems thinker must "start at the gap—the discrepancy between what is desired and what exists ... then look at the actions being taken to correct the gap" (p. 112). The leader must then translate the understanding into action. Senge also emphasizes that the "bottom line of systems thinking is leverage—seeing where actions and changes in structures can lead to significant, enduring improvements" (p. 114)

Framing and Reframing

Framing and then reframing refers to the leader's ability to switch attention across multiple perspectives, frames, mental models, and paradigms in order to generate new insights and options for actions. Typically, individuals reach for frames when they are trying to understand new, complicated events and how communications, goals, and initiatives could be perceived. However, the manner in which leaders frame a situation is crucial to their understanding and public reasoning. It enables them to sort through problems and opportunities, to see problems in ways that allow them to map out different strategies, and identify trends before others see them.

Framing and then reframing provides the advantage of multiple perspectives. It is a conscious effort made by leaders to generate new insights and options for actions. By rotating through appropriate conceptual models, activities and events observed, new usable knowledge can be produced. Using these cognitive skills, leaders can overcome Bolman and Deal's (2003) assertion that using singular frames filters out some things and allows others things to pass through quickly. "The ability to reframe experiences enriches and broadens a leader's repertoire and serves as a powerful antidote to self entrapment" (p. 4). Reframing a problem involves a conscious effort to size up a situation using multiple lenses. Bolman and Deal assert that:

> Managers who master the ability to reframe report a liberating sense of choice and power. They are able to develop unique alternatives and novel ideas about what their organization needs. They are able to tune in to people and events around them and are less often startled by organizational perversity, and they learn to anticipate the turbulent twists and turns of organizational life. The result is managerial freedom—and more productive, humane organizations. (p. 17)

Strategic leaders use framing and reframing to recognize when information is presented from only one perspective. They also demonstrate a willingness to seek different viewpoints on complex problems, to ask those around them what they think is changing, and to discuss solutions with critics and challengers as well as supporters.

Reflection

Reflection gives the leader the ability to see why certain choices work and others do not. Reflection is a cognitive skill that involves careful consideration of any belief or practice that promotes understanding of situations and then applies the newly gained knowledge to these situations. It relies on subjecting evidence, perceptions, and experience to critical scrutiny in order to make sense and meaning of situations prior to weaving the thinking into a theory of practice. By reflecting on both successes and failures, leaders begin to unpack the assumptions and values that lie beneath rules, regulations, and skills in work and everyday life. This constant effort of reevaluation and interpretation is an integral part of how leaders make sense of situations. Even though the leader is without all the information needed, the use of reflection offers the best possible option for action and prediction. Senge (1990, p. 2) uses the three types of reflection when he describes professional practice based on reflective thinking in terms of levels. He says,

> The first level is technical reflection, which is concerned with examining the efficiency and the effectiveness of means to achieve certain ends. The second level, practical reflection, involves examining not only the means but also the ends, questioning the assumptions and the actual outcomes. The third level is critical reflection, which considers the moral and ethical issues of social compassion and justice along with the means and the ends, encompassing the first two levels. (p. 2)

Of the three types, critical reflection is the most necessary for transforming oneself and one's organizations. As Mezirow (1990) points out, "we become critically reflective by challenging the established definition of a problem being addressed, perhaps by finding a new metaphor that reorients problem-solving efforts in a more effective way."(pp. 12–13).

Reflection refers to the leader's ability to weave logical and rational thinking together with experiential thinking through perceptions, experience, and information to make judgments as to what has happened and then creates intuitive principles that guide future actions. When leaders reflect they use perceptions, experience, and information to make judgments as to what has happened in the past and is happening in the present to help guide their future actions.

Strategic leaders using this cognitive skill are able to understand the past, the present, and perhaps the future by recognizing why certain choices worked and others did not. They demonstrate a willingness to question their assumptions and test whether their behaviors actually result in desired outcomes. Reflecting allows strategic leaders to use their perceptions, experiences, and knowledge to understand situations and inform their action.

What We Know So Far

Strategic thinking enables leaders to build a reservoir of insights and intuitions that they can call upon when confronted with ambiguity, complexity, and dilemmas. I assume that leaders who possess the ability to think strategically will be more effective than those who possess it in lesser quantities. To test this assumption, my colleagues and I constructed the Strategic Thinking Questionnaire (STQ).[12] Several studies have been completed that suggest that successful leaders think differently than less successful leaders. Pisapia, Reyes-Guerra, and Yasin (2006) studied 138 for-profit and not-for-profit managers and executives. Pang and Pisapia (2007) conducted a study of 543 school principals in Hong Kong. Zsiga (2008) studied 540 YMCA directors in the United States. Pisapia, Pang, Hee, Ying, and Morris (2009) studied 328 students preparing for educational management roles in Hong Kong, Malaysia, Shanghai, and the United States.

Six major impressions were left from statistical analyses presented in these studies. First, the use of strategic thinking capabilities distinguishes significantly between more and less successful leaders. Second, there is a cumulative impact when the three capabilities which form the strategic thinking construct are used. Third, the strength of the relationship between strategic thinking and leader success increases as leaders use the three dimensions in tandem. Fourth, the use of these skills is similar in the United States and Malaysia. Fifth, there is a significant relationship between strategic thinking capabilities and self directed learning. Sixth, the use of these skills improves with age and experience. My overall conclusion is that successful leaders use the three strategic thinking capabilities more often than less successful leaders.

These findings present several practical implications for management. They have special significance in terms of the rapid transformation leaders must undergo to be effective in the postmodern organizational environment. From a leadership selection point of view, the established differences presented here between successful and less successful leaders give us further criteria and measurement tools to use in considering who gets selected and promoted. From university-based training and professional development perspectives, the results of these studies indicate that in order for any organizational leadership program to be effective, it must contain an emphasis on the understanding, practice, and assessment of cognitive capabilities.

Table 3.4.   Samples of Specific Skills Strategic Leaders Use When Thinking Strategically

Reframing

1. Seek different perceptions of complex problems.
2. Track trends by asking everyone "what is new."
3. Ask those around you what they think is changing.
4. Discuss solutions with critics and challengers.
5. Engage in discussions with those who hold a different world view.
6. Seek other viewpoints before trying to solve a problem.
7. Using different viewpoints to map out different strategies.
8. Recognize when information is presented from only one perspective?

Reflecting

1. Review the experience of past decisions when considering current situations.
2. Understand why things worked base on the results of your decisions.
3. Reconstruct experiences in your mind.
4. Acknowledge the limitations of your own perspective.
5. Ask "WHY" questions to develop an understanding of problems.
6. Set aside specific periods of time to think about why you succeeded or failed.
7. Accept that your assumptions could be wrong.
8. Consider how you could have handled a past situation.

Systems Thinking

1. Seek a common goal when two or more parties are in conflict.
2. Seek the cause of a demand for your product or service before taking action.
3. Include those affected when creating a policy governing the use of limited resources.
4. Find that what you do influences what the organization does.
5. Find that one thing indirectly leads to another.
6. Define an entire problem before breaking the problem down into parts.
7. Try to understand how facts in a problem are related to each other.
8. Try to extract patterns in ambiguous information.
9. Seek feedback for to help the organization self-correct.
10. Identify and try to control external environmental forces which affect your work.

Source: Pisapia and Reyes-Guerra (2008). *The Strategic Thinking Questionnaire.*

In terms of the leaders themselves, the data produced by the use of the STQ provides the necessary feedback for their professional development on an important and hereto untouched set of skills. The addition of these skills promotes a wider use of strategic thinking throughout the organization and aids in turning the Leadership Wheel.

I have selected eight sample items in each of the three skill sets of strategic thinking from the STQ to demonstrate specific skills that when learned will enable you to think strategically. (See Table 3.4)

CLIFF NOTES

Habit 2. Agility: Developing the Strategic Mindset

This chapter began by establishing the importance of context to those who practice leadership. The tenets of the *old* and *new* science were specified and compared. Lessons from the new science were extracted and their relationships to acquiring a mindset that enables one to think strategically were established. The chapter concluded by presenting specific examples of each of these skills and discussing the research that supported them. In Appendix A, readers are offered the opportunity to take the STQ and use the results to first compare themselves to benchmark leaders before developing a plan of action to strengthen their use of the mental skills of systems thinking, reframing, and reflection.

The takeaways are that strategic leaders should: (a) learn those lessons of the new science which are learnable, (b) develop a strategic mindset by honing their ability to think strategically so they can lead in the post modern condition, and (c) The lessons of the New Science are learnable. Acquire and strengthen them. Strategic leaders can use the following strategies, actions and tactics to turn the Leadership Wheel.

- Leaders need to shift from an over reliance on the hierarchical skills of the twentieth century to a greater respect for the horizontal skills necessary in the twenty-first century.
- The status of mission and aspiration, and values and guiding principles must be elevated if they are to operate as a steering mechanism for organizational activity. Leaders should organize around simple rules and empower colleagues to adapt their work processes.

- Leaders following the old science tenets tend to over specify when they create visions and plans to guide organizational work.

- Planning must be a learning activity where results and processes are annually reviewed, unintended consequences are identified, and new strategies are developed.

- Organizations should get stuck *at the edge of chaos* since most observers believe that is where creativity and innovation occur.

- Coherence can be encouraged in times of uncertainty through the application of *generative processes* in which strategies, tactics and actions emerge from dynamic interactive relationships inside and outside of organizations

- The way to make a complex system work is to begin with a small working system, have multiple goals, strive to make good enough choices, and grow by *chunking*.

- Focus on the strategic implications of the information and allow others to work out the specifics

- The three strategic thinking skills should be used in tandem:

  o *Reframe* situations so they become clearer and understandable,
  o *Reflect* and develop theories of practice which guide actions
  o Use *systems thinking* to approach issues in more holistic ways.

- The use of strategic thinking skills are significantly related to leader success.

NOTES

1. Review the work of German political economist and sociologist Maximilian Weber (2002). One of the founders of the modern study of sociology and public administration His most famous works were his essay *The Protestant Ethic and the Spirit of Capitalism* and his studies on *bureaucracy* and on the classifications of *authority* to what he described as the inevitable move towards rationalization and capitalism, bureaucracy and the rational-legal state.

2. Edward Norton Lorenz (1917) is an American mathematician and meteorologist, and an early pioneer of the chaos theory. He discovered the strange attractor notion and coined the term *butterfly effect*. See also Butterflies, tornadoes, and time travel (2006). *American Physical Society.* Retrieved June 6, 2006, from http//www.aps.org/publications/apsnews/200406/butterfly-effect.cfm

3. See Stacey (1996); Stacey and Parker (1994); Kauffman (1995); Holland (1995); and Bak (1996)

4. Karnani (2006); and Porter (1996).

5. Name changed to protect privacy

6. Cited in Grimmett and MacKinnon (1992).

7. Covey (1989); Senge (1990).

8. For example, Bonn and Christodoulou (1996).

9. The mental processes necessary to work in ambiguous, complex, and conflictual situations have been described as analytical-logical or emotional-intuitive (Cohen et al., 1993, (Kets de Vries, 2001); conceptual (Chilcoat, 1995; Magee & Somervell, 1998); strategic thinking (Bonn, 2001); holistic thinking (Senge, 1990); sensemaking (Weick, 1995); ecological thinking (Capra, 2002); practical thinking (Fallesen, 1995); contextual thinking (Capra, 2002); process thinking (Capra, 2002); creative thinking (de Bono, 1996; Kendall, 1990); and opportunity or obstacle thinking (Godwin, Neck & Houghton, 1999; Neck & Manz, 1992).

10. Such as: chunking (Agor, 1988; Newell & Rosenbloom, 1981; Simon, 1947, 1999); cognitive reduction (Simon, 1947); cognitive heuristics (Stanwick, 1996); cognitive maps/schemas (March & Simon, 1958; Simon, 1947; Stanwick, 1996); mental imagery (Anthony, Bennett, Maddox, & Wheatley, 1993; Stanwick, 1996; creativity (De Pree, 1989); mental models and schemas (Riedel, Morasth, & McGonigle, 2000; Senge, 1990; Weick, 1995; critical thinking (Baron, 1994; Cohen et al., 2000; Halpren, 1996; pattern recognition (Cohen et al., 2000; Simon, 1947, 1999; reframing (Bolman & Deal, 2003; Morgan, 1986; reflection (Argyris & Schön, 1978; Dewey, 1933; Schön, 1983; and systems thinking (Senge, 1990).

11. Cited in Tedlow (2006).

12. *The Strategic Thinking Questionnaire* (STQ). A briefing sheet, found in the appendices, describes its development and psychometrics. See also Pisapia (2006a, b, & c), and Pisapia and Reyes-Guerra (2007, 2008), Pisapia, Reyes-Guerra, and Coukos-Semmel (2004, 2005).

CHAPTER 4

HABIT 3

Anticipating the Future

When the rate of change on the outside exceeds the rate of change on the inside, the end is in sight.

—Jack Welch, CEO of General Electric

Context matters and must be understood, sensed, interpreted, and acted upon. This chapter sketches the look -listen-learn sequence that guides leaders as they scan and interpret environmental trends. Externally, environmental change and turbulence presents both threats and opportunities which must be interpreted to determine the appropriate responses. The chapter uses the Strengths, Opportunities, Weaknesses, and Threats (SWOT) analysis tool to develop a clear understanding of the external environment. Internally, followers are seen as the

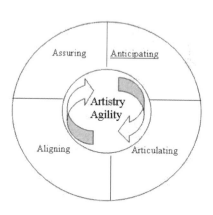

Figure 4.1.   The Leader's Wheel.

The Strategic Leader: New Tactics for A Globalizing World, pp. 73–98
Copyright © 2009 by Information Age Publishing

facilitators or inhibitors of change efforts. Hence they must be understood and identified to provide the leader information needed in the implementation of organizational changes. Several tools are described that can be used to gather the social intelligence necessary to understand different types of followers, their social networks and their readiness for change.

CONTEXT MATTERS!

Leaders of all genres—managerial, public, and governmental—feel the tensions from a globalized society with local constraints. They are confronted with multiple demands emanating from various stakeholders. They face pressure from customers and consumers to provide more value. In some respects, all organizations are asked to deliver the product at a lower cost and a higher quality, in less time. Profit-based organizations must become more profitable. Schools must provide better educated students. Drug companies must become more cost effective. Government must protect consumers without stifling growth. The list of pressures and expectations is endless. The challenge is how to maneuver in a world with few easy answers, yet with great expectations.

Unfortunately some leaders don't think about the context. They treat every organization the same way and act accordingly. In reality, some contexts are stable and secure, while others are wild and evolving. The strategic leader must understand both, to determine which one is providing the underlying psychology of the context they are working in, and then make the context work for them and their organization.

One thing is evident. Understanding context has become absolutely essential to grasping what is taking place in society, no matter what the area of examination. Unfortunately many leaders are unable to identify critical messages coming from their environment.

Consider Ferdinand de Lesseps, the builder of the Suez Canal. At the early age of 28, he served as the French vice-consul in Alexandria, Egypt and made many friends. At the age of 44, after several other diplomatic postings and a few missteps, de Lesseps found himself out of work. However, his dream to build a canal that crossed the strip of land connecting the Mediterranean to the Red Sea persisted. It was an ambitious project that would reduce sailing to the far western countries on the Pacific Rim by 10 thousand miles right at the time when short trade and supply routes were in demand. Returning to Egypt, de Lesseps reacquainted himself with the Turkish governors who ruled Egypt at the time and received a 'firman' or decree by Viceroy Said to run the Canal for 99 years after its completion. By 1859 the finances were in hand and the work of joining the two seas, by building a sea level canal without locks, began. The flat desert strip next to the Sinai Peninsula proved easy to excavate and the canal was finished and functioning in less than 10 years.

Emboldened by his success, de Lesseps next held the Isthmus of Panama in his sights. The task seemed similar; create a direct route between the Atlantic and Pacific oceans, thus eliminating the need to navigate the thousands of miles around Cape Horn. Married to the strategy he used at Suez, he proposed a canal without locks, even though the terrain in Panama was hilly compared to the flat topography of the Egypt desert. He *anticipated* that the task in Panama was similar to the one he faced in Suez.

Unfortunately, unlike Suez, this new venture was a massive failure. De Lesseps and his team failed to correctly estimate the excavation needed for a sea level canal without locks in the hilly Panamanian terrain. By the time he agreed to install locks the project was over budget and behind schedule.

De Lesseps might have salvaged his name and legacy if he had understood that leadership is a situated practice. The situation or context does not simply affect what leaders do, it constrains and enables what leaders can do and how they can do it. de Lesseps would have been better served if he had identified aspects of the situation that were critical—like terrain, corrupt politicians and malaria—before he attempted to exercise leadership. The lesson de Lesseps offers leaders of all types is to appreciate the patterns and power emanating from the environment, apply interventions judiciously, and recognize that a limited set of strategies, actions or tactics cannot be relied on.

Like de Lesseps, most leaders confronted with postmodern challenges find themselves caught between the need for change and the need for stability - between order and chaos. On one hand, their organizations and people require order. On the other hand, their organizations must change to meet new environmental pressures. Is it any wonder Ron Heifetz, (1994) Director of the Leadership Education Project at Harvard University's John F. Kennedy School of Government, characterizes leadership as adaptive work where leaders create organizations that can adapt to environmental changes quickly and in an orderly fashion. Leaders face a dilemma of how to provoke change without undermining the need for organizational stability. In order to do so they must first understand that in complex, ambiguous environments, flexibility and adaptability are the only sustainable leadership attributes.

THE HABIT OF ANTICIPATING

The pressures for change often stem from forces outside of the leader's control. Strategic leaders, therefore, must develop the antenna that enables them to understand threats and opportunities stemming from their internal and external environment. During my seminars and classes, I find little resistance to my use of the term *postmodern condition* to describe the environment surrounding organizations. Perhaps we are losing our innocence about how the world we live in works. There is a growing understanding that, while in the past things were sure, today they are less certain. The trust we placed in our old maps has dissipated. Strategic leaders understand that it is impossible to predict long term changes. They know that direction emerges without prior planning and that they need new maps to sail through uncharted waters.

In the movie the *Dead Poets Society* (Weir, 1989) Robin Williams advised his class this way:

> Why do I stand up here?... I stand upon my desk to remind myself that we must constantly look at things in a different way. The world looks very different from up here.... Just when you think you know something, you have to look at it in another way, even though it may seem silly or wrong.... Now, when you read, don't just consider what the author thinks, consider what you think.

There are many other examples. For instance, Bill Gates and Andy Grove periodically took sabbaticals from their organizations to gain an understanding of contextual changes and how they might affect their organizations' positioning and product lines.

A habit of anticipating helps strategic leaders learn about their context. In business schools, long range planning which is analytic, linear explicit, and emotionally neutral is promoted. It represents the hard side of anticipating. I suggest that an inductive process of gathering external and internal information by using scanning tools to look for patterns and relationships, then drawing conclusions, will be more effective in turning the Leadership Wheel in the postmodern condition. By being *alert* to the themes stemming from the environment, strategic leaders are better able to navigate through it. They can also identify power networks which can stifle or facilitate their efforts to move the organization from A to Z

Eleazer Hull, the crafty old seaman, and Superintendent Wilson, both introduced earlier, understood the connection between *anticipating* and *artistry*. They thought like artists most of the time and scientists some of the time. They tried to figure out how things really work, not how they theoretically work, by seeing, experiencing, learning and only then acting.

In my consulting and teaching I encourage leaders to use the look-listen-learn[1] sequence to understand the internal and external demands of their organization and then create a statement of strategic intent. Look outside and listen, look inside, and listen; from these activities learn and envision necessary changes. The look-listen-learn sequence pictured in Figure 4.2 is a simple, predictable, and uncomplicated sequence strategic leaders can use to anticipate changes in their context that allows them to sense change in the environment, gather and interpret relevant information about the change, and suggest significant changes that the organization must address.

The conclusions reached by going through the look-listen-learn process enables leaders to call on parts of the organization to act upon suggestions, introduce new processes and services, monitor internal changes and the impact of those changes.

Strategic leaders are usually early adopters of ideas—they have the knack of recognizing the value of a new idea. While some leaders look internally for a vision to guide the organization, the strategic leader first looks externally for threats and opportunities that the organization might need to address. Looking, in this context, refers to examining the current strategic situation, including first external opportunities and threats and then internal strengths and weaknesses. It is primarily used to reduce uncertainty found in the postmodern condition. It allows strategic leaders to assess where they are by looking into the future for threats and opportunities that could be significant.

Strategic leaders are information junkies. This is a good thing since they are constantly and continuously bombarded with ambiguous information

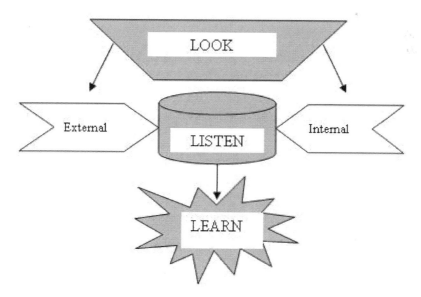

Figure 4.2. Anticipating tactics.

that tends to overload their cognitive processing behaviors. The information comes from people both inside and outside their field, reports, hearings held by public bodies and conclaves where information about the future is discussed. Rather than looking for information that confirms what they expect they look for information that refutes their expectations. Rather than collecting information and then interpreting it, the post modern condition requires that it be interpreted as it is collected. This eliminates the paralysis by analysis reported by several researchers.[2]

Information in its raw form must be processed, analyzed, synthesized, and interpreted. Interpreting is the most difficult skill to acquire. It takes specific expert knowledge of the industry and the wisdom that comes from experience. It is difficult since there is no way leaders can divorce their interpretations from their values, risk propensity, decision-making style, and their locus of control. Scholars, such as Bluedorn, Johnson, Cartwright, & Barringer (1994), suggest that cultural and functional homogeneity, tenure, and external locus of control are negatively related to desire and ability to adapt to one's environment. However, higher educational attainment, heterogeneity and internal locus of control are positively related to adaptation.[3] Many leaders try to overcome these blind spots by interpreting the information through some combination of the validity of their intuition, the wisdom of their peers, and performance.

Structured Planning Tools

Successful leaders supplement these three beliefs with structured scanning tools. In the 1980s, the ability to look back and look ahead to gain perspective and anticipate trends and challenges, took a leap forward with the development of sharper analytic tools. These tools helped leaders make better sense of their environment. The honor roll includes; situational analysis; scenario development; market segmentation and product life cycle analyses; industry structure analysis; Porter's (1979, 1996) five-force analysis of buyers, suppliers, entry/exit barriers, substitutes for the customer, and competitor rivalry, Strengths, Weaknesses, Opportunities and Threats analysis (SWOT); Strengths, Opportunities, Aspirations, and Results analysis (SOAR), and Political, Economic, Sociocultural and Technological factors (PEST).[4]

The SWOT analysis is still the gold standard and most widely used method strategic leaders use to examine the current strategic situation in an organization. It provides a useful lens to anticipate the impact of the environment on an organization. The technique usually proceeds by performing an inventory of an organization's strengths and weaknesses, followed by an assessment of potential threats and opportunities. In the strategic leadership framework we reverse the order since in the post modern condition the organization has strengths and weaknesses only in the context of emerging external trends, demographics, and competitor strategies. So, strategic leaders start by identifying the opportunities and threats found in the external environment then proceed by identifying the organizations strengths and weaknesses in relationship to external needs.

SWOT analysis is useful for summarizing findings from the internal and external environment. It enables leaders to ask "what-if" questions and create an issue agenda that can be further interpreted. It is a categorization method of interpreting information by placing it into four categories: strengths, weaknesses, opportunities and threats. One method of performing this analysis is to:

1. Self-administer a set of questions found on Table 4.3 about first external current or potential opportunities and threats and then internal strengths and weaknesses.

Table 4.1. Questions To Ask When Conducting a SWOT Analysis

LOOK

The SWOT Analysis

STRENGTHS	WEAKNESSES
• What is your strongest asset?	• What can be improved?
• Do you consider your team strong? Why?	• In what areas do competitors have the edge?
• What do you offer that makes you stand out from the rest?	• What necessary expertise/manpower do you currently lack?
• What unique resources do you have?	• Do you have cash flow problems?
• Do you have any specific marketing expertise?	• Are you relying primarily on just a few clients or customers?
• Do you have a broad customer base?	• What additional weaknesses are impeding your organization's growth or effectiveness?
• What additional skills does your organization possess that you believe are difference makers?	
OPPORTUNITIES	THREATS
• What trends to do see in your organization's environment?	• What obstacles do you face in taking advantage of the opportunities the environment offers?
• What trends might impact your organization's environment?	• What is the competition doing that you are not?
• What external changes present interesting opportunities?	• What challenges can be turned into opportunities?
	• Are economic forces affecting your bottom line?
	• What are the additional threats?

2. Ask people in various parts of the organization a similar set of questions.

3. Compare and analyze the results.

4. Keep your answers short, simple, specific, and realistic.

Finding opportunities involves identifying beneficial trends, new technologies, and new needs of customers. Threats can be thought of as vulnerabilities and obstacles to overcome which come from aggressive competitors, successful competitors, negative economic conditions, government regulation, changing attitudes, and in general areas in which you are vulnerable. Don't forget to consider such items as price wars, technology shifts, mergers and joint ventures as you interpret your information.

SWOT-like framing can help uncover useful insights but sometimes the process can be constrained by an organizational emphasis on mandates and mission. Similarly, when used with a group rather than by an individual leader, it can become a political process through which the values of key stakeholders determine what is a strength or a weakness. Nutt and Backoff (1995) suggest that as a rule of thumb, strategic leaders working in the private sector are pulled toward opportunities. Leaders working in public sector organizations are more apt to see threats.

LOOK OUTSIDE THE ORGANIZATION

After conducting a seminar on strategic thinking in New Delhi, I reflected on my experience. I came away from India with a sense that this land is where chaos and opportunity is king. This conclusion was primarily drawn from observations I made while being chauffeured from New Delhi to Agra to visit the Taj Mahal. The roadway was crowded with bicycles, auto rickshaws, small cars, tractors, motorcycles and anything else that could carry people from one place to another, even a wagon pulled by camels and another by water buffalos. The two wheelers particularly caught my eye. Men in helmets drove the bike with their spouse sitting side saddle on the back and without a helmet; often they were holding a baby. Sometimes a small boy or girl sat western style in front of their father.

It was interesting to see how the logistics worked themselves. There were plenty of police along the route but instead of directing traffic they stood back and watched it. There were traffic lights but they went unheeded except in the city itself. When I inquired of my driver if the chaos created problems for the safety of the travelers, he replied, "they will adjust." I sat back for the rest of the ride and observed people *adjusting* and listened to my driver tooting the car's horn every time we passed a car because the road was so congested and narrow that many vehicles did not have side mirrors. It was as if there was an inner force guiding them. Little did I know that while I enjoyed the pleasures of the Taj Mahal a revolution was in the making!

Ratan Tata ascended to the chairmanship of the Indian based Tata Group in 1991, after having served on the conglomerate's top policy making group since 1974. At the time the Tata Group (a holding company for 150 companies at the time) was a personality driven, loosely knit group of seemingly independent companies. It was a small version of India—huge, sprawling, complex, and full of heritage. It had evolved over 53 years of stewardship by Ratan's uncle, the revered J. R. D. Tata.

After consolidating power, Ratan sensed that the business environment was changing from a seller's to a customer's market. For Ratan the charge was clear; the Tata Group would have to transform itself fast by being more concerned with its customers, the quality of its products, and its brand image in the marketplace. His growth dicta was to compete with global benchmarks by focusing on knowledge based industries and market branded products to double revenues every four years and net profits every three. The company, he stated, should globalize, be skill intensive, and be among the top three in an industry or exit. He suggested the Tata Group had been inward looking, seeing only India as its market, and focused on getting bigger there rather than overseas. His main concern was with mindset and attitudes. He saw his most important tasks as creating a new mindset, allowing empowerment down the line, and encouraging sensitivity to customers' needs. The changed mindset started with him.

By 1990, the Tata Group accounted for two-thirds of all trucks sold domestically. In 1991, Ratan made a move into passenger cars with the introduction of a station wagon and a sport utility vehicle. He said that passenger cars were chosen because India was a country of 700–800 million people but the incidence of ownership of the passenger car was extremely small. By 1999, Ratan noted that the country was consuming about a million cars and 5 million scooters and motorbikes annually. The population stood around a billion plus, with 18 million people added each year, and 40% of the population under the age of 16. Ratan concluded that there had to be a growth potential in personal transport, not so much at the high end as at the lower end of the market.

Based on his synthesis and interpretation of the opportunities afforded by the market in India and the strengths the Tata Group had displayed after their first foray into the passenger car market, Ratan invested $400 million in the development of a four door hatchback that sold for just $4,100. The car was officially named the Indica but informally it was known as *Ratan's folly*. The Indica was positioned to compete with Suzuki as well as Ford, General Motors, Hyundai, and Daewoo. Ratan Tata staked his reputation on it and therefore gave the project much of his time; often spending weekends at the factory to help with the rollout. The Indica V2 became the third-biggest seller in India.

Ratan did not rest on his laurels for long. He had already seen the same potential customers on the motor bikes that I observed during my travels. He knew that India has approximately 65 million scooter owners, mostly men, and that only 58 million Indians, out of the country's one point one billion population; earn more than $4,400 a year.[5] In 2003, he reframed the challenge to make the potential consumers at this low income segment of the market into car owners. He announced plans to build a car costing approximately $2,500 dollars, with four doors so it could transport a family of five.

Dubbed the *People's Car* by the media, the car was meant to be within the reach of everyone who had ever dreamed of owning a car, not just the people who could afford one. When asked, Ratan explained;

> launching an automobile is a risky endeavor, as you point out. But we have been satisfied with the success of the Tata Indica and are undertaking the 1-lakh ($2,500) car with an even stronger base of competence. We are confident that the investment will prove a wise one.[6]

On January 10, 2008, at the New Delhi Auto Show, and with the immortal words "a promise is a promise," Ratan Tata unveiled the world's cheapest car—the $2,500 Tata Nano. For Ratan, the event capped a 17 year quest to transform the Tata Group into a world brand.

Ratan Tata suggested the following in the epilogue to Lala's (2006) book *The Creation of Wealth*, about the Tata Group's emergence as a global company:

> If I reflect on what these 10 years have been for me personally, they have been a mixed bag. There is some satisfaction that I've seen the group come together in many ways, but at the same time there is a sense of frustration at the resistance to change from many of my colleagues that I have seen through this period of time ... it has been a hard and sometimes unrewarding experience.

The case of the "People's Car" provides a solid backdrop to understanding the role of anticipating in strategic leadership. Ratan Tata scanned the environment and found opportunities in the form of a growing economy and population. He also found threats in the form of foreign corporations in the market place that had a significant head start in the design and engineering needed to manufacture cars. Knowing his penchant for strategic planning, I am sure Ratan used some formal analytic tools to collect, synthesize, and interpret the data found in the case.

LOOK INSIDE THE ORGANIZATION

Strategic leaders also look inside the organization for strengths and weakness relative to the opportunities and threats presented by the external environment. Assessing strengths includes understanding your advantages, core competencies, profit centers, and in general where you do well. To uncover areas needing strengthening you might look into areas you are avoiding such as lack of resources, and in general where you are doing poorly. Don't forget to consider such areas as Web presence, company image, quality, service, pricing, and work culture.

Scanning also requires an internal look to determine the feasibility of any response to changes that are needed in your organization. Strong corporate cultures have just as powerful affect on the behavior of people working in the organization as strong work cultures. Yet, while organizations try to create a strong corporate culture, the work culture is the important determinant of resistance to change so it must be anticipated and understood before change strategies are attempted. The process is not easy.

Strategic leaders must develop the social perceptiveness, intelligence if you will, to understand the essence of followers.[7] Why do they behave the way that they do? Why are some energizers and others energy sappers? How open are they to change? What motivates them? When strategic leaders answer these questions they are building social intelligence.

Acquisition of social intelligence leads to understanding. Understanding leads to alignment which enables leaders to build trusting relationships, norms, and supportive networks externally and internally. While the acquisition of social intelligence is important for leaders in all organizations, it is more important in public organizations where direct tactics such as edicts or interventions are less available. Therefore, where external constraints are numerous, indirect tactics such as cooptation must be used. (Nutt & Backoff, 1993) In the following paragraphs I offer several tools for gathering the social intelligence that enables the leader to understand the nature of followers, their social networks and readiness for change. The intelligence that stems from use of these tools enables leaders to create a sound understanding of the internal strengths and weaknesses as they relate to the opportunities and threats their external scanning uncovered.

Colleagues and Other Followers

In seminars and classes, I often begin the discussion on followership with this question, "What kind of followers do you want to work with?" I get similar answers from students and practitioners alike. They want people who can work autonomously, work without supervision, be self directed, take initiative, and solve problems; people who are committed to working together for change and will help establish a continuous learning mechanism that allows individuals and their organizations to rapidly adapt to changing conditions. These responses are true to the reality of most modern organizations' use of project-based work which requires followers who can be self-leaders or at least self-managers.

Follower self direction brings with it the paradox of empowerment. Are initiatives from above seen as a demand or an opportunity? The leader must identify the members of the organization who will accept and seek responsibility, exercise self-direction and self control, and take initiative. Too many times followers have interpreted efforts to empower as a license to do what they want to do. When leaders use the word empowerment they mean freedom to do the organization's work.

Good followers, like good leaders, are self motivated; they exercise critical thinking, give constructive criticism, assume ownership, and take initiative. Why are some followers exemplary? Robert Kelley (1992) proposes a useful taxonomy that strategic leaders can use to understand the motivations and goals of followers. He says followers can be characterized by performance on two dimensions; independent critical thinking and active engagement. Independent critical thinking means they think for themselves and give constructive criticism. Active engagement means that they take initiative and assume ownership. Kelley uses these dimensions to create four follower types: exemplary, alienated, passive, and conformist.

As seen in Table 4.2, I define the generic concept of followers more specifically as colleagues, competitors, subordinates, and laggards. Seven categories of followers can be teased out of the descriptions rather than the four pictured. Every category, except colleagues, has a positive and a negative side.

Competitive followers are mavericks. They think for themselves and carry a large dose of skepticism. At one time they might have been colleagues who became disenchanted with the current direction or practices. Positive competitors relish the role of the devil's advocate and stick up for the unheard voices. Destructive competitors can be troublesome. They assume the role of the "rebel without a cause." They are headstrong, lack judgment, and many times they are adversarial to the point of being hostile. They are certainly not team players and can drain the spirit of the organization.

Positive laggards rely on the leader's judgment and thinking. They take action only when the boss gives instructions and they let the people who get paid to handle headaches handle them. Negative laggards put in their time and little else. They follow the crowd without thinking about why,

Table 4.2. What Type of Follower Are You?

	Independent Critical Thinking	
	Competitors	*Colleagues*
	Think for themselves	Think for themselves
	Give constructive criticism	Give constructive criticism
	Dodge responsibility	Task initiative
	Require constant supervision	Assume ownership
Passive	*Laggards*	*Subordinates*
	Don't think	Take direction
	Must be told what to do	Don't challenge leader
	Dodge responsibility	Get job done without supervision
	Require constant supervision	after they are told what to do
	Dependent Critical Thinking	

Passive ... *Active*

Note: Adapted from *The Power of Followership* by Robert Kelley copyright 1992 by Consultants to Executives and Organizations, Ltd. Used by permission of Doubleday, a division of Random House, Inc.

and they require close supervision. They lack ideas, are flattering and self deprecating. They are unwilling to take unpopular positions and are adverse to conflict.

Subordinate followers accept assignments and gladly do the work. They are team players who trust and commit to the leader and the organization. They stay tuned to the shifting winds of organizational politics. They know how to work the system to get things done. They play by the rules and are adept at keeping things in perspective. They often stop the organization from going overboard. On the other hand, negative subordinates play political games. They bargain to maximize their own self interest. They are adverse to risk and are adept at covering their backside. They carry out their responsibilities with the enthusiasm of the bureaucrat who adheres to the letter rather than the spirit of the rule.

Colleagues think for themselves. They find and contribute to the critical path of the organization while innovatively and creatively working around barriers. They actively give constructive criticism and wholeheartedly apply their skills for the benefit of the organization. They don't hesitate. They take action, assume ownership, share information and go above and beyond their duties. They are tuned into the statement of strategic intent and are able to work towards its direction independently and with low supervision. Unlike the previous categories, colleagues have few negative characteristics.

Organizations populated with a majority of exemplary colleagues will be more successful than those who are not. Thomas Jefferson is an excellent example of a colleague. At 33 years of age he was asked to be the junior member of a self-managed committee tasked with drafting the American Declaration of Independence. The committee was made up of two notable individuals, John Adams and Benjamin Franklin, whose senior status and outspoken manner made them prominent leaders in the Congress. The committee, which also contained delegates Roger Sherman and Robert R. Livingston, asked Jefferson to be the scribe because of his reputation with prose.

Jefferson completed his draft of the declaration in late June of 1776. A gifted and proud writer, he watched as first Adams, and then Franklin, made 47 alterations to his draft before it went to the full committee. The amended document made its way to Congress on June 28 of 1776 as a committee report. The debate that followed began on July 1 and lasted 3 days. Congress made another 39 alterations, some substantive, before agreeing on the morning of July 4, 1776 to endorse the Declaration of Independence. Most of the alterations to the document are in Jefferson's hand. Later he wrote about the process as a painful and humbling experience.[8]

This was a powerful lesson in followership for Jefferson. He learned that the best efforts of followers may not be what are most needed or expedient for a given situation. Colleagues accept this fact and continue to make significant contributions because they want what is best for the organization rather than what will satisfy their ego. Through the painful experience described above, Jefferson learned about the difficulty of working with other powerful or dogmatic personalities, the value of building consensus, and the importance of accepting rejection. Today, Jefferson is rightly credited as the author of the Declaration of Independence, yet few people comprehend how what he learned as a follower in the Congress helped him become one of the most successful leaders of his nation and the world.

Using the follower categories, strategic leaders can examine the numbers of followers in each category and see if clusters appear. They can then determine the potential strength of support or non support and begin coalition building. Certainly organizations that contain large numbers of followers like Jefferson have an internal strength that would be helpful in addressing the opportunities and threats emanating from the environment.

Social Networks

Every leader and organization is affected by social relationships and informal, rarely visible, communication networks. One of the hardest things for leaders to learn is that, as they assume more leadership responsibility, they must depend on the help of others whom they do not know very well. Who are these people? What characteristics do they have? How can they be supported? Social network and opinion leader research is a useful tool to ferret out these relationships and make them visible.

A social network is a group of people who are connected through friendships, families or work in the organization. Relationships formed through the network can limit the leader's ability to influence success since much of the network exists below the surface. Many leaders and managers believe they understand the networks around them. However, studies show that the accuracy of their network perceptions varies widely. Some researchers estimate that leaders and managers only know the social links of the five or six people closest to them. Inaccuracy increases dramatically as they move to the periphery of their followers.[9] In contemporary times organizational structures are more flat, flexible, and team-oriented. It becomes critical to map the flow of information, including who shares knowledge with whom, because these relationships play a critical role in determining how problems are solved and how successful leaders will be in achieving goals. The map serves as a good tool for; communication of ideas, preparing for organizational change, selection of leaders, creation of taskforces, and unit or organizational mergers.

Network analysis is particularly helpful when the leader assumes a new position or plans a new project. It helps avoid the fragmentation of established and productive networks. Developing a map of individuals and the social ties that link them can provide useful information. How does information flow within the organization? To whom do people turn for advice? Who do they respect? Who are just the carriers of information? Are there cliques of followers who are not sharing what they know as effectively as they should? By such analyses, leaders can know the likelihood of success before they start.

Social networking that develops superior connections among followers explains why some people are successful in a particular setting. However, while a cohesive network with no subgroups splitting off is thought of as healthy, it can also create a downward leveling of norms because such cohesion can exclude new information and people, limit member freedom, and place excessive claims on group members. The leader's task is to understand the social network present in their organization so they might use or attempt to change it to achieve positive outcomes for the organization.

The informal network tends to be a series of small multiple networks that overlap and are linked together by some individuals who serve to validate information and others who span boundaries. Katz and Lazarsfeld (1955) and Katz (1987) called the former individuals opinion leaders and proposed a two-step hypothesis to explain that those followers with most access to media develop an understanding of the issue and then explain and diffuse the content to others.

Everett Rogers (2003) also reported the presence of opinion leaders and used the two step hypothesis in his studies of innovation diffusion. He found that most initiators of change mistakenly broadcast their messages to all receivers believing this is the quickest way to encourage the adoption of innovations. Like Katz and Lazarsfeld, he found that messages are received by intermediaries who, in turn, retransmit them to the members of their network. Rogers was also able to differentiate between opinion leaders and communicators.

Rodgers (2003) discovered another phenomenon among followers. When some people talk, others listen, and are influenced by the talker's interpretation of events. Opinion leaders have a great deal of influence on the interpretation of events, communications, and activities. They broker opinion within and across social boundaries and between groups. Opinion leaders may be found in official positions, but they may also be staff members without any official authority. More than likely they are trusted coworkers, valued friends, or respected individuals with similar values. Opinion leaders are important because they either provide or withhold support for management directives. Organizational members take their cues from them. Some opinion leaders work just with internal issues and people. Others serve as bridges from their group to other groups internally or externally.

Rogers (2003) called people who talk, but do not validate, communicators. Communicators have little influence on the interpretation of information. Communicators serve as conduits in the information pipeline. They fill the structural holes in an organization by connecting one network to another.

Look at the social networks of the two organizations presented in Figures 4.3a and 4.3b. In the diagrams two individuals are connected if they regularly talk to each other. Some of these people are considered opinion leaders if one of the participants believes the other or acts on their conversations. For instance, in organization #1, position 44 is the only opinion leader in the organization—opinion leadership is centralized. If 44 is removed or damaged, the network would quickly fragment into unconnected sub-networks. A network centralized around a well connected hub can fail abruptly if that hub is disabled or removed. Consider what happened in Nazi Germany when Hitler and his cabinet were isolated and then destroyed.

In a less centralized network, like organization #2, there is no single point of communications failure. Many nodes or links can fail while allowing the remaining nodes to continue to reach each other over other network paths. Consider the continuing survival of al Qaeda in the face of

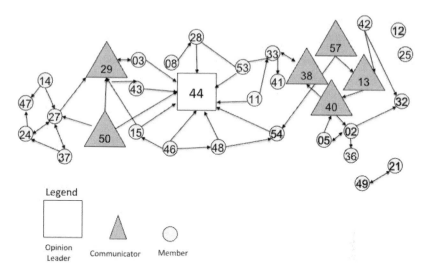

Figure 4.3a. Network analysis of organization 1.

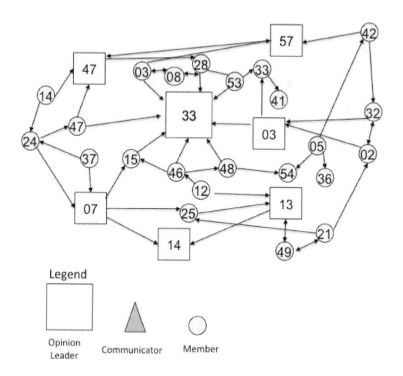

Figure 4.3b. Network analysis of organization 2.

the capture of many of its leaders. Networks of low centralization fail gracefully and slowly.

In organization #2 there are many opinion leaders: positions 33, 47, 07, 14, 13, 03, and 57. Review the diagrams and answer these questions. Which organization will be more open to new ideas and opportunities? Which would be more difficult to change?

The shape of the social network helps determine its usefulness. Look at the relationship among organizational members 27, 14, 47, 24 and 37 in organization #1. Individuals in relationships such as these, for instance a group of friends who do things together, already share the same knowledge and opportunities. Now look at the location of member 57 who has connections in the organization and also outside the immediate network. Member 57 might be a boundary spanner who has connections to other social worlds and thus is likely to have access to a wider range of information. The opinion leaders and power wielders can be identified by understanding their centrality to people and information. Member 44 in organization #1, and member 33 in organization #2, offer good examples of centrality.

For individual and organizational success, it's better to have connections to a variety of networks rather than many connections within a single network. Woodrow Wilson, the 26th American President, understood this phenomenon. When Europe plunged into war in 1914, like most Americans Wilson believed the country should remain neutral. He saw America's role as that of peace broker. However, on May 15, 1915, the ship Lusitania was torpedoed by a German submarine with 1,265 passengers aboard (128 Americans) and the dream of neutrality for many Americans was shattered. Wilson tried to stem the flow of events by demanding an apology from Germany. He stayed his neutral course as long as possible. His position was that America's interests where better served if he maintained connections with both the Germans and the allies. Wilson's restraint now seems remarkable given the wave of American anger over the sinking of the *Lusitania* and later the White Star liner *Arabic*. He held to his position of neutrality until the start of 1917, when British intelligence intercepted a secret German communication to Mexico promising United States territory in return for supporting the German cause. On April 2, 1917, Wilson finally relented and asked Congress for a formal declaration of war.[10]

Boundary spanners like President Wilson can exercise influence or act as brokers within their social networks by creating a bridge between two networks that are not directly linked. However, power within organizations has been found to come more from the degree to which an individual has created a web of influence internally.

In organization # 1, member 44 has the most direct connections in the network, making him/her the most active in the hub that the organization moves around however others regard him or her. If they value 44's opinion, then 44 is an opinion leader for them. So, if 44 nods his/her head up and down, a lot of others will nod their head up and down.

While member 44 has many direct ties, 50, 57, and 38 have few direct connections; less than the average in the network. Yet in many ways they have the best connections in the network. They play a broker role by connecting two important constituencies which puts them in an excellent position to monitor the information flow in the network. They have the best visibility as to what is happening in the network and they can have great influence over the information flow. Without 50, 57, and 38, member 44 would be cut off from information and knowledge. These boundary spanners are more central than their immediate neighbors whose connections are only local and within their immediate cluster. Boundary spanners are also well-positioned to be innovators since they have access to ideas and information flow in other clusters. They are in a position to combine different ideas and knowledge into new products and services.

Most people would consider those on the periphery of a network as not very important, yet peripheral people are often connected to networks that are not currently mapped. Peripheral members 12 and 25 may be contractors or vendors that have their own network outside of the company, making them a very important resource for fresh information not available inside the company.

Strategic leaders who want to use the power of internal and external networking must develop an accurate picture of the capability (skills and experience) and capacity (ability to do real work) of networks in their organization. With this information they can choose those people with whom they want to network, and then blend their goals with members already in the network. If leaders identify the types of followers who disproportionately impact a group, they can manage them by controlling information and withholding support so the group as a whole becomes more important. Furthermore, understanding peripheral players in a network, and crafting ways to engage these followers, is an important means of ensuring that network expertise is being effectively utilized. It is increasingly important in today's age of job turnover and change to get followers networked more quickly so that they are productive within an organization.

Readiness for Change

Strategic leaders must understand how ready the organization is to change if it is to successfully meet the threats and opportunities posed by the external environment. Conventional wisdom says that when 30% of followers are on board and supporting an idea in a visible, vocal, consistent and persistent way success is inevitable. This is particularly true if those supporting the change are on board faster than the critical mass of those in opposition can coalesce against the desired change. Rogers' *Diffusion of Innovations* (2003) theory, Gladwell's (2000) popular *The Tipping Point* and Quinn and Rohrbaugh's (1981) competing values framework are all useful tools to gauge the organization's readiness for change.

The Rogers (2003) model begins with the premise that in any normal distribution followers in organizations will fall into five categories; innovators, early adopters, early majority, late majority, and laggards. Innovators compose 2.5% of the normal population. They are seen as cosmopolitan, venturesome and willing to accept risks. They are generally younger and of a higher social status. They have closest contact with new scientific information sources. They interact with other innovators, and are adept at using impersonal sources. However, their opinion leader status is tentative.

Early adopters compose 13.5% of the normal distribution. They are held in high esteem in the organization and are seen as role models. Early adopters are generally found in large or specialized operations of the organization and come into closest contact with innovators and other local change agents. They are very local and are the greatest source of opinion leadership in the organization. In a sense they hold the keys to change. If they do not buy in to the idea it's unlikely that the rest of the organization will.

Early majority adopters compose about 34% of the normal distribution. They are deliberate, and willing to consider innovations only after peers have adopted them. They have considerable contact with local change agents and early adopters.

The late majority adopters compose about 34% of the normal distribution. They are skeptical and require overwhelming pressure from peers before they adopt. They secure their ideas from peers who are mainly late or early majority adopters themselves.

The laggards compose about 16% of the normal distribution. They are oriented to the past and to tradition. Their main contacts are with neighbors, relatives and friends with similar values. Often they are organizational isolates and may never adopt a new practice. The key to understanding the placement in each category is that the term applied— laggard, early adopter, innovator—only applies to a particular innovation. Laggards in one instance may be early adopters in another instance.

The problem confronting leaders is that organizations are seldom composed of normal distributions of people. Vibrant organizations will have more innovators and early adopters in their ranks. Stale organizations will have more late majority adopters and laggards in their ranks. Therefore, before introducing major change leaders must understand the makeup of the organization's followers and act appropriately. If the organization is ready, go full steam ahead. If not, the task is to till the soil and get the organization ready before the introduction of change. Consider the readiness for change of the two organizations pictured in Figures 4.4a and 4.4b. Which is more ready to change?

At the beginning of any significant change it has been estimated that around 10–15% of the affected organizational members are wildly supportive of the idea and another 10–15% are equally wildly antagonistic towards it.[11] Whichever end of the new idea adoption continuum doubles in size first, is likely to win out. This suggests that leaders should focus primary attention on those in favor of the idea, and encourage the next level of acceptors to join in, rather than trying to fix the hard-core resistors' stance, which may only drive the skeptics into more vocal resistance!

Like Rogers' diffusion theory, the competing values framework (CVF) is one of the most important organizational analysis models available. The framework, advanced originally by Quinn and Rohrbaugh in 1981 and developed in successive stages by several collaborators,[12] looks at culture as a way to help leaders identify the current status of an organization and its ability to support change and high performance.

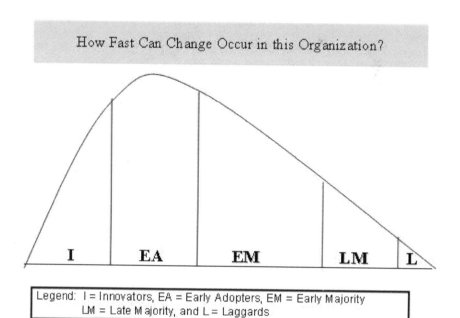

Figure 4.4a.   Organizational readiness for change: Organization 1.

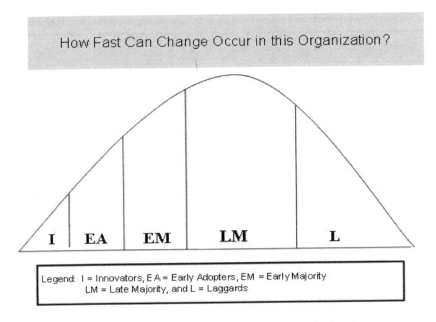

Figure 4.4b.   Organizational readiness for change: Organization 2.

The basic CFV framework consists of two dimensions resulting in a two-by-two figure which contrasts four sets of values. (See Table 4.3) The first dimension of the framework is a continuum that ranges from flexibility, discretion, and dynamism on one end to stability, order, and control on the other. The second dimension of the framework is a continuum that ranges from internal orientation, integration, and cohesiveness on one end to external orientation, differentiation, and independence on the other. An internal focus means that the organization emphasizes maintaining and improving the existing organization, whereas an external focus means that the organization focuses on competing, adapting to, and interacting with the external environment (Quinn & Spreitzer, 1991)

These dimensions result in four ideal types of culture: a group culture, a developmental culture, a rational culture, and a hierarchical culture. Each type represents a different orientation toward values, motivation, leadership and strategic orientation in the organization. The results of analysis using this framework capture the fundamental values that exist in the organization and enable strategic leaders to understand the degree to which their organization emphasizes each of the four cultural orientations. The analysis will also reveal whether conflicts exist between the

Table 4.3.   The Four Culture Patterns of the Competing Values Framework

	Flexibility and Adaptability	
Group Clan Orientation		*Developmental Adhocracy Oriented*
Flexibility and internal focus Affiliation/Belonging Information sharing trust/Nurturing Participation		Flexibility and external focus Growth External support and Resource acquistion Adaptation and Entrepreneurship
Hierarchically Oriented		*Rational Market Oriented*
Stability and internal focus Structure and control Clear rules and documentation Continuity and control		Stability and external focus Results oriented Competition and productivity Efficiency and accomplishment
	Stability and Control	

Internal Focus and Integration ← → *External Focus and Differentiation*

Note: Adapted from *Diagnosing and Changing Organizational Culture: Based on the Competing Values Framework,* by K. S. Cameron & R. E. Quinn, 1999, Reading, MA: Addison-Wesley.

apparent cultural values of leaders and managers and those enacted daily by staff and other stakeholders (Denison & Spreitzer (1991)

The upper left hand corner represents a group culture focused on flexibility and internal integration. Organizations emphasizing a group culture tend to value belongingness, trust and participation. The upper right hand corner represents a developmental culture emphasizing flexibility and external orientation. Organizations with emphasis on this cultural orientation tend to focus on growth, resource acquisition, creativity, and adaptation to the external environment. The bottom right hand corner represents a rational culture focused on the external environment and control. Organizations with emphasis on a rational culture encourage competition and the successful achievement of well-defined goals. The bottom left hand corner represents a hierarchical culture that emphasizes stability, internal integration, centralization, and regulations. The strategies emphasize clear rules, close control, and developing routines.

The CFV provides critical lessons for strategic leaders. The originators of the CFV indicate that there is no one type found in every organization. They also advise that a combination of the four cultural orientations should be strived for. Other researchers say that while all cultural types are important to understand, not all cultures are equal when it comes to implementing change.

Group, rational, and developmental cultures seem to have the greatest effect on implementation of change. The effect of group culture on change efforts can be explained by its focus on participation, trust and concern for human resources which creates a supportive environment for continuous improvement. The rational cultural type, with a focus on control and goal achievement, has a supplementary role to play if the change is accountability oriented, while the development culture type plays a supplementary role if the change is innovative oriented. Results indicate that the hierarchical culture has a negative effect on change readiness and little impact on change implementation. What this suggests is that strategic leaders should strive to create a culture that has strong group, developmental, and rational aspects. They must empower their followers while also ensuring that the organization's need for stability during change is addressed.

The *anticipating* habit begins the learning cycle the organization goes through to invent or reinvent itself. Through it leaders gain perspective; seeing not only the big picture but changes in that picture. Henry Mintzberg (1995), a preeminent scholar of strategic thinking and management, nicely summarizes the importance of the habit of anticipating. He describes strategic thinkers as;

> visionaries with the ability to see ahead, and behind (an understanding of the past) and above (able to see the big picture) and below (able to dig out "gems") and beside (able to think laterally and creatively) and beyond (able to put ideas in context) and, finally, able to see it through (implement the strategy). (pp. 79–83)

CLIFF NOTES

Habit 3: Anticipate the Future

Strategic leaders use Habit 3 to gain perspective and see not only the big picture but changes in that picture. The future may be largely determined by forces outside our control but by becoming skilled at anticipating, leaders can use images of the past and future to make changes in the present.

The takeaway is that strategic leaders can use a look-learn-listen sequence to scan for and interpret environmental trends. The successful use of scanning tools such as a SWOT analysis, the gathering of internal social intelligence about the number of colleague type followers in the organization, and an understanding of the organization's readiness for change, allows leaders to gauge responses to signals stemming from the environment. Strategic leaders:

1. Understand leadership is a situated practice. The situation or context does not simply affect what leaders do - it constrains and enables what leaders can do and how they can do it.

2. Proceed by identifying the opportunities and threats found in the external environment then identify the organization's strengths and weaknesses in relationship to external needs.

3. Understand that high performance is easier to achieve when colleagues followers outnumber other types of followers in the organization.

4. Map the flow of information, including who shares knowledge with whom, because these relationships play a critical role in determining organizational performance levels.

5. Develop an accurate picture of the capability (skills and experience) and capacity (ability to do real work) of networks in their organization.

6. Understand the organization's readiness for change and act appropriately.

7. Develop an understanding of the organization's external environment and be prepared to shift gears rapidly by combining planning with entrepreneurship.

NOTES

1. Attributed to a statement by Governor Franklin Roosevelt (1932) when he declared his candidacy for President of the United States.

2. Most notably—Peters and Waterman (1982).

3. See Nutt and Backoff (1993).

4. See Armstrong (2006) and Chermack and Kasshanna (2007) for fuller descriptions.

5. Data acquired from Delhi's National Council of Applied Economic Research

6. After becoming aware of Ratan Tata during my work in India I pieced together his story from sources such as Pete Engardio (August 2, 2007); Lala (2006); http://www.telegraph.co.uk/news/worldnews/1575181/ Ultimate-economy-drive-the-andpound1,300-car.html http://www.accessmylibrary.com/coms2/summary_0286-33768505_ITM; http://www.indiacar.net/news/n73529.htm

and a series of interviews with Ratan Tata (http://www.tata.com) including those by Christabelle Noronha (January, 2008) and (August, 2006).

7. See Zacarro, Thor, and Mumford (1991) for a full discussion.

8. See Cunningham (1987); Ellis (1995).

9. For example, see Casciaro (1998); Cross, Parker, and Borgatti (2002); Krackhardt (1987, 1990); Krackhardt and Hanson (1993).

10. See Bailey (1935); Clements (2004); and Powaski (1991).

11. See Adams (1988, 2003) and Beer and Nohria (2000).

12. The CVF framework has been empirically validated in a variety of settings and provides a body of empirical literature from which lessons can be learned in related contexts. Validation sources include: Berrio (1999); Buenger, Daft, Conlon, and Austin. (1996); Goodman, Zammuto, and Gifford (2001); Hooijberg and Petrock (1993); Kalliath, Bluedorn, and Gillespie (1999); Sendelbach (1993); Quinn (1988); Quinn and Kimberly (1984); Quinn and Rohrbaugh (1981); Quinn and McGrath (1985); Quinn and Rohrbaugh (1983); and Quinn and Spreitzer (1991).

CHAPTER 5

HABIT 4

Articulating Strategic Intent

The winds and waves are always on the side of the best navigators.

—Edward Gibbon, English historian

This chapter focuses on the strategic leader's most important function: finding the future. They utilize a generative process to develop a common understanding of the challenges and opportunities presented by the external and internal contexts in which they work and begin to create cohesion. Strategic leaders use two tactics to steer, guide, and maneuver the process. They *light the way* by creating a statement of intent that provides a vehicle to describe the organization, what it stands for, what it wants to become, and how it

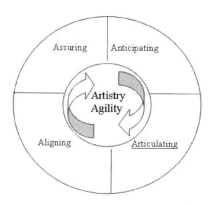

Figure 5.1.   The Leader's Wheel.

will work toward its intent and a flexible set of priorities. Then they look for windows of opportunity to open and they *run for daylight*. This chapter

---

The Strategic Leader: New Tactics for A Globalizing World, pp. 99–120
Copyright © 2009 by Information Age Publishing

deals with the first step: creating direction. It examines the leader's role in articulating direction and the tactics and tools used to develop a shared direction.

THE ARTICULATING HABIT

Articulating a statement of intent is one of those consequential decisions strategic leaders make—and it is an important one! It can be used to create direction that either works to alter the environment to conform to their point of view, or changes the organization to conform to environmental demands. The first step is to create a statement of intent that articulates what the organization stands for and aspires to, and what initiatives will lead to success. The second step is to convey this intent throughout the organization via electronic media, online venues, speeches, and one on one and small group question and answer sessions. The first step is dealt with in this chapter. The third and fourth steps are described in the next two chapters on *aligning* and *assuring*.

THE LEADER'S ROLE IN ARTICULATING INTENT

Strategic leaders listen, synthesize, seek patterns, and verify information to search for clues to the future. As Mintzberg (1994a, p. 107) says, they capture what they have learned

> from all sources (both the soft insights from his or her personal experiences and the experiences of others throughout the organization and the hard data from market research and the like) and then synthesize that learning into a vision of the direction that the business should pursue. (p. 107)

In a sense, strategic leaders act like Captain Richard Burns during the Vietnam War. Burns (2002) was a member of the 14-man 101st Pathfinder Detachment. He operated in live-or-die situations, risking his life so that other men and women could keep theirs. He acted as air-traffic controller, keeping call signs, frequencies, and aircraft locations in his head as he orchestrated takeoffs and landings, often under heavy enemy fire. He guided in helicopters filled with disembarking troops, directed medivacs to retrieve the wounded, parachuted into areas, supervised the clearing of landing zones and pinpointed enemy targets. While strategic leaders do not normally operate in life or death situations, much like Captain Burns they do establish direction and create and maintain momentum.

The strategic leader's role is find the future and set future can be in the direction that the organization is alre this case, frame-sustaining action is necessary and the le tilt the "Leadership Wheel" in the direction of manageria holding to a preexisting strategic course, they reinforce the existing belief and value system. When the organization's course cannot be supported, it is no longer working and must be changed. In this case, a complete restructuring of the value system and then the structural system is required. This is the more difficult type of change because it requires a shift in fundamental beliefs and actions. In such a case, the strategic leader must conduct a carefully calibrated process of change leadership, ultimately leading to substantial cultural and structural change.

In the past, strategic plans were drawn up for 5- to 10-year periods. They worked because the future was controllable. However, in postmodern times, we have become disappointed and disillusioned with efforts to plan for a long-term future. Mintzberg (1994a, 1994b) says that the process is so complicated that planning loses its meaning. Sometimes it becomes more important than the results and requires preparation of a large document culled from a mixture of data. Furthermore, the utility of the plan is often called into question because it has been prepared by specialists with little knowledge of practical matters related to people and budgets.

Consider the example of Henry Ford. First, he created a mass-produced car in an environment where mass production was not understood. This one strategic decision allowed Ford to dominate the new automobile market and make it conform to his point of view. However, as the environment changed he refused to change with it. He continued to believe that the Model T, and later the Model A, were all that the market needed and should need. He wound up losing his monopoly to leaders of companies who understood that the consumers were not just concerned with usefulness but also with fashion and niches. Ford's success was making correct strategic decisions that led to an altered environment. His failure was that once the environment changed, he failed to recognize the need to change and adapt. He did not continue to keep his organization at the edge of chaos.

In these fast days, strategic leaders recognize that complex environments do not yield to prediction. They resist this trap by providing a general sense of direction and allowing enough autonomy for members to self-manage and adapt over time. They view planning as a flexible tool that requires analysis, and then synthesis. When strategic leaders set direction, they rely on an inductive synthesizing process of gathering external and internal information. They look for patterns and relationships found in the information. Then they craft a vision, values, and beliefs that guide the organization and allow the leader to engage in flexible planning. Under conditions of ambiguity, complexity and chaos, no specific plan can last for very long. It will either become outmoded due to changing external and/or internal pressures. Yet incrementalism in the form of *muddling through* is not the answer. A better approach is to cycle back and forth between efforts to set a shared direction of what the organization intends to become and the themes and strategies it will pursue.

In postmodern times, strategic leaders can employ the new science tactics of *organizational fitness, generative relationships, minimum specifications* and *flexible planning*, to create sustainable visions. These tactics, described in the following paragraphs, suggest that leaders would be better off replacing elaborate strategic planning with simple documents that describe the general direction the organization should take and then identifying a few priorities to get there. Of course, this method is difficult for traditional managers to accept since their training prioritized analysis rather than synthesis. It is also difficult for the organization's dominant coalition because they are used to organizational decisions and choices being based on their values.

Organizational Fitness

The strategic leader is guided by the concept of organizational fitness when establishing the parameters of a high performing organization. Organizational fitness is a term given to organizations that are more in tune with themes emanating from the environment. The degree of fitness can be expected to change as the environment changes. Therefore, the application of this principle necessitates a continual scanning, rethinking, revising, and restructuring of the organization so that it stays connected to the environment, and the establishment of a learning process to insure that organizations are in continuous development.

Strategic leaders create fit organizations by *anticipating* where the opportunities and threats are and *articulating* a direction to travel. As Wayne Gretzky (1990), the hall of fame hockey player says, "the key to success is skating to where the puck is going to be, not where it is." Mary Parker Follett,[1] the mother of modern management, suggested the same thing in a more expanded way when she said,

> the most successful leaders see a picture not yet actualized. They see things that belong in the present picture but are not there yet. They make co-workers see that it is not their purpose that is to be achieved but a common purpose born of the activities of the group and that drives the organization toward the picture not yet actualized. (as cited in Metcalf & Urwick, 1941, p. 24)

Generative Process

The strategic leader employs a generative strategy to cr
sense of purpose throughout the organization. While a strong sense of
purpose and direction is essential in order to *articulate* organizational
intent, there is disagreement in the leadership literature as to who determines the future to which the group or organization aspires. For some,
the picture not yet actualized can come from the personal vision of the
leader. For others, the vision comes from an external authority and the
leader's role is to focus followers' attention and help them understand
and pursue it. For still others, it can be created through an inclusive process. Each of these versions brings different results in the depth and width
of the response from organizational members. Whichever version is used,
the strategic leader's role is to be active not passive in providing focus and
to facilitate and galvanize action.

A dominance-driven process has a strong internal planning orientation and occurs at the upper levels of the organization. The resulting
plans use pre-identified goals to decide on resource allocation and the
actions necessary to achieve specified goals. The dominance strategy
starts fast, but generally loses power over time and can result in a loss
of productivity. Its success depends on the ability of top leaders to push
change through the organization. The dominance tactic fosters compliance by organizational members. It appeals to followers who seek stability and order and who feel little responsibility to change behavior other
than what is called for within their contractual relationships. Leaders
using this approach are able to bring about structural organizational
changes to improve current conditions by imposing their personal
vision or by the directives of senior managers. The approach works best
when the leader has full authority to hire, deal with low performers and
command commitment to goals. The downside of this strategy is it loses
its momentum when the leader leaves.

Direction setting through a generative strategy calls for gathering, synthesizing and sharing external and internal information by top level management and members of both the dominant and less dominant
coalitions in the organization. They look for patterns and relationships
found in the information, and produce a statement of strategic intent that
guides organizational decision making and behavior over the next 5 to 7
years. The upside of the strategy is that it has the best potential for creating coherence and counters fragmentation of effort in the organization.
The downside is that it takes longer to produce a shared direction than
the dominance method.

Minimum Specifications/Flexible Planning

The strategic leader uses *minimum specifications* to create a stage which enables followers to self manage and become accountable for the organization's outcomes. Operating under minimum specifications, strategic leaders create a simple tablet which describes the general direction to pursue and a few basic principles to guide how to get there. They are then free to look for opportunities to exploit. A strategic plan under conditions of minimum specifications should be able to fit on one page, front and back.

LIGHT THE WAY

The van carrying my evaluation team and me entered the gate of the school in the Colombian mountains at around 7:30 A.M. We had arrived in the compound 15 minutes earlier on a plane from Barranquilla because rebels controlled the roads. We were there to review the school's strategic plan and recommend its accreditation.

Laura Horbel (the principal) and Luis Cortez (the president of the company that owned the school) were standing there with big smiles on their faces. They greeted us like visiting potentates from some distant country. I was immediately struck by the message on the welcome banner. It read, "Together We Light the Way." Through that day and into the night the words moved noisily through my mind. What a wonderful way to describe the purpose and values of the school. Moreover, what a fitting description of what strategic leaders do. They light the way for their followers and together they light the way for their clients, consumers, and customers.

Like a good vision statement, the phrase "Together We Light the Way" is compelling, it says a lot in one sentence. My Italian ancestors had a saying for women giving birth; *dar a la luce*. Translated it means *give them to the light*. That is the challenge before strategic leaders—they must hold up the vision, aspirations, and values to the light and let them be the bridge that leads others to the picture not yet actualized. Strategic leaders build the bridge and light the way for others to follow. As discussed earlier, there are many ways to light the way, but the process should be uncomplicated in order to create a strategic and sustainable direction. The first step begins with the strategic leader facing the consequential decision of direction setting style. Does he or she follow an authority-dominance or a leadership-learning driven direction setting process?

The Strategic Process

The strategic leader's tasks are to sense shifts in the internal and external environments, find the paths to the future and create a statement of strategic intent that lights the way for others to follow. In simple terms, strategic leaders look-listen-learn, and then they lead. Strategic leaders commit to the following criteria to guide the process. They:

- Are responsible for putting in place a process that supports generative relationships
- Lead and participate in the process and use the results to drive the organization.
- Facilitate, rather than judge, the creation of ideas.
- Provide just enough structure (minimum specifications to launch the initiative on its way. They do not propose any grand designs or possible solutions at the beginning of the process.
- Pose structured questions rather than offering definitive answers.
- Suspend judgment and are willing to follow initiatives that emerge from the process as long as they move the organization toward its aspiration.

Imagine the differences in behavior between leaders who operate with the idea that leadership means influencing the organization to follow the leader's vision and those who operate with the idea that leadership means influencing the organization to face its problems and act on its opportunities.

As a guide to creating strategic intent, I extend the look-listen-learn sequence by adding the leadership component as seen in Figure 5.2. The four L sequence begins by following Covey's (1989) advice. Strategic leaders seek to understand before seeking to be understood. From these new understandings, they force their organizations to face reality by leading their colleagues through the same sequence of understanding that they went through. Then, they lead! Together they develop a shared organizational direction that identifies their purpose, aspirations, and the values and behaviors necessary to be successful. As the organization moves in this direction, strategic leaders continuously adapt their strategy to the changing environment.

This four L theory of leadership is a predictable uncomplicated sequence strategic leaders' can use to engage followers at the emotional level but allows the leader to remain in control of the original vision. Strategic leaders employ the sequence to:

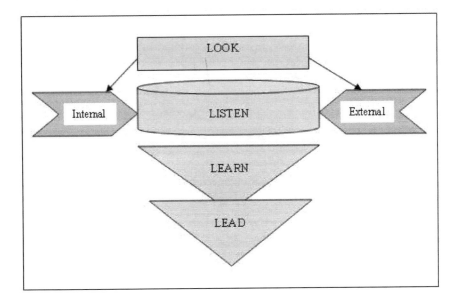

Figure 5.2.   The stages of creating a statement of strategic intent.

- Sense change in the environment—*Anticipate*
- Gather and interpret relevant information about the change—*Anticipate*
- Suggest significant changes which the organization must address—*Articulate*
- Introduce new processes and services which are more in line with the originally perceived changes in the environment—*Articulate*
- Call on parts of the organization to act upon the suggestions—*Align*
- Monitor internal changes and the impact of those changes—*Assure.*

The goal of the four L process is not just to change procedures, systems, and authority relationships. The goal is to establish conversations that generate a coherent statement of strategic intent by bringing differing viewpoints together or selecting a viewpoint to follow. Some of these conversations will be dialogue oriented, an open-ended process in which resolution is not necessarily a goal. People come to the table without an agenda and review the gathered information and then throw out ideas for understanding and consideration. A particularly useful leader tactic is simply asking short questions and listening such as: What has to happen here? What is precious and what is expendable? What can be modified? How can we make it happen? How do we keep making it happen? Avoid the urge to answer these questions quickly and then tell colleagues what to do. It will take time and patience to reach consensus. This course of action continues for at least 5 months (or six full day meetings spaced out so integration of ideas can take place). Although the process is time consuming, long term benefits such as orderly change, common direction and agreed upon values will accrue to the organization. The leader uses the emergent sense of purpose, values, and beliefs as screening devices for adopting or resisting new procedures and to promote self-management by staff and teams.

Some organizations attempt to create direction simply by empowering the leadership team or a small group of interested individuals. While they may achieve immediate success, it is seldom sustained. Creative, self-managed, and self-renewing sustainable organizations cannot be built through dominance. They are built through the establishment of generative relationships in which strategic direction emerges from ongoing interactions inside and outside of the organization. The central point of investing time and energy in a generative process is to ensure that a compelling and meaningful direction emerges that leaders try to embed as deeply as they can into the hearts and minds of their followers.

Todd Lanier[2] the CEO of a software company explains the process he used every time he moved to a new company.

> I always began each new job with an emergence strategy. I always reserved the dominance strategy for operational decisions not substantive ones. I used a *whither* committee to guide the principle of generative relations. You know *whither we go*? Some of my peers call it the guiding coalition, or simply a transition management team. The makeup of the whither committee is crucial. It should be composed of those with (a) position power (i.e., leaders and managers), (b) informal leaders, and (c) expert knowledge so informed decisions are possible.
>
> I charge the whither committee with developing a one page draft statement of strategic intent that stretches our company to meet future needs of our customers and our environment. In three months, the draft of the strategic intent is presented to our board of directors and company wide for their input and then revisions if necessary. The draft should cover our mission, aspiration, core values and initiatives. Our aspiration statement should focus on what we wish to become not what we are. In particular, the core values should clearly define how we wish to work together. Once we adopt the statement no level of personnel may be exempt from accountability to these. Examples of values that are needed are collegiality, acting civilly, sustainability, use of data in decision-making and delivering profit and shareholder value. The process should also result in a few (no more than 5) initiatives that will move us closer to our aspirations. Once agreed upon, this statement of intent will be articulated throughout the company, and be used to make hiring decisions, develop working relationships, and resource allocations.

I work in tandem, teamwork style with these powerful people, make sure the important questions are asked and discussed, but I do not give up the pen. By working in this fashion with this committee, trust developed and I have been able to maintain the support of these colleagues through the execution stage.

I believe that since the statement of strategic intent will affect everyone, everyone should be involved in its development. It is extremely important that all staff members get the same information. I do this by setting up information sharing sessions where the whither committee and staff members receive the same information. The purpose of these invitations is to expand the knowledge available to members of the organization both from a future and present perspective. At each meeting I present small pieces of objective data so everyone gets the big picture and the little picture. I limit the amount of white papers, data analyses and predictions, and focus more on the testimony of experts who provide their particular advocacy or inquiry view of the environment, the challenges, and opportunities it presents. The whither committee attends all information sharing activities, engages in conversation and listens to the conversation of their colleagues.

As the workforce begins to understand the challenges presented by the environment and the ways they can address them, a common understanding of the challenges and opportunities should grow.

A week after each of the meetings the whither committee engages in a private conversation and tries to make sense out of the new information and the reactions of their colleagues. This process is largely social. Its success depends on the credibility and standing of an idea's champions, the evidence that supports their case, and the way others in the organization responded. Then, the conversation shifts to examining how current assumptions and work processes constrain the action required for the necessary changes. After the process runs for several months, the whither committee shares a draft statement of strategic intent with the rest of the organization and the board of directors. Each member is charged with providing feedback to the whither committee members who in turn prepare a final draft for adoption. It generally takes us several other meetings to get a solid understanding and agreement of the direction we will move in.

There are several strengths to be found in Todd's strategy. The way he set up his whither committee insures that the members will have creditability and their decisions will engender support from other organizational members. The mix of people he chooses for membership satisfies a number of preconditions for emergence to occur. The committee has heterogeneity, powerful individuals outside the chain of command and both leaders and managers are involved. Furthermore, if the strengths of this group can be united as a collective force, they can determine what needs to be done and how quickly. Nevertheless, even with a powerful coalition there must be some dissatisfaction with the status of the organization if frame-breaking change is the goal.

A generative process such as Todd's is necessary to develop the int... commitment to sustain change and reduce resistance. To capture th... attention of their workforce, strategic leaders must get followers to think about what things they think are important. The best way to do this is by increasing the flow of information to soften some calcified assumptions. For example, a college dean could invite in the provost and president of the university, key policy researchers in the specialty of the college, and some organizations that employ graduates of the college. A business manager might invite in a university professor, a regulator, a company president of a partnering company, a stock analyst, and experts who are on the cutting edge of changes in the economic, political, societal, and technological aspects of society. Whoever is invited, the process ensures that challenges, problems, and dilemmas facing the organization become part of every staff member's reality through presentation, debate, dialogue, and critique of objective and political reality.

The generative process is more easily accomplished in small organizations (up to 350 people in the same location) than in large organizations such as Ford motor company with its 340,000 employees in 200 countries or the giant IBM. Nevertheless, it has been done in these organizations. Jacques Nasser, the former Ford CEO, and Lou Gerstner, the former CEO at IBM, both noted that when they arrived as new CEOs, far-flung divisions had their own *fiefdoms*. They guarded their own privileges and did not share information or ideas, which drove up costs. Nasser and Gerstner, each in his own way, set out to help employees view the company in its entirety.

At Ford, Nasser[3] created a teachable point of view about what it takes to succeed in the automobile business. He involved the Ford workforce in conversations around the world to understand the way business should be conducted at Ford installations. At IBM, Gerstner noted that change could not be accomplished with a couple of speeches, or by writing a new credo and then mandating it. He set out to create the conditions for transformation, provide incentives, and insure that the entire workforce had the information they needed to understand the direction, challenges, and opportunities that faced IBM.

With these caveats, following the look-listen-learn-lead sequence should result in a sustainable direction *fitted* to the strategic context of the organization. This shared sense of direction motivates and coordinates the kinds of actions that create transformations. When a shared sense of direction is clear it provides a framework for how people direct their energy, judge organizational performance, and foster self-management. Everything else—practices, structures, systems, policies and procedures—are negotiable.

...egic Intent

...trategic intent is the leader's platform from which ...sion transcends into organizational vision as mem- ...on make their own commitments to it. Gary Hamel, ...don Business School, and C. K. Prahalad, a University of Michigan professor, introduced the term "strategic intent" in 1989 as a future oriented strategy. They argued that when Western companies faced complexity and ambiguity they focused on trimming their ambitions to match resources. Hence, they searched only for advantages they could sustain. By contrast, Japanese corporations faced the same conditions; they leveraged resources by accelerating the pace of organizational learning and tried to attain seemingly impossible goals. They concluded that "it is not the cash that fuels the journey to the future, but the emotional and intellectual energy of every employee" (Hamel & Prahalad, 1994, p. 127) When what you choose for your future is more important than what you know about your past or present capabilities it's time to develop a statement of strategic intent.

Strategic intent as they saw it stakes out an organizational purpose and long term aspiration which eliminates ambiguity, creates coherence, and lets all organizational members see the big picture. The statement of intent should concern all organizational levels, command the respect of every employee, and offer many alternative means of achieving it. The statement of intent serves the purpose of clarifying the long term objective of the organization, motivates people to take action guided by a strong sense of what they are ultimately trying to achieve, and helps coordinate action of members throughout the organization. The statement of strategic intent is clear about ends, flexible as to means, and leaves room for creativity.

The statement of strategic intent is composed of four components; mission, aspiration, guiding principles, and priorities. These four components clarify the vision and inform all organizational members about how it will be realized. In effect it is more than a vision that is crafted and displayed on every bulletin board and work station. The four components of the statement of strategic intent will impact everyone in the day to day work.

The statement of strategic intent enables strategic leaders to articulate any potential misfit between current position and organizational aspirations. It provides a framework of values and priorities to enable organizational members to generate ideas. In this way, unplanned strategic initiatives emerge. It establishes the expectations and behavioral norms that guide the work of the organization and the individual over time. The process of developing a statement of strategic intent is emergent, flexible, and at times, erratic and fuzzy. However, the statement of strategic intent itself is none of these.

When properly crafted, a statement of strategic intent serves as an orienting device that articulates the organization's position, provides a sustaining direction around which organizational members can cohere, *lights the way* for others to follow and allows organizational members to *run for daylight*. It does not focus on today's problems but on tomorrow's opportunities. The statement of strategic intent contains an aspiration, or hope, for what the organization wants to become. It also contains the blueprint for organizational behavior, and the priorities that will move the organization toward their aspiration. When the statement of strategic intent is generatively created it guides people's work and attracts the best talent. When it is shared, it can be institutionalized. When it is institutionalized, it can be sustained.

Table 5.1 illustrates the components of the Statement of Strategic Intent with examples from Southwest Airlines, Intel, Japan Airlines, the Department of Educational Leadership at Florida Atlantic University, General Electric Corporation, and the University of Illinois at Springfield. There are several keys to capturing the statement of strategic intent. The statement should fit on a single page front and back. The goal is not a planning book with goals, objectives and sub objectives that will sit on the shelf. It is a simple statement of what the organization aspires to, what it believes in, and how it will allocate resources when the appropriate opportunities present themselves. This simple tablet enables strategic leaders to use principles rather than rules to align the organization and its members.

A second key is to have the creators sign the statement of strategic intent as artists sign their work. The importance of work attribution is illustrated by Andy Hertzfeld (2004, p. 82) a key member of the original Apple Macintosh development team during the 1980s. He relates:

> The Mac team had a complicated set of motivations, but the most unique ingredient was a strong dose of artistic values. First and foremost, Steve Jobs thought of himself as an artist, and he encouraged the design team to think of ourselves that way, too. The goal was never to beat the competition, or to make a lot of money; it was to do the greatest thing possible, or even a little greater. Steve often reinforced the artistic theme; for example, he took the entire team on a field trip in the spring of 1982 to the Louis Comfort Tiffany museum, because Tiffany was an artist who learned how to mass produce his work.
>
> Since the Macintosh team were artists, it was only appropriate that we sign our work. Steve came up with the awesome idea of having each team member's signature engraved on the hard tool that molded the plastic case, so our signatures would appear inside the case of every Mac that rolled off

Table 5.1.   Examples of the Components of a Statement of Strategic Intent

Mission

Definition—A purpose statement which provides a crisp, clear image of why you exist and who you serve—in one sentence with no more than three themes.

Examples:

- The mission of Southwest Airlines is dedication to the highest quality of Customer Service delivered with a sense of warmth, friendliness, individual pride, and Company Spirit.

- The mission of the Department of Educational Leadership (EDL) at Florida Atlantic University is to prepare and support the leaders in public and private educational institutions at all levels.

- The mission of Intel is to do a great job for our customers, employees, and stockholders by being the preeminent building block supplier to the worldwide Internet economy.

Aspiration

Definition—A picture not yet actualized that concretely defines a desired future which challenges and inspires people; enrolls colleagues to reframe their thinking and reorganize their priorities, and guide their subsequent actions.

Examples:

- EDL aspires to develop a growing national and international reputation for the preparation and support of leaders.

- Southwest airlines' aspiration is to be the low-fare airline.

- The University of Illinois at Springfield aspires to be recognized as one of the top five small public liberal arts universities in the United States.

Guiding Principles

Definition—Permission statements which describe how the organization intends to *behave* as it tries to accomplish the mission/aspiration and in working with each other and customers and other stakeholders.

Examples:

- *GE* leaders … always with unyielding integrity.
    - Are passionately focused on driving customer success.
    - ensure that the customer is always its first beneficiary … and use it to accelerate growth.
    - Insist on excellence and be intolerant of bureaucracy.
    - Act in a boundary less fashion … always search for and apply the best ideas regardless of their source.
    - Prize global intellectual capital and the people that provide it … build diverse teams to maximize it.

- Above all, employees will be provided with the same concern, respect, and caring attitude within the organization that they are expected to share externally with every Southwest Customer.

- EDL—The faculty is committed to maintaining a cohesive, respectful, and supportive work environment that stimulates collaborative and continuous learning.

Priorities

Definition—A set of flexible priorities that describe how the organization intends to allocate resources to accomplish the mission/aspiration over time and provide focus to organizational aspirations.

Examples:

- Intel—extend silicon leadership; deliver architectural innovation for consumers; pursue opportunities worldwide.

- EDL—Infuse technology and interactive methodologies such as distance learning, case studies, and simulations into instructional practices; Nurture national, regional, and international partnerships and alliances.

- GE—Digital Connections, Infrastructure Technology, Origination Financial Markets, Emerging Growth Markets, Environmental Solutions, Meeting Demographic Demands

---

the production line. Most customers would never see them, since you needed a special tool to look inside, but we would take pride in knowing that our names were in there, even if no one else knew.

We held a special signing party after one of our weekly meetings on February 10, 1982. Jerry Mannock, the manager of the industrial design team, spread out a large piece of drafting paper on the table to capture our signatures. Steve gave a little speech about artists signing their work, and then cake and champagne were served as he called each team member to step forward and sign their name for posterity. Burrell had the symbolic honor of going first, followed by members of the software team. It took forty minutes or so for around thirty-five team members to sign. Steve waited until last, when he picked a spot near the upper center and signed his name with a flourish.

The test of an agreed upon direction is not how well it stands up to external events. The test is how well it enables the organization to gain coherence and momentum in changing priorities and behaviors. A properly crafted statement of strategic intent meets the organization's need for order and change. The driving forces for stability and order are the mission statement, which grounds the organization, and the guiding principles, which provide guidance on how to act while pursuing the mission. The driving forces for growth and change are the aspiration and priorities statements. Aspiration points the direction. Priorities connect the enterprise to its external environment.

The third key relates to how the strategic intent statement encourages solidarity. The best strategic leaders prepare their organizations for change by creating shared aspirations, flexible priorities, and guiding principles. By articulating direction in this way, aspirations and values are fixed, and priorities and initiatives are flexible. Flexible priorities enable leaders to induce followers to join in a common purpose. Principles, and not written policies, guide organizational members. Strategic leaders are now armed with the tools to turn the Leadership Wheel.

Mission statements should be central characteristics of successful organizations. Yet these statements are rarely specific enough to provide organizational members clear guidance. Can your recite your organization's mission? How does it influence the way you carry out your day to day duties? If you answered in the negative you can begin to see the difficulty with mission statements. In many organizations they change nothing and are used only for annual reports or posters. Mission statements must do more than cover up spots on the wall to facilitate the organizational change process.

The key to a good mission statement is to focus on the core of why the organization is in business. These statements should contain no more than three crisp, clear, and compelling themes. For example, Southwest Airlines focuses on friendly service, speed, and on-time departures. A police department's mission might be to protect and serve. A university department's mission might be to prepare and support students. Anything over one sentence turns a mission statement into a political statement.

Aspiration statements have the capacity to orient organizational members to a future state not yet articulated. They are statements that specify a measurable end but not the means. They *stretch* human ambition and generate creative tension in the organization. Aspirations need to challenge, inspire, and enroll colleagues to reframe their thinking and reorganize their priorities. Aspirations guide subsequent action and decision-making. Aspirations are differentiated from vision when they are compelling enough that people can feel them in their heart, as the following examples from John F. Kennedy, Southwest Airlines, and University of Illinois are.

In 1961, Kennedy aspired to land a man on the moon and return him safely to earth before the decade was out. Southwest Airlines' aspires to be the low-fare airline. And the University of Illinois at Springfield, aspires to be recognized as one of the top five small public liberal arts universities in the United States.

Guiding principles define what the organization stands for and how it will act in the daily flow of activity. They function as permission statements which enable followers to act on their own or through self-managed teams. They act as transmission rules that guide organizational members as they move toward the organization's aspiration. They serve as a shaping force for organizational life. To some extent they represent core values that form the building blocks of a new cultural orientation. They can suggest standards for individual ethical behavior. Consider General Electric (GE) when it was managed my Jack Welch. GE's aspiration at the time was to build the most competitive company on earth. This aspiration was supported by the following values that would guide employee decision making.

GE leaders ... always with unyielding integrity:

- Are passionately focused on driving customer success.
- Live six sigma quality ... ensure that the customer is always its first beneficiary ... and use it to accelerate growth.
- Insist on excellence and be intolerant of bureaucracy.
- Act in a boundary less fashion ... always search for and apply the best ideas regardless of their source.
- Prize global intellectual capital and the people that provide it ... build diverse teams to maximize it.
- See change for the growth opportunities it brings ... for example, "e-Business."
- Create a clear, simple, customer-centered vision ... and continually renew and refresh its execution.
- Create an environment of "stretch," excitement, informality, and trust ... reward improvements ... and celebrate results.
- Demonstrate ... always with infectious enthusiasm for the customer ... the "4-E's" of *GE* leadership: the personal Energy to welcome and deal with the speed of change ... the ability to create an atmosphere that Energizes others ... the Edge to make difficult decisions ... and the ability to consistently Execute (extracted from Welch, 2001)

Priorities focus the organization on what it needs to do to achieve its aspiration. They are not pre-identified goals. Instead they are best guesses of the areas the organization should explore to work toward its aspiration. They provide a sense of discovery and are not established in priority order. They are flexible enough so leaders can adroitly identify initiatives in each category as opportunities are presented.

RUN TO DAYLIGHT

Leaders should be visionaries but they must also be able to maneuver through the issues presented by realistic interpretation of the possibilities and opportunities they face. Therefore, it is important that commitment to the statement of intent includes short term initiatives that establish momentum and give the organization a sense of success. This can be difficult because organizational members are trying to redirect their energies toward new directions while managing the old initiatives which still remain. Metaphorically, it is like flying a propeller driven plane while rebuilding it into turbo jet power.

The strategic intent is fixed, while the means to its attainment are opportunistic. Strategic opportunism permits the leader to pick and choose his or her way, by using certain events as catalysts for action, turning constraints into opportunities, and blunting or minimizing other impositions that do not make sense. In other words, the leader does not jump at every opportunity that presents itself. Rather, they select those opportunities that are the best fit for achieving their aspirations and initiatives. As Eleanor Roosevelt (1961) said, "If you prepare yourself … you will be able to grasp opportunity for a broader experience when it appears" (p. 261).

I learned this lesson by watching the Green Bay Packers football team during the Vince Lombardi era of championships. Lombardi, Green Bay's Hall of Fame coach, wrote a book called *Run to Daylight* that chronicled the Green Bay football dynasty. In the book (Lombardi & Heinz, 1963) he described a play that became the signature play for the team. The play was called the Packer Sweep (sweep right or left.) It was a simple play but when executed in the Green Bay fashion it was unstoppable. The play was designed for the quarterback to turn and hand the ball to the halfback who was told to run laterally toward the sidelines but keep looking at the goal line. All the linesmen were also instructed to run laterally and block the first person in a different colored jersey. In effect, the whole Green Bay team ran laterally toward the sideline. The running back was coached to cut up the field and straight to the goal line when he saw daylight between the linemen.

Think about this play for a moment. It was guided by simple rules. A general direction—the goal line—was established as the aspiration. The running back was told to *run to daylight*. The linemen were told to run laterally and block the first person with a different colored jersey. The success or failure of the play was dependent on circumstance and opportunity. What I took away from the example was the importance of pre-planning and being prepared for opportunities to arise, and then swiftly taking advantage of them.

Another observation early in my career implanted the *run to daylight* tactic in my brain. I observed that certain people or units were always the first ones to take advantage of new resources or opportunities to grow their operations. It was the same people over-and-over again, so I studied their behavior. They all pre-planned a direction and established initiatives they thought would help create a stronger organization. They did one other thing. They fleshed out plans in broad terms that would help work toward the initiatives. When opportunities presented themselves, they were the first one through the door while the rest of us were still planning to take advantage of the opportunity. Being ready means being first when opportunities present themselves. Being first means getting the best locations and installing your product before the competition gets theirs out of the research lab. Being first means market share and profits.

Later in my academic career, I found the Isenberg (1984, 1987) opportunistic model of planning which assumes that:

> the plan develops incrementally, there is jumping around within the planning space, several unrelated specific sequences are planned without lining them together, ... priorities may be ignored at any one point, and each new decision produces a new situation.

The strength of strategic opportunism is that it permits the leader to pick and choose their way, as they attempt to use certain events as catalysts for action, turn constraints into opportunities, and blunts or minimize the impositions that do not make sense.

Lighting the way and *running to daylight* are powerful tactics of strategic leadership. Consider how Antonio Davis, principal of Sherman Hill High School[4] used them when he was appointed to the position a few years ago.

> Sherman Hill was a school that had the reputation of a fallen star when I was selected to become its principal. The school had been a star in the school district for many years but had lost its star image when changes occurred in its environment. The community was growing fast, students were becoming more diverse, the faculty was a capable but lethargic group of individuals, and few discretionary resources were available. I knew these conditions existed when I took the position. I also knew that the challenges of the future would be different from the past.
>
> Soon after I accepted the position, I sent a memorandum to each staff member saying that I was pleased to have been appointed and anxious to meet them individually to gain an understanding of their aspirations for and perspectives on the school. Throughout the summer I was able to meet with each staff member to gain an internal perspective of the school. I also made appointments to meet with individuals at the central office and in the community who, in one way or another, would be involved with decisions at the school. I even stopped by to introduce myself to the Mayor and some key business people in the community as well as influential parents. I had several conversations with members of the central staff who would be reviewing my budget proposals and program plans. At these initial meetings, the focus was on getting to know one another, nothing substantive on my part. However, I did ask for their perspectives on the school. From these visits, I concluded that those individuals inside and outside the school held

different perspectives about the value of an education from Sherman Hill. It seemed to me that my primary mission was to help the school community search for its shared future.

One of the positive benefits of my visits was that a positive relationship had been established internally and externally. I also was able to identify the movers and shakers in the Sherman Hill community. During the teacher workdays prior to the opening of school in the fall, I presented my entry plan to the faculty. I appointed a 'rising star' committee which included those individuals who would have to agree before any real change occurred at the school. I also explained that once a month for the first five months I would be inviting different individuals to share with us their perspectives of changes in the educational and school environment. For example, our guests included the president of the school board, the superintendent, the mayor, the deputy to the state superintendent, the president of the state teachers association, and the president of the local taxpayer's association. I explained that the purpose of the committee was to listen to faculty comments and discuss the implications of information provided by our guests for Sherman Hill.

At the end of the five months, I led the committee through a dialogue about Sherman Hill's future. After several meetings, the committee developed a set of values and a vision to address the school's strategic context. They were discussed with the faculty in work groups and then in full session after which they were adjusted where necessary.

At the end of the seventh month, the statement of values was agreed upon and the focus of the committee turned to the strategic initiatives that would enable the school to fit with its environment. The initiatives were rather broad by design. One priority was to network teachers in each discipline with their peers in other schools and school districts. Another priority was to infuse teaching with technology. As I said, they were rather broad. In all, the committee agreed on seven initiatives. At the end of the school year, when graduation was over, our faculty voted unanimously to pursue the aspirations, guiding principles, and initiatives proposed by the committee. The general understanding was that over the summer, each of us would assess ourselves against the guiding principles we espoused and the seven initiatives.

During the summer, I shared our initiatives with the central staff and key individuals in the community. As the new school year started, we began to prospect for opportunities to further our initiatives. It took a while for things to get started but, when I received a call from the district's technology coordinator in November, I knew we had hit pay dirt. She said that the state department was looking for a school to pilot a program to connect teachers of mathematics through the internet so that they could share ideas on how to carry out the NCTM standards. It was the opportunity our staff was looking for and we submitted a successful bid. Three years later I look at that proposal as the turning point. It seemed that once we were successful, other opportunities presented themselves to further our strategic intent. Each year new ideas are generated as we evaluate our school's performance against our statement of strategic intent. We definitely are on the way to our future!

CLIFF NOTES

Habit 4: Articulating the Strategic Intent

Some leaders, like moths, take dangerous paths. They fly toward whatever light they see, become dazzled by the light and even burned. Other leaders are like beetles. They take a back and forth flight which is erratic and directionless. The take away is that strategic leaders are like fireflies, rather than like moths or beetles, they illuminate their own way and also that of others. With the aid of their colleagues they push back the darkness. They *light the way* and *run to daylight* to rethink, revise, and reform their organizations. They create organizational fitness and the ability to thrive.

- There are many ways to light the way, but the process should be generative, uncomplicated and based on minimum specifications. Setting direction is done through an inductive synthesizing process. External and internal information is gathered. Patterns and relationships in the information are discovered.

- Strategic leaders light the way by *anticipating* the forces vital to their organization's and/or their personal survival and success. From these understandings they *articulate* a statement of strategic intent which captures the organization's mission, aspiration, and guiding principles.

- A statement of strategic intent is produced that allows strategic leaders to engage in flexible planning and enables them to lead through principles not rules.

- The statement of intent should be a simple one page tablet that engages followers at an emotional level and provides a framework guiding how people direct their energy, judge organizational performance, and foster self-management.

- Strategic leaders do not plan; they create a shared reality that is neither too rigid nor too chaotic; it doesn't over control the change process or allow it to fall apart.

- Strategic leaders run to daylight by creating a flexible plan of initiatives within the statement of strategic intent that enables leaders and organizational members to seek out, create, or wait for opportunities that advance the initiatives to appear and exploit them. Leaders further this ability when they think like entrepreneurs and adopt a strategic opportunistic, rather than linear planning strategy which enables them to experiment with a variety of low cost probes.

- Strategic leaders use the intent statement as a torch to illuminate the future and guide action for organizational members at every level of the organization.

NOTES

1. Mary Parker Follett (1868–1933) was honored as the Prophet of Modern Management by Peter Drucker. She worked as a management and political theorist, introducing such phrases as "conflict resolution," "authority and power," and "the task of leadership." Follett suggested that organizations function on the principle of power "with" and not power "over." She recognized the holistic nature of leadership and advanced the idea of "reciprocal relationships." Follett advocated the principle of integration, "power sharing." She criticized hierarchical organizations and celebrated nonlinearity; she detested competition, bullies and the "command and control" leadership style, favoring instead more "integrated," democratic forms of management. (See Metcalf & Urwick, 1941, for fuller information.)

2. Name changed to protect privacy.

3. To facilitate communication and market awareness, Nasser instituted a program that provided home computers and Internet access to employees. Workers gained the power, in a very hierarchical company, to make decisions both small and large. Nasser's downfall is attributed to his abrupt style and external communications particularly as the point man in the dispute with tire maker Bridgestone/Firestone Inc. over which company was responsible for the safety problems and the hundreds of deaths linked to Ford Explorers equipped with Firestone tires.

4. Name changed to protect privacy.

CHAPTER 6

HABIT 5

Aligning Colleagues With Intent

The greatest leader in the world could never win a campaign unless he understood the men he had to lead.

—General Omar Nelson Bradley

Strategic leaders do not just establish direction for the organization. They also influence the alignment of values, followers, processes and structures with the organization's strategic intent. This chapter describes how leaders use their social intelligence to lead in ways that link the organization's intent to the people who work in the organization and the organizational processes which support their work. It offers two tactics that leaders can use to mobilize followers; building relationships and reaching for power.

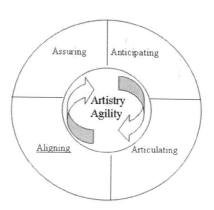

Figure 6.1.   The Leader's Wheel.

The Strategic Leader: New Tactics for A Globalizing World, pp. 121–154

Consider the following scenario. You and your leadership team just spent months developing a statement of strategic intent which proposes a new direction for the organization. In all modesty, you and your governing board think it is brilliant. There's just one problem. The people who run the place know you have been working on it but have little idea of what you are up to. In fact, they have been sitting on the sidelines, nit-picking the latest senior management scheming. In short, they don't know what you did or why you are recommending a change for the organization. They don't know what you want them to do differently, and they don't know if they have the capability or aspiration to do it.

You've just learned the simple but painful lesson that every leader of change stumbles upon sooner or later—you can't do it without the support of a critical mass of followers! Once the strategic intent is defined it does not implement itself. I had that truth reinforced when, after consulting with a country club to develop their statement of strategic intent, the staff members were asked to list the club's 5 highest priorities. Alarmingly, they listed a total of 23 priorities; only 2 appeared on every staff members list and only 7 were on the lists of more than three staff members; indeed 10 of the 10 priorities appeared on only one list. This illustrates a severe case of misalignment and management failure. In management terms, the club's leadership team did not use the statement of intent to align the organization.

Developing a direction, plan, or policy is the easiest part of a change process. Executing the change is the hardest. It involves mobilizing individuals and groups who have an interest in the organization's future. The strategic leader is not only active in creating the direction but also in establishing a process for achieving the organization's strategic intent.

THE ALIGNING HABIT

Alignment is the process through which the organization's intent comes to life. It influences thousands of big and small decisions made throughout an organization. Alignment means that our resources, our projects, our values, and our daily activities are allied with the goals and objectives of the organization.

Everyone who drives knows when their car is out of alignment. The car shakes at certain speeds and pulls to the left or right. Just like the car, organizations also shake and pull to the right or left when they are misaligned and run smoothly when they are aligned. Sounds simple, doesn't it? Yet Collins and Porras (1994, pp. 7–11) found that only visionary companies were able to constantly emphasize and achieve alignment. In fact, they described alignment as the central definition of organizational effectiveness. Without alignment organizations wander, focus is lost, and people waste energy by following different purposes.

Often leaders believe their work has been accomplished when they set the direction for the organization. The reality is that when the statement of strategic intent is completed, their work is just beginning. Strategic leaders must use the social intelligence they gather to understand followers, and emotional intelligence to foster colleagues and lead them towards organizational goals.

The ancient game of curling is a game of stones and brooms where two teams of four players each slide 44 pound polished granite stones down a sheet of ice toward a target at the other end. Each team tries to get more of its stones closer to the center of the target than the other team. The key to understanding curling is to know that when the curler throws a stone down the ice it will curl one way or the other, depending on the rotation applied; like when a baseball pitcher throws a curveball, except the curler does not have as much control of the bend as the pitcher. In baseball, the control comes from the pitcher. In curling, control depends more on the playing surface. To influence the speed and bend of the stone as it travels down the sheet of ice, the surface has to be influenced. Sweeping the ice is the only way to influence the stone once it has been thrown. Sweeping, which in fact melts the ice in front of the stone, is the most unusual aspect of the game. The player who furiously runs with the stone with broom in hand is in fact influencing the ice, which will either make the stone bend less and travel further or will allow the stone to slow down and get into the right position.

In the strategic leadership paradigm, we can substitute *leader* for player, *strategic intent* for stone, *follower* for ice, *relating, reaching,* and *persuading* for brooms, and *trust* for melted ice. Sweeping the ice (creating, gaining, and developing trust) creates the momentum needed to set sail. With trust at the center, leaders can create momentum to move the organization along its critical path.

Strategic leaders must master melting the ice—it's that important. Trust is not just the glue that binds the sails, it helps strengthen the wind that fills the sails and it always ensures a breeze. This assertion has support from those who study and practice leadership. In Kouzes and Posner's (2003) longitudinal studies, followers rated trust in their leaders as number one by a significant margin over other items. Peter Drucker (1999) reinforces the work of Kouzes and Posner by adding that workers must be committed. Organizations can force compliance or build commitment; but commitment cannot exist without trust. Therefore, organizations must foster trust to gain commitment. Kotter (1996, p. 61) says "when trust is present you will usually be able to create teamwork. When it's missing, you won't." More importantly, Podsakoff, Niehoff, Moorman, and Fetter (1990) found that the willingness of followers to go beyond the minimum requirements of their job descriptions may be linked to trust in the leader.

Leadership gurus like Jim Collins (2001) advocate a focus on human capital, that is, get the right people on the bus and in the right seats. The egalitarian dream notwithstanding, some people enjoy higher incomes than others. They are promoted faster and take the lead on more important projects. The human capital explanation is that inequality results from differences in individual ability. Hence, leaders driven by this theory focus energy on hiring and developing *the right people*—those with the knowledge, skills, and capabilities needed by the organization. On the other hand, we have all seen examples where buying the most talented individuals, as the New York Yankee's do in baseball, does not equate with ultimate success all of the time.

When people work together bonds develop which can further or limit organizational aspirations. Sociologists explain this phenomenon through social capital theory. Social capital theorists and practitioners focus on the quality of the relationship between people. In Collins' (2001) terms, they get people into the *right seats*, to which I add *on the right bus with the right bus driver*. Putting people in the right seats encourages the development of mutually trusting relationships, opportunity, and a collegial quality between people's relationships.

Leaders connect people and activities with goals and values in different ways. Some leaders focus on the leader's perspective and follow Jim Collins' advice or that of Lou Gerstner (2002) who did not tolerate senior executives *pushing back* when he was revitalizing IBM. Some organizational thinkers say we need visionaries; others say we need professionals who can bring order to the organization. The need for aligned, dedicated followers is seldom mentioned. Yet, followers facilitate or constrain the leader's room to maneuver.

LEADERS, FOLLOWERS AND COLLEAGUES

In an age of changing workforce demography, the importance of followers is not heavily debated among theorists. Some of Peter Drucker's most insightful contributions hinge on the value of effective workers. For instance, in 2002, he noted that employees are people first. Successful organizations create the conditions that enable people to do their best work. In a similar vein, James McGregor Burns (1978) advised that interpreting and reacting to the behaviors of followers is a key aspect of leadership. Furthermore, Steven Covey rested his theory of the individual's movement from independence to interdependence on the assertion that, "the single most important principle in the field of interpersonal relationships is this.... First, seek to understand and then to be understood." Most people, he says listen, "not with the intent to understand, but with the intent to reply" (p. 28). Drucker, Burns, and Covey are saying much the same thing; that the importance of leaders understanding the nature of followers is crucial to organizational success.

Leaders need followers as much as followers need leaders. The relationship is symbiotic and reciprocal. If a leader wants to get more from followers they must give more to followers and vice versa. In many ways followers are similar to leaders. Both leaders and followers exert influence which can impact the achievement of desired outcomes. Howard Gardner (1995, p. 35) says that they may also have some common needs. Leaders and followers need mission, common values, and structure. When followers pick leaders, they tend to choose those with characteristics and social backgrounds similar to their own. Historically, many successful leaders served apprenticeships early in their careers and/or were mentored by leaders who influenced them during their developmental years. Examples of such apprenticeships include: Aristotle and Plato; Carl Jung and Sigmund Freud; Dwight Eisenhower and Fox Conner; Thomas Jefferson and John Adams and Benjamin Franklin; Mahatma Gandhi and Jawaharlal Nehru; Gordon Moore and Andy Grove; J. R. D. Tata and Ratan Tata; and Lovie Brown and Tony Dungy.

Followers differ from leaders in several ways. Gardner (1995) believes that leaders are more apt to challenge authority at an early age whereas followers tend to search for an authority figure for security. Followers take the lead only on matters related to technical or professional expertise. Leaders, on the other hand, might hand off to followers several times during the same meeting when both technical and organizational matters are at stake.

The long-standing view that good leaders establish direction remains sound. Leaders, not followers, are at the helm for goal setting, work distribution, resource gathering, and organizational interfaces with other organizations or groups. They serve as the reality check for followers as to whether or not ideas will work within the organization. They let the people who make up the organization know what the needs and limits are. Moreover, successful leaders have learned to achieve not only their own and the organization's goals but also the significant goals of their followers because they understand that the relationship between them is symbiotic.

With few exceptions, most leadership research has been undertaken from the leader's perspective; ignoring the fact that followers have their own motivations. Rarely mentioned is the fact that followers also have the need for power, achievement, sociability, rewards, incentives, equity, and meaning in varying degrees. Many leaders consider only their own actions without considering what their followers might do. They don't understand follower behavior well enough to choose the best course of action. Examining the leader-follower relationship exclusively from the leader's perspective leaves a vacuum in trying to understand the phenomenon. In essence, before leaders can effectively engage followers, they must learn something about them and eliminate a potentially destructive blind spot.

In my leadership journey I learned that organizational alignment was easier to achieve when my organization contained colleague type followers, or when I was successful in turning followers into colleagues. As I explained earlier, working with colleagues is different from working with subordinates. Colleagues interact with leaders, as opposed to just reacting and responding to them. Distinguishing between these two terms might seem to be semantics to some, but it's a necessity if leaders are to integrate the organization's strategic intent into daily work routines.

Colleagues want to believe in their leaders. They seek leaders who provide direction not through orders and commands, but through shared values, inspiration and a shared vision. Above all, colleagues also want an honest interpretation of the future—one they believe is worthy of their investment. Leaders transform followers into colleagues by facilitating the development and pursuit of common goals and by linking follower awareness of the needs of the organization and their needs for self-development. While some followers come to this naturally, others must be helped to develop this awareness. Three overarching concepts—the zone of acceptance—social capital—trust—are at the center of assisting leaders to understand the importance of their relationships with followers.

The Zone of Acceptance

In his powerful and seminal treatise on the functions of the executive, Chester Barnard (1938), the former CEO of American Telephone and Telegraph Company, proposed an "acceptance theory of authority" in which he suggested that the decision as to whether an order has authority lies with the person to whom it is addressed, not in the person who issues the order. He further proposed that for an order to be authoritative the follower must understand it; accept that it is consistent with organizational or personal goals; have the ability to comply with it; and believe the rewards outweigh the costs in complying. He explained what he called the *zone of indifference* in the following manner:

If all the orders for actions reasonably practicable were to be arranged in the order of their acceptability to the person affected, it may be conceived that there are a number which are clearly unacceptable, that is, which certainly will not be obeyed; there is another group somewhat more or less on the neutral line, that is, either barely acceptable or barely unacceptable; and a third group unquestionably acceptable. This last group lies within the "zone of indifference." The person affected will accept orders lying within this zone and is relatively indifferent as to what the order is so far as the question of authority is concerned. Such an order lies within the range that in a general way was anticipated at the time of undertaking the connection with the organization. (pp. 168–169)

Herbert Simon won the 1978 Nobel Prize in economics for his pioneering research into the decision-making process within economic organizations. In 1947, he offered a complementary theory to *the zone of indifference* which he referred to as the *zone of acceptance.* The zone of acceptance is the area in which organizational members accept decisions without question. As seen in Figure 6.2, the zone of acceptance (ZOA) can be wider or narrower depending on the degree to which the inducements exceed the burdens and sacrifices which determine the individual's adhesion to the organization. It is important to remember that the ZOA expands and contracts. The more decisions that fall inside the zone, the

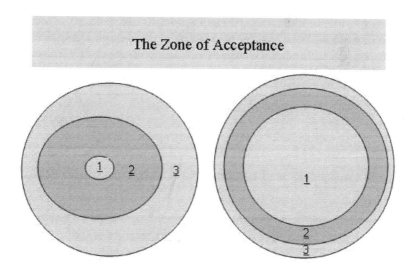

Legend: 1 = Acceptance, 2 = Indifference, 3 = Resistance

Figure 6.2.   Why do followers resist change?

more trust builds between leaders and followers, and the zone widens. If leader decisions fall outside the zone, followers will resist. When leaders are new the zone is understandably narrow. Their goal should be to widen the zone and gain acceptance from followers.[1] Leaders as well as managers want to expand the ZOA as much as possible to make the tasks of leadership easier.

Strategic leaders can work to widen the ZOA through a number of influence strategies. They enforce their role legitimacy, create a sense of obligation, and develop a reputation as an expert in key areas, get people to publicly commit to requests, map the political terrain and build coalitions of influential stakeholders. They can also manipulate through fear of retribution; or reinforce through charisma, loyalty, or approval ratings. Furthermore, they learn to bargain, negotiate, and recast situations to create responsible compromises.[2] I suggest that strategic leaders try to stay in the ZOA during the important first months on the job. The ZOA tends to be narrower at this stage so it requires a period of time during which each participant foregoes the opportunity to exploit the other for their own advantage.[3]

The Elephant in the Room

Trust is the connective tissue that enlarges the zone of acceptance and binds the leader-follower relationship together. Before followers align with the strategic intent, they will ask rhetorically. Is this leader truthful and ethical? Does the leader have character and conviction? Is the leader worthy of our trust? The second set of questions they ask focus on leader capability, productivity and efficiency. Does the leader communicate in ways that challenge and inspire us? Is the leader decisive, positive and optimistic? Does the leader have a sense of direction, a strong vision of the way the organization will look and feel in the future?

When employees lack trust in their leaders, stress and divisiveness prevails, performance erodes, and talented workers leave for more motivating environments. Trust is crucial to the leader's ability to move organizations and causes. It creates a safe present and a willingness to explore future possibilities. It enables leaders to make decisions when they do not have full knowledge of consequences.

Some leaders fail to establish trust because they remain tied to the old science. It goes against the leadership paradigm many current leaders and some followers grew up with. Classical managers did not trust employees to do the right thing. They trusted the system to make employees do the right thing. Hierarchical relationships have never been built on trust. For that reason the old maxim "if you want something done right, you do it yourself" has become a part of our culture.

We feel trust. Trust is visceral. Emotions associated with trust include companionship, friendship, love, agreement, relaxation, and comfort. Trust allows belief in a person's ability to perform a specific task under specific circumstances. From the leader's perspective, it is a positive statement about a relationship that says, "I believe you are capable of taking this action."

In one of my seminars I was extolling the virtues of building trust when the CEO of the host organization said, "I give trust, I don't build it." He was signaling to me and his staff that he was worthy of trust. While I agreed that to gain trust you have to give it, upon reflection I understood that his premise was faulty. One cannot give trust; one must earn the trust of followers. It is created (or destroyed) by leader competence, benevolence toward followers, reliability, honesty, and consistency in following a set of desirable principles.

Leader behavior is critical in developing trusting relationships with followers. Leaders who monitor too closely; fail to delegate significant work, do not support follower decisions, and constantly change their minds are not showing trust in their followers. If leaders want to reap the benefits of empowered staff, they must be willing to trust their staff to get the work done. It is difficult for leaders to trust when they retain the responsibility for job success, but they must. From a follower perspective, trust has a greater chance of being established when the leader is honest with them; is perceived as doing the right thing; respects their privacy; helps them keep their promises; and stands firm on decisions based on principle. The key benefit to the leader of the use of these actions is that they can trust with comfort. Trust is both an emotional and logical act. Emotionally, it occurs when we expose our vulnerabilities to people believing they will not take advantage of our openness. Logically, we assess the probabilities, calculate expected gains and losses based on hard performance data, and conclude that the person in question is worthy of our trust. In practice, trust occurs because we have experienced the other person's trustworthiness and because we have faith in human nature.

Some say a broken bond of trust cannot be mended. It is difficult but given enough time, a willing heart and a great deal of effort, it is possible. Some beginning attempts to mend trust might take the form of: "I was not clear about my expectations." "How can I make this work?" "I am beginning to understand what is going on, here is what I can do." Mending trust involves reestablishing the relationship through transparency and personal connection. Most of that is done by immediate recognition of mistakes followed by the creation of a sense of inclusion for the resolution and/or absolution of those mistakes.

The benefits of trustworthy relationships to organizations are many. In a trusting relationship followers have confidence in their leaders. Trust improves task effectiveness because it reduces the need for close monitoring. A trusting relationship supports interdependence. Great teamwork requires trusting relationships so that coworkers feel confident that everyone is fulfilling their shared commitments as they work interdependently toward a goal. When people have confidence in one another, they are willing to lead and be led by the team. They do not have to second-guess, double back, or duplicate other people's work. They communicate more easily, frequently, and transparently. They catch problems quickly and take bolder steps to fix them because they don't worry about embarrassment or punishment. Consequently their energy is directed to achieving goals rather than to self protection.

In a trusting relationship we can relax, communicate openly and celebrate the successes of others. Trusting relationships help us achieve more than we can on our own. Trust is an important missing ingredient for bringing about frame-breaking or frame-sustaining change. For these reasons it serves as the tightly strung strategic leadership glue that binds the organization together.

Social Capital

The presence of accepting zones of acceptance and trusting relationships is achieved with the development of social capital. Coleman (1988) defines social capital as—the personal network of individual and group relationships. It is the wind that unfurls zones of acceptance and leads to the full utilization of the organization's human capital. Without it, the organization's strategic intent has less of a chance of making its way into the everyday work processes and behaviors, and eventually results in greater efficiency and performance. Social capital stems from trusting relationships, communications (active listening, dialogue, and storytelling), norms of reciprocity, as well as from bridging, networking, and bartering, and sometimes temporarily from the use of hierarchy or force.

There are many ways strategic leaders can build social capital. For instance, since they are strategically positioned in an organization leaders can develop more rewarding opportunities for their followers. They serve as role models, provide intellectual stimulation, give individualized support, recognize accomplishments, and manage information through task cues.[4] I have categorized these concepts into three tactics—relating, reaching for power, and persuading—strategic leaders can use to become more adept at building great teams and producing committed followers. In Table 6.1, I have captured the three tactics. Supportive *relationships* are

Table 6.1. The Tactics and Levers Leaders Use to Build Social Capital

Tactics	Levers	Related Leader Actions That Followers Associate With Aligning Tactics*
Bonding	• Social Capital • Active Listening • Storytelling	• Is honest with us. • Does the right thing. • Can be trusted to do the right thing. • Helps us try to keep promises. • Respects our privacy. • Makes decisions by following policy Ensures that procedures are followed. • Stands firm on decisions based on principle
Bridging	• Reaching	• Develops alliances with people from outside of the organization. • Maintains alliances with people of power and influence. • Strengthens his/her position by gaining the allegiance of others inside the organization • Develops alliances with people from inside the organization. • Uses influence to advance his/her agenda. • Has access to people who have influence over getting things done. • Associates him/herself with individuals who have influence. • Allocates resources to influence his/her purposes.
Bartering	• Motivational Levers • Bartering • Social Influence	• Willing to barter to make deals. • Gives something in exchange for help. • Gives rewards when s/he is helped. • Promises rewards to get what s/he wants • Compromises to make deals.

Source: The Strategic Leadership Questionnaire

created when they are built on common interests, normative bonds, listening, and understanding the power of story are central aspects of building strong relationships with colleagues. *Reaching for Power* is accomplished by building internal and external alliances. *Persuading* enables relationships and alliances to cohere and is mastered through understanding the motivating levers, bartering, and application of social influence principles. As Kouzes and Posner (2003) reported from their studies, "on balance, we found that by sharing power and allowing followers to influence them, leaders can foster leadership skills in others, as well as achieve other gains through their greater participation and involvement" (p. 279).

BONDING

As I drove home from Miami International Airport one Wednesday morning I listened to a radio interview with Colleen Barrett, Southwest Airlines' President. The piece discussed the steady growth of her company, which consistently turns a profit in an industry marked by failing companies. The most intriguing part of the interview was President Barrett's description of the internal workings of Southwest Airlines, a company that has a vision of employee satisfaction as the most important aspect of their success. She described the culture of the company as one of collaboration based on human relations, emphasizing the point by describing her "family of 35,000 employees."

My subsequent research of the company suggests that President Barrett's description of her relationship with employees of the company is a reality.[5] Apparently she has a wall of pictures, changed every 2 months, of a few hundred employees doing whatever they like to do—playing with pets, sailing, and working—whatever they want to submit. She walks by the photographs every day, pauses to look and adjusts them. In the radio interview she talked about an office party being held, a pot-luck event for an entire office to which both the company president and chairman were invited. There they were, the big and not so big wigs, chit chatting around and gobbling up chicken wings. From her description it would have been difficult to tell who was who in the hierarchy.

Having heard many company propaganda pitches in my day, I went to the Southwest Airlines Web site where I found a picture of three casually dressed employees and the maxim, "we are a company of people, not planes—ind out more about us." A click on the second half of the sentence reveals a biographical description with another picture of each employee. I looked up the mission statement of Southwest Airlines[6] and found: The mission of Southwest Airlines is dedication to the highest quality of Customer Service delivered with a sense of warmth, friendliness, individual pride, and Company Spirit.

To Our Employees

We are committed to providing our Employees a stable work environment with equal opportunity for learning and personal growth. Creativity and innovation are encouraged for improving the effectiveness of Southwest Airlines. Above all, Employees will be provided the same concern, respect, and caring attitude within the organization that they are expected to share externally with every Southwest Customer.

Notice one thing; this mission statement is 19 years old! More importantly, the second sentence describes a learning community. It is obvious

29 years later that Southwest was far ahead of the competition—ready and waiting for a new paradigm for the twenty-first century.

Southwest Airlines is not alone in recognizing that organizational alignment is gained through trust and commitment to the people who make up the organization. Consider companies like Ritz-Carlton and its employee promise:

- At the Ritz-Carlton, our ladies and gentlemen are the most important resource, and our service commitment to our guests.
- By applying the principles of trust, honesty, respect, integrity and commitment, we nurture and maximize talent to the benefit of each individual and the company.
- The Ritz-Carlton fosters a work environment where diversity is valued, quality of life is enhanced, individual aspirations are fulfilled, and the Ritz Carlton mystique is strengthened. [7]

Ritz-Carlton nurtures employee loyalty by fulfilling "the employee promise" and encouraging employee innovation. Nowhere was the Ritz-Carlton's employee promise more evident than the days that followed Hurricane Katrina.[8] Immediately, the CEO made contact with their employees in the New Orleans area, indicating that Ritz-Carlton was there to help them. He promised that they would find employment at other Ritz-Carlton's, while the damage was being addressed in New Orleans.

Companies like Southwest Airlines and Ritz-Carlton have it right. They have developed a trusting culture by pledge and deed. Trust is the key to the door of other people's minds. If they don't trust you, then you haven't a hope of persuading them. If they do trust you, it doesn't necessarily mean you can persuade them, but at least they will listen to you and take you seriously.

What about the competitors? I found that United Airlines had a huge amount of employee ownership in its own company, and the new CEO[9] came in thinking that this meant that United would make some great deals with their unions and bring together a cohesive airline that would become number one in no time. As it turned out, the major barrier to every initiative was what was described as a lack of trust among differing factions. The ideas were great and the reforms palatable, but in every instance they were stopped by this lack of trust between the various groups and management.

At its core, bonding is about ensuring that trust is an attribute of the system and not just something developed among individuals. Strategic leaders connect with followers, and connect followers to the organization. From an alignment perspective, leadership is not as much about the leader's goals and priorities as it is about the connections made with colleagues who are organizational superiors, subordinates and peers. Leaders bond with followers by first creating meaning, and then by cajoling and persuading followers through social influence tactics. There is no more powerful force than human connection to foster organizational bonding.

It is important that good leaders bond with followers, but it's more important that followers bond with the organization. This connecting tactic focuses on developing close emotional ties between followers and building emotional commitment from followers to the organizational aspiration and values. The barbecues at Southwest Airlines and the morning line up at Ritz-Carlton help create a bond between a critical mass of employees who share common values. These are practical ways leaders build commitment and community and can be described as methods for building internal social capital.

Leaders and followers bond in different ways. Some bond around shared interests. For instance, in studies of 32 negotiation experiments involving more than 5,000 participants, Leigh Thompson (1996, 2003, 2005) of the Kellogg School of Management found that rival negotiators failed to identify shared interests 50% of the time. She concluded that looking for shared interests was the factor that distinguished the excellent negotiators from less successful ones.

Armand Hammer, the industrialist, art collector, and philanthropist, understood the relationship between common interests and advancing one's career. At the age of 23, with a newly minted medical degree from Columbia's College of Physicians and Surgeons, he considered two paths to the future. The first path led to a prestigious medical career in New York, the other led to a medical career as part of the American delegation to assist Russians after their revolution.

The New York offer was a prestigious internship, one of two offered each year, with the Bellevue Hospital. The internships were the gift of Dr. Van Horn Norrie, a renowned diagnostician at the time and also the person who selected the interns. In his autobiography, Hammer (1987) said he did everything he could to make Dr. Norrie aware of him. As he said, "I wanted to make sure that he would remember my name" (p. 87). In his characteristically meticulous way, the young Hammer did extensive research on Dr. Norrie and found that etchings were by far his greatest passion. Never having owned an etching and not being very knowledgeable about them, he studied everything he could find about etchings. When he was finally sure that he had sufficient knowledge, he approached Norrie on one of his hospital rounds and said, "I understand you are a great collector of etchings, Doctor." Norrie replied, "How did you know that?" To which Hammer replied, "well I am interested myself in art, especially etchings, and I've frequently come across your name in the literature as one of the great collectors ... I'd love to see your collection someday." Norrie, who always looked for ways to explore his passion, replied "why don't you come to my home on Sunday afternoon and I'll be glad to show you the whole collection." After the viewing, which was accompanied by tea and conversation, Hammer commented that Dr. Norrie knew "exactly who I was." When awarded the celebrated internship Hammer added "I never knew if he was influenced by my examination marks or having found what he thought was a brother collector." Hammer would use this technique of influence many times during his long career.

Leaders and followers also bond through common goals. Armand Hammer turned down the internship at Bellevue to take the second path of practicing medicine with victims of the typhus epidemic that broke out after the Russian revolution. He returned to the United States an entrepreneur and a rich man. Walter Cronkite noted that Hammer embodied a unique bridge between communism and capitalism. His journey was aided by none other than Lenin. Hammer (1987) recalls their first meeting as one of "getting to know you." Lenin asked, "shall we speak in Russian or English?" Hammer replied that he would prefer English since Lenin "spoke so perfectly." While refuting the compliment, Lenin offered that most foreigners find Russian a difficult language to learn. Hammer replied that he was trying to master 100 words per day. To which Lenin replied, "I used the same method myself when I was in London ... at first it was not so bad, but the more you learn, the more difficult it is to retain." Lenin then explained that "our two countries, the United States and Russia are complementary." Russia, he said, was like the United States during its pioneering stage. It was backward but possessed enormous undeveloped resources. Russia could provide the raw materials and markets for machines and goods in exchange for American technology, spirit, machines, engineers and instructors. Hammer left the meeting with the first American concession (contract) and a relationship that Hammer cemented by gifting Lenin with a bronze monkey contemplating a human skull. He noted that "Lenin gave orders that the bronze was not to be removed from his desk and is still there today, in his Kremlin office, which is a national museum" (p. 139)

Consider another example of the way common goals bind followers to the organization. In 1968, Robert Noyce and Gordon Moore left Fairchild Semiconductor to found Intel. They brought along Andy Grove. When Noyce moved to the board room he was replaced as CEO by Gordon Moore. When Moore moved to the board room he was replaced by Grove. When it was Andy Grove's turn, he was replaced by Craig Barrett (another of the early defectors from Fairchild to Intel).[10] This line of succession led to extraordinary financial results. It also created a culture of trust that survives to this day.

There are lessons to be learned from these examples. First, bonding requires developing or recognizing a common interest, a commitment to a goal, and the nourishment of long term relationships. At the heart of the Noyce, Moore, Grove, Barrett handoff is a bonded relationship built on trust, common goals and interpersonal exchange. Development of trust began when the quartet took the risk to leave Fairchild Semiconductors. Some left as founding members (Noyce and Moore) others as colleagues (Grove and Barrett) but the bond was cast. Through the turmoil of the next four decades, when the company had to reinvent itself three times to maintain its position in the market place, the interpersonal exchanges and mutual obligations among the quartet were augmented by a work environment that valued dialogue, cooperation, and collaboration. When it came time for each to pass the torch they passed it to a member they trusted and respected.

The Hammer and Intel stories illustrate the elemental relationship between bonding and network building. Colleagues bond when trust and reciprocity are prominent features of their relationships and networks.

Active Listening

Many leaders view their communications role as information givers rather than listeners. Strategic leaders, however, should be much more listeners and information seekers than givers. But, listening is not hearing (Gamble & Gamble 1994). Listening to hear requires understanding, analyzing, and evaluating ideas. It requires active listening.

Strategic leaders use active listening to process both verbal and non verbal content as well as feelings and to monitor communication channels. There are three active listening skills leaders use to listen in a way that the persons know you understand what they are saying (a) reflecting content, (b) reflecting feeling, and (c) summarizing. Active listening is improved when the leader also displays proficiency in fundamental behaviors such as paraphrasing, clarifying, elaborating, reframing, self-disclosing, questioning, and summarizing. Table 6.2 describes these essential communication skills.

Review the active listening skills presented in Table 6.2. Which active listening skills are leaders demonstrating when they ask the following questions or make the following statements?

"You seem to be saying." "Are you saying?" "Did I hear you right, what you said was...?" "My attention wondered on the last point—can you hit me again with it?" "You seem upset with something, have I said something to offend you?" "What you are saying now is…. What I heard you

Table 6.2.   Communication Skills—Active Listening

Active Listening is a method which focuses entirely on the speaker's communications, internal frame of reference (often their feelings and interests), and then reflects back to the person what has been heard, attempting to "check" what has been said. In active listening the focus is not on the listener's view or opinion, but rather on the speaker's content and nonverbal clues. Three skills are essential to listening in a way that a person knows you understand what he is saying: (a) reflecting content, (b) reflecting feeling and (c) summarizing

Reflecting Content is the ability to understand the meaning of the message through the listener's response by elaborating, clarifying, and reframing responses to clear up confusion or create common understandings.

Paraphrasing is a skill that helps the listener interpret, or reflect ideas or suggestions to clear up confusion, indicating alternatives and issues, and giving examples.

Reframing is a skill that involves changing the wording, concept, or description of any piece of information. For example, the painting remains the same, but the matting may change. Reframing provides new view to an old problem.

Questioning is a skill that uses direct and indirect questions to seek specific answers, requesting facts, relevant information, or opinions, suggestions, and ideas.

Brainstorming is a skill that aims to generate possible solutions to a problem that has already been defined in terms of interests and other supporting facts.

Reflecting Feeling is the ability to listen sensitively to expressed and unexpressed feelings, in order to create a sense of trust between the speaker and the listener.

Sensitivity is a skill that enables you to perceive the needs, concerns, and personal problems of others. It is useful in resolving conflicts; dealing with people from different backgrounds; dealing effectively with people concerning emotional issues; and knowing what information to communicate and to whom.

Encouraging is a skill that generates a friendly, warm and responsive reaction to others. It helps you to accept others in order to understand rather than appraise or refute their contributions.

Self-disclosing is a skill that focuses on the speaker's feelings, thoughts, or beliefs, including: Information or opinion giving - offering facts, providing relevant data, stating a belief, and giving suggestions or ideas.

Confronting is a skill used to encourage one or more of the parties to stop a particular behavior that is destructive to the communication process. It is typically done in face-to-face conferences, though in some cases will occur in group settings where the risks are higher.

Summarizing is the ability to pull related ideas together and restating suggestions after discussion, then sending up trial balloons to see if nearing conclusion or agreement has been reached. Summarize what you think the other person has been saying and obtain his or her reaction periodically during the communication episode.

say 5 minutes ago was…. Can you clarify the difference in these two statements for me? Or, do they mean the same thing?" "Your last statement suggested that you didn't have a clear idea of what I said. Can you repeat it to me?" "Let's review the alternatives and what you think are the strengths of each?" "Let me see if I can summarize the main points I heard you say…. Do you have anything else to add?" "Here's what I heard you say…." "I hear you saying…." "Before we proceed, let me check on whether I really understand that…." "Let me run that one through the machine again." "What I got from that was…. Is that the whole idea?" "Can you summarize what we've been discussing for the past 5 minutes?" "I need to check to see that we are both saying the same thing before we proceed to the next issue. Would you summarize our agreement to this point?" "You know I have had similar feelings about it." "Hey, you look happy all of a sudden."

Storytelling

Storytelling is another important communication skill in building relationships. While it is true that strategic leaders are much more listeners and information seekers than givers, they also play an important role in shaping the mindsets of followers. They engage in what David Cooperrider (1986, 1987) calls appreciative inquiry—the art of valuing possibilities. They center on positive conversations of hope and inspiration rather than deficit-based conversations of disappointing experiences. When leaders and followers look at a certain priority as a "problem," they constrain their ability to effectively address the priority. Strategic leaders move conversations away from problems and toward possibilities by offering new and unconsidered alternatives. In a way they provide intellectual stimulation that creates room for movement and authorship. Deficient discourse is not empowering. It erodes trust, creates cynicism, and depletes energy. From an appreciative inquiry perspective, strategic leaders draw out and highlight ideas that otherwise would remain unexpressed.

Strategic leaders are also skilled at telling a story of why change is needed and what the role of everyone will be in a way that resonates throughout the organization. They always talk about the same things. They sell the company, its aspirations and its contribution to the stakeholders. Strategic leaders talk about the values that hold members together in a common cause. They talk about the challenges the organization faces and what they are doing about it. They honor the collective contributions of individual followers as well as their unique contributions. They put followers at the center of things not on the fringe. Finally, they talk about the future. They provide the expectation of success coupled with a belief in the ability of followers to make the change work. They frame the change by appealing to followers' needs for achievement and growth. They make sense out of information that does not support or threaten the direction the organization is taking. Through a continuous formal and informal dialogue which reinforces a sense of community, purpose, values, and commitment, they move the organization in the right direction.

Strategic leader talk is distinctive. They talk through analogy, story, metaphor, and aphorisms. Confronted by a new problem or opportunity they think about how they solved similar problems or exploited similar opportunities in the past. In a simple example of such a spin off, McDonald's, the originator of the McBurger, followed it up with the McPizza, McChicken and the McMenu. In a more indirect situation, Circuit City created CarMax because someone saw the used car market as analogous to the electronics market. It's easy, however, to overlook the limits of analogies. Strategic leaders make sure the similarities are more than superficial. They ask, "Will it work in the new context?" They remember de Lesseps's miscalculation of the similarities of the topography of the Suez and Panama Canal surroundings and the resulting disastrous campaign.

Strategic leaders rely on vivid, emotionally engaging, and compelling stories which are told and retold to make their points. Antoine Marie-Roger de Saint-Exupery, the French pilot, poet, and author makes this point when he says, "if you want to build a ship, don't drum up the men to gather wood, divide the work, and give orders. Instead ... teach them to yearn for the vast and endless sea." Like the image created by Saint-Exupery, there is something surreal about the relationship of a great leader and their colleagues. Though the context is different, Jack Welch, the former Chairman of General Electric, highlights the intensity and focus he brought to the repeated communication of ideas he thought the company should adopt:

> I was an outrageous champion of everything we did—from our early need to face reality and change the culture to our major initiatives that reshaped the company. Whenever I had an idea or message I wanted to drive it into the organization, I could never say it enough. I repeated it over and over and over, at every meeting and review, for years, until I could almost gag on the words. I always felt I had to be "over the top" to get ... people behind an idea. (Welch, 2001, p. 393)

It seems, however, that the common wisdom of repetition, repetition, repetition is only half right. If directed at management levels, Welch's strategy would be effective in developing a commitment. But for repetition to stick where the work gets done, communication of a major change must be undertaken by managers and supervisors, rather than just top executives or the public relations office.[11] Repeated communications, as Welch employed, will not by themselves make the ideas stick. The problem is that leaders at the top do not encourage two-way communications that provide a common discussion ground, nor do they eliminate ambiguity. There must be a conscious effort to weave the key points of the strategic intent into organizational conversations at all levels.

Chip and Dan Heath (2007), the coauthors of *Made to Stick*, suggest that

> if your frontline employees can talk about your strategy [intent], can tell stories about it, can talk back to their managers and feel credible doing so, then the strategy [intent] is doing precisely what it was intended to do, guide behavior. (p. 153)

The Heath brothers used British Petroleum's (BP) vision of having "no dry holes" as a concrete way to make an idea stick. The "no dry holes" aspiration was formed in 1991 after BP studies estimated that it cost $4 million to drill a small well, a sum that could well expand to $40 million for large wells, which they considered to be too much risk. They studied the problem by asking their drillers to predict the chance of success prior to drilling. They found that drilling opportunities with a predicted success of below 20% rarely hit! Oil drillers were systematically overestimating the chance of success. In an effort to avoid these dry holes, the head of exploration suggested that instead of considering dry holes as a cost of doing business, they should be considered a sign of failure. He declared that the new standard should be "no dry holes."

The new standard was definitely out of the drillers' zone of acceptance. They believed that the only way to know if there was oil was to start drilling, and then gather information so they could sharpen their prospects on the next site. However, the "no dry holes" standard required the drillers to don their geologist hats and evaluate the geological data about the ability of the substrates to form oil. The new standard caused them to systematically aggregate the information they had. Heath and Heath report that:

> the language of discussions at BP also shifted. Before "no dry holes," BP tended to rely on Expected Monetary Value (EMV) to talk about decisions. As an analytical model, EMV is flawless, but the assumptions feeding the model were subject to manipulation. Crafty explorers who wanted to drill a high-risk well would just increase the numbers assessing the potential payoff of the field.... "No dry holes" created common ground that brought more people into the conversation—it shifted the conversation from numerical risks to geological risks. (p. 20)

The phrase "no dry holes" is a great example of strategic communication. It created a competitive edge for BP against other energy companies because it was concrete, unexpected and easy to communicate in conversations around the coffee pot, the conference room, and the board room. It was also an effective guide to behavior. By 2000 BP's hit rate was an astonishing 2 in 3 hits, rather than the 1 in 10 hit rate before "no dry holes." Think of the savings! The lesson for strategic leaders is that dense statements of intent can't unite followers in the way concrete language and stories can.

BRIDGING

Strategic leaders build relationships but they also *reach* for power to multiply support for their goals. Bridging is a tactic used by strategic leaders to develop alliances with people of power and influence from outside and inside the organization; they use social influence and available resources to advance his/her agenda. From a follower perspective they are seen as associating him/herself with individuals who have influence and as having access to people who have influence over getting things done.

Bridging is the key tactic strategic leaders use to reach for power. They bridge to influential members of their community and organization to further their own interest and/or to develop external social capital. The purpose of bridging is to gain insights, support, and potential availability of resources from either the different levels within the organization, or from the complementors and competitors external to the organization. Of course the bridge must also carry the weight of negotiating, defending institutional integrity, and improving public relations. Reciprocation, alliances, commitments, and obligations are the building blocks of a bridging strategy. The exchange centers on skills, experiences, information, technology, and political support in return for the same. Whereas social power deals with the relationships of individuals and groups, bridging tactics are used to maximize the power of the leader or the organization through a process of networking, partnership and coalition building.

The strategic leader needs to be a skilled networker who is able to identify and establish a mutually beneficial relationship with those complementors and competitors that are either blocking or supportive of the goals and interests of the organization. Internal and external bridging builds capacity. Leaders who can detect crucial powerful social or political networks are a long way down the path to understanding their environment which allows them to lead more powerfully. When charged with mobilizing efforts successful leaders call on their network for support (if they have cultivated one).

Networking can be employed as an individual strategy through which leaders adopt and create an individual supportive network. It can also be used to link a critical mass of organizations into a supportive network so that power is maximized. At the individual level networking can be seen as a support group. For example, the network helps when leaders are looking for new work. The same concept is in action when cancer survivors take cancer patients out to lunch, to the doctor, or to purchase a wig. The bond established by the disease is acted upon by those who are connected to it. The motto of the Cheers Bar, "where everybody knows your name," captures another important benefit of supportive friends. At another level networking allowed Bill Gates and Warren Buffet, two of the wealthiest men on the planet, to become allies in the fight to eradicate disease worldwide. They had the common purpose and flexibility necessary to adapt as their bridge was built.

At the organizational level, strategic leaders recognize that informally constructed networks of opinion leaders and people with resources or political clout are the true structure of the organization. They must be engaged to make things happen. Furthermore, strategic leaders understand the personal and organizational benefits of networking and encourage their followers to develop and seek out such relationships. Don't we all value a friend in the right place when a favor is needed? Didn't Armand Hammer benefit from his relationship with Lenin? As strategic leaders up and down the line develop bridges, the entire organization benefits from the insights, support, and potential availability of resources tapped into by the joint efforts of all. The result is a dynamic organization with multifaceted relationships at all levels within, and external to, the unit.

The story of heroic Bertha Calloway story provides an example of the failure to bridge. Mrs. Calloway was an Omaha civil rights activist and black history buff. She harbored a dream for an archives and interpretive center that chronicled the seldom told story of black pioneers. Beginning in 1976 she forged the museum from her own imagination and determination. It became a storehouse and a source of Black pride chronicling Kwanza, Black History Month, the Black cowboys, the Black homesteaders, and the Tuskegee Airmen. The center revealed a history that has been withheld.

Mrs. Calloway is famed for her comment that "we cannot direct the wind, but we can adjust the sails." She obviously did not follow her own advice because her grand vision for the museum was never fully realized. Bertha wanted to keep the museum in the hands of grassroots Black people. However, it was already in fiscal trouble in 1993 when a benign tumor diminished her faculties. When Jim, her son, finally closed the museum in 2001, he summed up her failure in these words: "The powers that be like to see some substantial, high-profile figures on your board. They want you to change to their ways so she's steered clear of them."[12]

Part of the failure stems from her wary, insular, defensive posture probably brought on by many injustices during her life. She valued her independence above all else. She was never one to go out to cocktail parties or fancy dinners. Few outsiders were brought into her inner circle. She was a strong-minded lady who found it difficult to work with other people. She would listen and say "thank you very much, but I'm going to go ahead and do what I'm going to do." Admirable as that maverick streak may be, it also isolated the museum and cost it valuable allies. Like Henry Ford and de Lesseps, Mrs. Calloway could not adjust to a new context. Like Napoleon and Henry VIII, whose leadership failures were caused partly by their reliance on decreasing groups of trusted advisors, she created a smaller and smaller inner circle.

When strategic leaders need resources they do not currently possess, they bridge to those who can assist them. Of course it always helps to build the bridge prior to crossing the stream. Bertha rejected informal socializing. She also failed to maintain contacts through visits, telephone calls, correspondence and attendance at meetings. Consequently she was not able to connect her dream to powerful forces in the external environment and sadly she failed to capture the support she needed to achieve her dream.

A happier ending was achieved by Alex Rodriquez, the New York Yankee superstar. In November, 2007, Rodriquez and the New York Yankees agreed on a record $275 million, 10-year contract. The deal would not have occurred without Alex bridging to Goldman Sachs' managing directors John Mallory and Gerald Cardinale who conducted some shuttle diplomacy.

The need for shuttle diplomacy was created when Alex's agent rejected the Yankees final offer and closed negotiations for a new contract. Yankee management then publicly moved to replace Alex. Yet, Alex wanted to remain with the Yankee organization. He solved the dilemma by taking over the negotiations himself. First he reached out to Warren Buffet, the head of Berkshire Hathaway. Buffet advised him to find a confident of Yankee management to intervene for him and open up the negotiations again. Alex then reached out to the Goldman Sachs executives with whom he had done business with before and they worked with Randy Levine, the Yankee President, whom they had done business with before. The rest, as they say, is history.

The bottom line is that strategic leaders reach out to those outside their normal work or social units in order to build partnerships and alliances that support their work, social life or even their self interests. Strategic leaders learn to bridge and network by observing and seeking advice from others. They learn from examples such as Bertha Callaway and Alex Rodriquez. They learn by identifying who networks well in their organization or community. They identify exactly what those networkers do and say. They invite them to lunch or to meetings and ask them to talk about their view of networking.

BARTERING

Bartering enables relationships and alliances to cohere. It is mastered through understanding the motivational levers, principles of bartering, and application of social influence principles.

Motivational Levers

Strategic leaders are better able to relate, reach, and persuade when they understand the levers of human action. In this sense motivation is a foundational form of influence that leaders can use to try to move individuals from point A to point Z. Scholars offer several ways that this movement happens; needs, norms, rewards, equity, and goals. For instance, in more colleague-driven organizations followers want to go from point A to point Z. In laggard-driven organizations, followers must be told to go from point A to point Z. In competitor-driven organizations, followers must be cajoled into moving from point A to Z. In subordinate-driven organizations, followers are willing to move to from point A to B. The central issues for leaders are: (a) understanding activating forces which stimulate follower behavior, (b) gaining awareness of their own beliefs about human behavior, and (c) creating nurturing social and psychic environments which reinforce the intensity and direction of individual motivation.

Activating forces such as needs, norms, rewards, equity, and goals stimulate movement by followers. There is a rich and large literature base related to each of these forces. However, while motivational theories can offer suggestions and techniques to improve practice, they are generally not thought of as precise enough to provide answers in an everyday world of complex environments. Leaders can, however, use the different motivational theories to frame their problems of practice and select the ones that seem to work best in the context they practice.

Abraham Maslow (1954), the clinical psychologist, proposed that human beings are motivated to satisfy certain universal innate needs. He classified these universal human needs in a hierarchy: physiological, safety, affiliation, esteem, and self actualization. The conceptual clarity and intuitive appeal of Maslow's theory has led to its wide acceptance, even though it has not been rigorously tested.

Important variations on Maslow's theory are provided by David McClelland (1955, 1975, 1976) and Frederick Herzberg (1959, 1987). Rather than try to improve the Maslow construct, McClelland observed that people vary in their need to achieve, the extent they are motivated by it, and how it is activated. He identified three needs that motivate human behavior; achievement (the need to excel in reaching goals), power (the need to influence, control or dominate one's surroundings), and affiliation (the need for positive interpersonal relationships). He proposed that each one can be activated by organizational structure and norms. McClelland's research on these same three needs in work environments is enlightening. He found that the most productive for-profit organizations are inhabited by large numbers of workers with high achievement needs that can be activated by organizational structures and incentives.

Frederick Herzburg's investigations into human work behavior concluded that Maslow's higher order need factors (challenging work, verbal recognition, achievement, responsibility and promotion) motivate followers. However, the lower level needs such as bodily functions, safety, and affiliation, must be present before the motivators can be effective. In essence, Herzburg agrees with McClelland that enriching work has the potential to satisfy the esteem and self-actualization needs of individuals which leads to higher levels of performance.

Need theories can be used to understand follower resistance of or support for change. For example, resistance to change may be simply understood as the result of a large number of followers with high safety needs (Maslow); mismatches of needs and organization context (McClelland); or dissatisfaction caused by lack of hygienic factors (Herzberg). Support of change may be understood as the result of the change providing for recognition and self actualization (Maslow); power or achievement (McClelland); or higher order needs (Herzberg).

Most leaders are concerned with the more positive question of how to motivate most of the people most of the time. The need theories mentioned above are often referred to as deficiency theories; if needs are not being met followers will not follow and/or organizations will not be successful. Vroom's (1964) expectancy theory and Locke's (1968, 1990) goal theory provide more encouraging view points. Three assumptions underline these theories.

First, individuals go through a cognitive process to determine how much expenditure of energy they will apply to a particular outcome, goal, task, or opportunity. Second, people anticipate that certain events will occur. Third, people rationally consider situations, alternatives and consequences, and determine the amount of effort they are willing to expend to achieve an outcome. In essence, expectancy and goal theories are decision making models that use different factors to explain individual motivation.

In expectancy theory (see Table 6.3), the anticipation of the reward is the motivator.[13] Followers must believe that if they expend energy to achieve a particular outcome, they will be successful and they will be rewarded. While making up their mind to commit they will seek answers to questions such as: Is the task difficult and do I have the ability to accomplish it? If I act, what level of accomplishment can I achieve? Do I have the time to work toward the goal? Do I have the ability to do it? How do I feel about the goal I am being asked to work toward? Managers must be able to determine what rewards induce higher expenditures of effort, and if they can provide them.

In goal theory, however, the intention to accomplish a goal is the motivator. This intent (a commitment to doing something) is strengthened by the nature of the goal and its value to the individual. The more important the goal is to the individual, the more likely it is to create activity. While making up their mind to commit, followers judge which goals are good or bad against their personal interests by reviewing the incentives available and anticipating if the outcome will occur. The primary question for leaders is; how can I influence follower intentions so they achieve prescribed goals.

Motivation is personal. In many ways it's intangible. Yes, leaders can provide incentives and organize experiences in a way that encourages the sorts of behaviors that achieve a certain goal; but can they motivate another person? As seen in the needs-based and cognitive-based theories, the actual motivators are in the hands of the followers. Leaders can activate those motivators by the way they establish goals, and by the way they organize, inform, and support the individuals on their staff. Their first task is to identify the motivators at play. Their beliefs about human nature will shape the activating forces they employ. Criticisms notwithstanding, McClelland and Herzberg's notions of redesigning the organizational context to enhance intrinsic work motivation which encourages positive psychological states among followers are not only valid, but practical.

Table 6.3.   Cognitive Steps in Expectancy and Goal Theory

Theory	Expectancy	Goal
Motivator	Anticipation of receiving a reward.	Intention of achieving the goal.
Step 1	Can I do it?	What is the nature of the goal?
Step 2	Will I be rewarded?	How committed am I to the goal?
Step 3	Is the reward something I value?	

A primary aim of strategic leaders is to mobilize followers so together they accomplish important organizational goals. To achieve this aim they reach for the motivational levers of goals and incentives to encourage followers to initiate and sustain effort. Therefore, leaders must design organizations that deliberately assist participants in satisfying their psychological needs for esteem, autonomy, competence, and belonging. They must motivate followers to expend energy towards organizational goals; otherwise their motivation will be little more than a response to rewards or uses of power. Furthermore, when attempting to develop followers into colleagues, leaders would be well served by combining intrinsic incentives with the human tendency to respond to what is morally correct.

Bartering

Bartering can be seen as the grease that lubricates relationships. Strategic leaders barter to strengthen the effectiveness of their relationship and alliance building efforts. They do it by being willing to promise rewards, compromise and barter as long as it is ethical and moral to make achieve the organization's goals. From a follower perspective, leaders are seen as giving something in exchange for help. They want to know if the leader is a "two way guy;" one that expects but is willing to give. Consider the use of bartering and social influence and bridging tactics used by Major Victor Joppolo, a man famous for his leadership in the Italian city of Adano at the end of World War II.

Major Joppolo was the civilian affairs officer stationed in Adano after it was liberated from the Germans in World War II. He was charged with organizing village life, food and medical supplies, generally restoring order and installing a democratic government. In both words and deeds, Joppolo demonstrated leadership by addressing, on the ground, the needs and aspirations of those over whom he had authority, while striving to elevate those needs and aspirations to a higher plane. He explained to village leaders that the difference between democracy and fascism is that in a democracy the government leaders are no longer the masters of the people. "They are the servants of the people.... And watch: this thing will make you happier than you have ever been in your lives" (Hersey, 1988, p. 45).

The Pulitzer Prize winning book, *A Bell for Adano*, tells the story of Joppolo's attempts to get the extremely anti-authority fisherman, Tomasino, to lead his fellow fishermen back to work by telling him:

You said I was different. You could be different too. It is possible to make your authority seem to spring from the very people over whom you have authority. And after a while, it actually does spring from them, and you are only an instrument of their will. This is the thing that the Americans want to teach you who have lived under men who imagined that they themselves were authority. (p. 78)

A third incident speaks to the rewards of leading through Joppolo's framework. During his performance review, a high-level occupation official arrogantly tells Joppolo, "we can't afford to be too sentimental, Joppolo. Can't afford to let these people be *too* happy, you know. Can't afford to let discipline get too loose." Joppolo explains that the official couldn't "see that happiness and discipline don't go together.... Every time I've done something for these people, I've found they did two things for me just out of thanks" (p. 134). Understanding individual motivators and influence actions assist the strategic leading in developing the bartering tactic.

Social Influence

Strategic leaders use social influence principles to coax, cajole, entice, win over, and move people or groups to their own will. Normally power is identified by what can be seen; decision-making and agenda setting, applications of authority or coercion. There are also, however, invisible applications of power that work through people and stem from normative preferences such as beliefs, values, and self-interest.

The key to understanding how to persuade is to first determine what you are after—compliance or commitment. Compliance and conformity are fairly easy to come by. Commitment is a different genre. When people commit, they form a deep personal and sometimes emotional relationship. Committed followers are the foundation of organizations that are aligned. They know what to do and are able to persist in doing it for a long period of time, even in the face of adversity. Strategic leaders need commitment not just conformity or compliance from in order to catch a full wind. Therefore, they need to understand the use of social power tactics and follower response to those tactics. Researchers French and Raven (1959) and their followers[14] provide a plethora of such power tactics which are summarized in the following paragraphs.

Coercive power—the capacity to force people to do something against their will—can lead to compliance, but is more likely to lead to resistance. When leaders issue orders, demand action, and threaten negative consequences they are leading through coercion. "If you do not comply I will fire you!" "Do what I ask or I will break your leg." In these cases, follower must believe that the leader possesses coercive power and that they will use it in order to induce compliance.

Legitimate power—granted by position in an organization—generally leads to compliance but not to commitment. When leaders provide direction they are using legitimate power based on position. People will follow if they believe that the leader possesses the authority granted by the organization to make decisions, assign duties and require conformity.

While there is some evidence that managers who lack self-confidence will more likely use coercion and legitimate power even when other strategies might be more effective. Strategic leaders are able to persuade followers without the use of force or authority. However, they do not take force or authority off the table. They understand that the unfettered use of coercive power or a *power over* approach can be dysfunctional at best and a disaster at worst. As a leadership tactic, power is better shared and leaders better served by allowing followers to influence them.

It's unlikely that commitment can come out of the use of coercive and legitimate power. Commitment is more likely to be gained through the use of combinations of referent, reward, information, expert and connective power bases. These influence sources persuade followers to comply and/or commit for different reasons. Some say, "I will follow because you know more about this subject than I do." Other people accept the decision because they like you, want to be in your sphere of influence, or want to be a manager some day. Some followers commit because they trust you, believe in your goals, and want to be a part of it. Other followers believe the leader has the power to reward in ways they value. As we saw in our discussion of bridging, some followers recognize that you are connected to the power structure of the organization or that the leader possesses scarce information. Leaders, on the other hand, might encourage these perceptions by cloaking themselves with symbols of power such as diplomas on the wall, pictures taken with important people, and forms of dress to indirectly influence followers. In conversation they may allude to their ability to control rewards and punishments, ingratiate themselves through compliments and favors, and manipulate the mutuality of interests and/or goals. They would refrain from negative influence applications such as minimizing another person through subtle put-downs. Strategic leaders are able to gain compliance and commitment without resorting to the use of force or threat. Like Victor Joppolo, they use their social influence to bridge and connect, form alliances, coalitions, and partnerships which result in internal and external social capital and access to resources.

Many social psychology researchers corroborate French and Raven's findings.[15] For instance, Robert Cialdini (1998) the Regent's Professor of Psychology at the University of Arizona, narrowed social influence down to six key principles that can be used to influence behaviors or thoughts and generate desirable change in the widest range of circumstances; reciprocation, commitment/consistency, social proof, liking, authority, and scarcity. These principles are briefly described in the following talking points:

1. **Reciprocation:** Followers are more willing to comply with requests (for favors, services, information, concessions, etc.) from those who believe they owe something. People tend to say yes to those they owe. Strategic leaders provide small favors and concessions first to establish a reciprocal relationship.

2. **Commitment/Consistency:** Followers are more willing to be moved in a particular direction if they see it as consistent with their existing commitment. They are inclined to comply with a leader directive because they share the organizational vision and they are convinced that their effort will assist the organization in reaching its goals. Strategic leaders work to develop shared goals and commitments in their statements of intent

3. **Authority:** Followers are more willing to accept the directions or recommendations of a communicator to whom they attribute relevant authority or expertise. Strategic leaders drill down into information so they can make sense of it and create a teachable point of view.

4. **Social Proof:** Followers are more willing to take a recommended action if they see evidence that many others, especially similar others, are taking it. Strategic leaders work to get early adopters and opinion leaders supporting a recommendation.

5. **Scarcity:** Followers find objects and opportunities more attractive to the degree that they are scarce, rare, or dwindling in availability. Strategic leaders emphasize what the organization and followers will lose rather than what they will gain in conversations with followers.

6. **Liking/Friendship:** Followers prefer to say yes to those they know and like. Strategic leaders work on developing trust so they can bond with followers before asking for a commitment of energy and time.

The application of social influence principles that Professor Cialdini identified can easily be seen as a manipulative activity. It can be. However, it is the nature of humans to connect, and it is the leader's responsibility to influence that relationship in support of the organization's intent. Used judiciously and ethically, leaders use the social influence principles to mobilize support within their organizations. It is only in this fashion that the influence process can be simultaneously effective, ethical, and enduring while enhancing a lasting sense of partnership between those involved in the exchange.

Taken as a whole, strategic leaders are more successful in aligning follower's hearts and minds with the organizations' strategic intent when they are able to bring to bear a variety of aligning tactics a situation. Leaders can gain acceptance in directives to which followers are merely indifferent. But for directives in which the follower is resistant, a wider array of tactics is needed to gain to broaden followers' zones of acceptance (ZOA) and trust, or develops the leader's social capital.

CLIFF NOTES

Habit 5: Aligning Followers With Strategic Intent

This chapter described how strategic leaders lead in ways that link the strategic intent to the work behaviors and decisions throughout the organization. An aligned organization moves more quickly and more efficiently and results in higher performance results when it is populated with committed colleagues capable of self management After creating direction, the leader's most important function is to develop followers into colleagues. Tactics such as bonding, bridging, and bartering are strong determinants of the leader's ability to accomplish this important task.

The takeaway is that when strategic leaders provide direction through shared values, inspiration and a shared vision they are better able to attract and develop followers into colleagues, and unite them a common cause. They unite by employing relating and reaching tactics.

- Strategic leaders build relationships by employing three strategies: bonding, active listening, and storytelling. They bond by:
  - Sharing interests and common goals.
  - Being more listeners and information seekers than givers.
  - Centering their communications on (a) positive conversations of hope and inspiration, (b) stories of why change is needed and what the role of everyone will be in it, and (c) values that hold members together in common cause.
  - Making early decisions that fall inside the zone of acceptance, develop trust and continually widen the zone.

- Strategic leaders *reach for power* by bridging. They reach by:
  - o Bridging to maximize the power of the leader or the organization through networking, partnership and coalition building.
  - o Creating horizontal and vertical bridges inside and outside of the organization to gain insights, support, and resources from either the different levels within the organization or from supporters and adversaries external to the organization.
- Strategic leaders barter by understanding motivational levers and using negotiating and social influence principles. They barter by:
  - o Activating follower motivators through establishing goals and providing rewards.
  - o Using nonauthoritarian based social influence tactics such as Referent-Reward-Expert-Connection and Information to gain compliance and build commitment.
  - o Giving something in exchange for help.

NOTES

1. Followers possess their own motivations as to why they comply with goals or commit to the organization such as: working on a highly visible project they think will gain them recognition; receiving admiration from peers and supervisors; recognizing that the directives are well-matched with their own value systems; and desiring to prove themselves and reinforce their self-concept. According to Shamir (1991) followers comply because they are committed to the goals of the organization, respect the leader's formal position, and desire to satisfy their needs for security. They look to leaders to provide order and meaning.

2. These influence strategies are further explained in Badaracco (2002); Barbuto (2002); Bolman and Deal (2003); R. B. Cialdini (1998); French and Raven (1959); Kotter (1998); and Pfeffer (1981, 1992).

3. Suggested by the work of Burt and Knez (1996); Gabarro (1978); Kramer and Tyler (1996); Lewicki and Bunker (1996).

4. Suggested by the work of Bass (1985); Conger and Kanungo (1987); Conger and Kanungo (1988); House (1977); Locke (1991); Kouzes and Posner (2003); and Yukl (1998).

5. See W. Goodwyn (2002) & www.npr.org for Colleen Barrett interview.

6. Southwest Airlines Mission Statement. (2006). http://www .southwest.com

7. *Ritz-Carlton employee promise*. http://corporate.ritzcarlton.com/About/ GoldStandards.htm.

8. Hurricane Katrina was the costliest and deadliest hurricanes in the history of the United States. It devastated the City of New Orleans and much of

the Northern Gulf Coast of the United States on August 23/24, 2005. Over 1,836 people lost their lives. Damage estimates exceeded 81 billion (2005) U.S. dollars.

9. United Airlines (UAL) C.E.O Glenn Tilton, despite his obvious lack of air-line-industry experience, was aggressively courted in 2002 by the directors of UAL Corporation, who reportedly hoped that the oil industry veteran's widely touted people skills and management expertise could help turn the troubled airline around. He was hired to halt the loss of profit and employee morale which began around 2000. Tilton's honeymoon was short as 9/11 severely damaged most of the airline industry.

10. Reported in Tedlow (2006).

11. See Larkin and Larkin (1996); and van Riel, Berens, and Dijkstra (2007).

12. Omaha Black Music Hall of Fame (2007). Retrieved March 1, 2007, from http://www.omahablackmusic.com/inductees/Calloway_Bertha.html

13. See also Campbell, Dunnette, Lawler, and Weick (1970).

14. See Ashforth and Mael (1989), Conger and Kanungo (1987); Hollander and Offermann (1990); Ireland, Hitt, and Vaidyanath (2002); Raven (1992); and Raven, Freeman, and Haley (1982). Note: The original French and Raven typology was seen as useful as a conceptual tool for consulting and teaching. However, it was challenged for its lack of conceptual consistency regarding the source or origin of influence, making it difficult to operationalize the construct and sample the domains of interest. These objections were overcome by Hinkin and Schriesheim (1989). They conceptualized the application of these powers from the follower's perspective (because power exists only if it is perceived to exist by followers). If the follower believes leaders control resources then the leader has reward power no matter what the reality. They also improved the theoretical definitions and made them practical for research efforts. Criticisms notwithstanding, the original framework has stood the test of time.

15. For example, Cialdini (1998); Kotter (1998). Steven Covey (1989) reported that "I have personally identified over 30 separate methods of human influence ... most people have only three or four of these methods in their repertoire, starting with reasoning, and if that doesn't work moving to fight or flight." Note: On the other hand, Mr. Hammer and Thompson's negotiators also practiced *WOOing*—winning over other people. Cialdini (2004) studied the way lovers try to bring about change in their relationship. He found that the coercive approach tried by some lovers was a recipe for disaster. Others attempt "to argue that theirs was the more reasonable view and that it only made sense for their partner to adopt it." He concluded that the most successful lovers use the relational approach. Before making a request for change from their partner, they merely made mention of their existing relationship. They might say, "you know, we've been together for a while now" or "we're a couple; we share the same goals." Then, they deliver their appeal incorporating the pronouns "we," "our," and "us" into their request. It's the human connection—the relationship itself—that influences compliance, conformity, or commitment. Strategic leaders using the relationship-raising approach

merely elevate awareness of the personal connection in the moment before making a request so that it will have due impact on the response.

CHAPTER 7

HABIT 6

Assuring Results

Nothing is possible without individuals; nothing is lasting without institutions.

—Jean Monnet

Strategic leaders are responsible for results. They get them by focusing themselves and their followers on executing the organization's aspiration, guiding principles and initiatives. Thus far, the centrality of the habits inside the leader's wheel—agility and artistry—to the four habits composing the learning cycle of the wheel was clarified. Then the use of the habits of anticipating and articulating to develop the strategy that drives organizational performance was explored. We noted that strategy alone cannot guarantee high performance, it must be executed! In the previous chapter the tactics of aligning were offered to develop the internal conditions and relationships

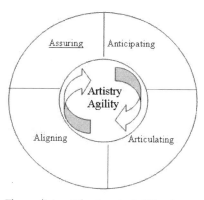

Figure 7.1.   The Leader's Wheel.

The Strategic Leader: New Tactics for A Globalizing World, pp. 155–181
Copyright © 2009 by Information Age Publishing
All rights of reproduction in any form reserved.

necessary to drive the statement of intent into the hearts and minds of followers throughout the organization. In this chapter the focus is on assuring results and high performance. One thing is certain, strategic leaders are responsible for results. What are the levers to "make it happen and how do strategic leaders keep making it happen?"

THE HABIT OF ASSURING

The road to high performance is built mile by mile by executing the strategic intent of the organization. The habit of *assuring* guarantees results and performance. It requires consensus, learning and accommodation. Strategic leaders assure by being more proactive than reactive. They are more than problem solvers; they rely on an adaptive and extrinsic motivation for change. They *assure* by relying on creative tension created by the statement of intent to focus internal motivation and a generative learning approach to build a high performing organization.

The statement of intent creates creative tension; the gap between the organization's aspiration and its current reality. Often this picture creates tension because it is at odds with prevailing norms and processes within the organization. Leaders are responsible for executing the plan, closing the gap, and assuring results. They address this responsibility by being crystal clear about the organization's aspiration (the bottom line), and its guiding principles and initiatives. They assure by developing deep understanding of the strategic intent throughout the organization and by using seven specific embedding levers to create a cohesive and fit culture focused on results. By assuring in this manner, leaders are able to embed the organization's strategic intent into the minds and spirit of the organization's stakeholders and cement lasting change in the culture. By assuring in this manner, colleagues throughout the organization are able to be empowered to make sound decisions in support of the organization's statement of intent.

PERFORMANCE BUILDERS

Some leaders are performance builders who attempt to influence performance directly. They focus on external adaptation priorities such as profits and exploring new markets in business contexts. In educational contexts, they center on improving learning gains and developing new instructional techniques. In all contexts, performance builders measure progress in a transparent way. They value data based decision making, face the hard facts, and build a culture of candor where people are encouraged to tell the truth, even if it is unpleasant. They motivate people through targeted compensation, competition, and pressure.

A singular focus on performance building can create toxic effects. By focusing all their attention on results in the short term, leaders may neglect to build a strong internal foundation for the future. A case in point is Al Dunlop, the infamous *chainsaw Al*, a no-nonsense executive famous for turning around struggling companies—and sending their shares soaring in the process. Dunlop was a self styled turnaround artist and downsizing champion noted for his successes at Scott Paper, American Can, Lily Tulip, and Crown Zellerbac. That is before he landed as the CEO at Sunbeam. John Byrne (1999) reveals Dunlap's entrance, tenure, and eventual downfall at Sunbeam for us to examine.

At Dunlap's first meeting with Sunbeam executives he asserted "You guys are responsible for the demise of Sunbeam! I'm here to tell you that things have changed. The old Sunbeam is over today. It's over!... This is the best day of your life if you're good at what you do and willing to accept change and it's the worst day of your life if you're not." Dunlap lost no time burying the old Sunbeam. He called for the elimination of half of the company's 6,000 employees and 87% of its products. He used pressure and reward tactics to demand that managers meet numbers that were increasingly not makeable.

Sunbeam managers had more than just their jobs at stake. The top 250 to 300 executives and managers received options that were vested over a 3-year period. Getting fired or leaving could mean losing out on more than $1 million in gains. The outsize rewards made it easier for employees to do things they might otherwise refuse to do. For a time, Dunlap's executives and managers met their quarterly numbers and outdid Wall Street's projections. However, the managing tactic of *kissing up and kicking down* took its toll as it became more difficult to meet the numbers. In an effort to hang on to jobs and options, some managers began using questionable tactics like withholding commissions to sales reps and not paying bills on time. The most controversial tactic was called *billing and holding*.

Anxious to boost sales in Dunlap's turnaround year, the company offered retailers major discounts to buy barbecue grills nearly 6 months before they were needed; all in the name of getting quick, bottom line improvements. The retailers did not have to pay for the grills, or accept delivery of them, for 6 months. After Dunlap's departure from the company, outside auditors forced a restatement of Sunbeam's financials, pushing $62 million worth of these sales into future quarters. A year later Sunbeam Corporation (now named American Household, Inc.) filed for protection under chapter 11 of the United States Bankruptcy Code. Unfortunately, questionable and rapid turnarounds often produce only short term benefits. Al Dunlop was a charismatic leader whose style was personalized. House and Howell (1992) define this style as "(a) based on personal dominance and authoritarian behavior, (b) serves the self-interest of the leader and is self-aggrandizing, and is exploitive of others" (p. 83).

Strategic leaders build performance by focusing on results which are the consequences of action; not activities. They use metrics and incentives but they don't overload on them. Instead they measure what matters. Often, a few dozen key metrics will serve to measure most of the economic value of the business. Problem indicators might include declining profits or learning, declining quantity or quality of work, increases in absenteeism or tardiness, and negative employee attitudes. Strategic leaders use their key diagnostic skills to identify conditions symptomatic of a problem requiring further attention. Carlos Ghosn of Renault and Nissan fame was this type of performance builder.

Ghosn's four keys to high performance are vision, strategy, commitment and results. I have framed his keys through four questions all strategic leaders must answer. Then, from the interviews, books and articles, I have paraphrased his words in answers to questions a strategic leader would ask.[1] What appears in the following paragraphs is my interpretation of Carlos's keys to high performance.

What Has To Happen Here?

Ghosn would say—establish with and within the company a very simple vision about the destination. When he went to Nissan he started without any preconceived ideas just a clean sheet of paper and set about, with his top team, evaluating the company systematically to find the problems that were limiting performance. He personally interviewed over 300 employees at all levels and scoured the financial and performance data. What Ghosn found was an unclear vision and vague goals. He set about to make sure that Nissan had the right priorities before sharing the diagnosis and clear vision and priorities. Then he set out to spread it throughout Nissan. Ghosn fondly quotes a former teacher's words: "If you find things complicated, that means you haven't understood them. Simplicity is the basis of everything." This affection led him to capture Nissan's vision in a concrete and measurable number; 180. The number is short hand for Nissan's aspiration; add 1 million global vehicle sales, achieve an 8% operating margin, carry zero debt over 3 years and the result is 180. So, Ghosn would say the first key is to establish a diagnosis; listen and interact with many people, and make sure you have the right priorities before you share this diagnosis and simple plan

What Is Precious and What is Expendable or Modifiable?

Ghosn would say, the company for the most part determines its own faith. It is the internal happenings that determine the company performance, not so much that of the economy. Develop a strategy, action plans, at every level of the company so everyone knows the contribution that is expected of them from the company. In Nissan's case, the point was not to change culture just for the sake of change. He wanted to change the culture for the sake of performance. In every step he took, he was very careful not to institute changes that were not based strictly on the advantages they give Nissan to improve company performance. By showing that every change made was for the sake of performance and benefit to the company, gradually these changes were approved and accepted.

How Can We Make It Happen?

Ghosn would say, draw executives from all ranks and locations and assign them to common company goals, to brainstorm and recommend solutions within 3 months. He used these cross functional teams to both empower and improve performance. The purpose of the team is to induce change from the bottom up rather than from the top down. These teams had the responsibility and freedom to choose the means to find the best suited way of reaching the target. He found that commitment was enhanced when all viewpoints are considered; and problems got solved faster. Nissan's workforce tended to be less satisfied with their own performance, and less assuming that poor results were due to someone else's inadequacies. He found that the essence of the power of cross-functional teams is that they force people to talk to one another, listen to one another, and exchange knowledge.

Ghosn is convinced that the biggest mistake you make is not connecting with people. You have to establish some kind of direct and indirect contact with them. He believes people need to feel a strong personal and team commitment coming from the top. You have to listen deeply—not only to direct reports—go deep into the organization. When you find something out of place act fast and empower as many people as possible to make decisions. Communicate not only what you are doing but the results also—then reward people.

He believes that leaders must feel the situation, understand the expectation of people, and, respond to them in ways to improve overall performance. That's the challenge: make improvements that lead to high performance! In the end results cement everything. They give you credibility—make people feel safe and want to sign on for the journey.

How Do We Keep Making It Happen?

Ghosn says that many times people make great speeches but frequently nothing happens. While words are important, they do not automatically translate into action. He believes that measurement pushes you into action. The only way you're going to make sure actions are going to follow talk is by measurement. He believes in straight talk focused on results from his managers and employees. But he also believes in having an appreciation for simplicity in setting up monitoring indicators and surveys—not just to see how our customers rate the quality of sales processes, but mainly also to understand what's going wrong. He believes that measuring objectively the way individuals and teams have contributed to the performance of the company (on a yearly or monthly basis) can be more useful for motivation than general raises based on subjective views.

As seen through the comparison of Dunlop and Ghosn's tactics, the best performance builders' focus on building a performance culture. They take a broader long term perspective when looking at the bottom line. They emphasize core values. They explore new opportunities to develop competitive products, and achieve results important to stakeholders. These performance builders focus efforts on asking questions that tell them if they have a positive performance culture; they ask:

1. Do we have an organization wide measure for productivity growth?
2. Do we demand the facts?
3. Can we identify how we're going to turn the initiatives into specific results?
4. How can the strategy be broken down into doable initiatives?
5. Which people will do the job, and how will they be judged and held accountable?
6. Do we have the right people in the right jobs?
7. Do we have strong frontline execution?
8. How, specifically, are we going to achieve our projected goals on a timely basis?
9. What are the milestones for progress of the plan and is there strict accountability of the people in charge?
10. Does every executive have a 90-day action plan and clear agreement on following through?
11. Have we done a good job of linking rewards to performance?

The best performance builders use the aspiration and initiatives found in the organization's statement of strategic intent as the focal point for improved performance. In this light, reconsider your own organization's statement of strategic intent. Is the aspiration clear, concise, and measurable? Review the initiatives. Do some have to be addressed before others can come on board? If so, focus on the critical few first by assigning a team to develop and execute the plan throughout the organization. Then assign the plan to the appropriate organizational units and individuals. Ask each team or team member to identify 2–4 things they need to move the organization and put it in writing. Make sure they identify the roadblocks that must be removed not just the resources they need.

The best performance builders also develop a scorecard so results are transparent and easily grasped. Which results are not being met, and which are on target, budget, and time. Meet with the teams and/or individuals to confirm what can be done and what can't be done. Strategize to overcome the things that cannot be done. Follow up with a 30-minute stand up monthly meeting with teams and individuals responsible for the results. Focus on the targets they are achieving and what should be done to keep achieving those results. When targets are not met, the discussion should be done to produce positive results, in what time frame, and what additional help is needed. In every discussion about results, be direct and candid but not abrasive with staff; let them know where they stand, what's needed, and when it is needed. Every quarter celebrate your wins; acknowledge your concerns and review the lessons learned with all of your direct reports. Ensure that those responsible for results are visibly rewarded.

INSTITUTION BUILDERS

Institution builders understand that the primary impediment to achieving the organization's strategic intent is the existing culture. Understanding this Schein (1992, p. 275) says they influence performance indirectly by developing a cohesive, adaptive, learning culture as the focus of their work. They institutionalize the values and systematize the processes by building a strong organizational culture and creating consensus among employees on a set of values that enhance performance. They use learning as a way to positively impact performance. Both motivation and learning have a positive impact on performance, but there is an important difference between them. Motivation affects performance within one's current capacity. People may try to work harder, but there is no guarantee that they will do anything differently. Learning, on the other hand, enhances capacity. Employees who learn from their empowered roles enhance their performance not by doing more of the same but by taking new and different approaches. The impact on performance should thus be more significant.

Institution builders are primarily developmental or person-orientated.[2] Many of them are mild mannered, as discovered in the research of Collins and Porras (1994) in their book *Built to Last*, and Collin's (2001) *Good to Great*. As institution builders, strategic leaders focus on internal integration schemes such as developing shared vision and values and encouraging the evolution of common goals, language and procedures. They focus on learning through empowerment, coaching, monitoring, teaching, and feedback as a way to create self managed teams and positively impact performance.

Institution builders ensure that the organization has the right people and the right skill sets to get the job done. They deliberately eliminate counterproductive values and structures while remembering that there will always be a need for structure and processes. The institutional culture strategic leaders seek is built on these principles:

- Achieving results important to stakeholders.
- Creating metrics and incentives to keep people focused on results.
- Focusing on the consequences of action or inaction; not activities.
- Measuring progress in a transparent way and ensuring it is continuous.
- Understanding the value of data based decision making, facing the hard facts, and making sure everyone in the organization is equally committed both to getting and to using the best facts.
- Developing a climate of community.
- Creating a learning culture based on sharing of experience, trust, honesty, and openness in which people are encouraged to tell the truth, even if it is unpleasant.
- Motivating people to have an impact on performance through commitment and empowerment as well as targeted compensation, competition and pressure.
- Being direct and forthright with people in every conversation, letting them know where they stand, what's needed from them, and when.

The "GE Way"

Consider the way Jack Welch, the legendary former CEO of General Electric, wielded the levers of super teacher, learner, and protector of core values to make sure every mind in the company was engaged with the company's strategic intent. Jack Welch worked at GE for 40 years; the last 20 as the CEO. This tenure gave him a profound grasp of the business and the people who worked for it. When he ascended to the CEO's position, Welch knew that the company's culture (which he came to refer to as its *social architecture*) was vital to its success. He set out to build an institution as well as focusing on performance. The teaching and learning levers he used; the Coffee Pot, the Corporate Executive Council, the Annual Get to Together, Session C reviews, and the Workout provided a rhythm for himself and the executives, managers and line operators.

Corporate Executive Council. Before the close of each financial quarter Welch met with his Corporate Executive Council (CEC) which was composed of GE's top 30 officers. At the meetings, Welch collected unfiltered information, challenged and tested his top players, and made sure that the organization's triumphs and failures were openly shared. Welch set precise performance targets with them and then monitored them throughout the year and at the end of each quarter in what has been described as a *free for all*. At the end of each year every one of them received a handwritten, two-page evaluation of their performance. Welch, who wrote the performance report himself, explained that "it gives me a chance to reflect on each business."

The Coffee Pot. Welch inherited the General Electric (GE) training center at Croton-on-Hudson when he became CEO. He called it "the coffee pot" because the center not only percolates but gives off aromas which draw people from all over the company. Every GE executive was required spend 3 weeks at the coffee pot in development courses directly linked to GE's strategic initiatives. Near the end of the 3 weeks, he arrived by helicopter from New York and engaged the minds of around 71 of GE's high potential managers and executives. They came face to face with Professor Welch who listened, lectured, and questioned; unscripted and without notes. He also expounded on some of his philosophy such as: "you can't have a long term unless you eat short term," and "anybody can manage short. Anybody can manage long. Balancing those two things is what management is about."

GE is a culture where there is a free flow of ideas. The managers were not hesitant to push back and question and disagree with Jack, particularly after being encouraged to do so by the executives they encountered in the previous three weeks. Something exciting happened during these sessions. Jack became human to his managers and he learned from them. After around four hours of give and take, Welch invited them to have a drink with him rather than hurry off to the heliport. Welch made the trip to the *coffee* pot at least 250 times during his tenure at GE.

The Annual Get Together. At the annual gathering of GE's top 500 executives in January of each year, Welch set the new year's agenda and celebrated the company's successes and its heroes. Some of the latter were asked to present the new ideas that allowed them to make the organization leaner and more profitable while Jack listened intently in the first row and took notes. Like *the coffee pot* managers, executives traded the secrets of their successes and looked for solutions to the challenges they faced. The soiree ended with Welch in front of the audience and cameras wrapping up the gathering with his list of warnings and challenges, and priorities for the year. Like many successful leaders, Welch found out that you can't just talk with the top layer of executives and expect change to happen. The message must go unfiltered to the shop floor. So when the executives returned to their workplace, a videotape of Welch's talk would be on their desk along with a guide on how to use it with their teams. Typically, in lock step order, each executive would use the tape to discuss what was learned at the session with his or her direct reports. Each direct report conducted the same briefings with their reports and so on until Welch's message had been sent unfiltered throughout the organization and became known to all.

Session C Reviews. Welch believed that his most important job was to identify, develop and acquire talent. He believed that weeding out the weak, encouraging the average to get better, raising the bar and letting the top people know how much you loved and cared about them was the game. Welch also believed that, "rigorous differentiation delivers real stars—and stars build great businesses." In his philosophy, everybody must feel they have a stake in the game, but not everyone has to be treated the same way.

Welch appraised individual performance through the annual Session C Reviews. Over a 2 month period in the spring, Welch and three of his senior executives traveled to each of GE's 12 businesses locations to review the progress of the company's top 3,000 executives. Typically Session C reviews were held with the CEO of the business and his senior human-resources executive. Welch and his executives were provided with a briefing book that contained every employee's assessment of their strengths and weaknesses, developmental needs, and short and long-term goals, together with their supervisor's analysis. Welch and his team inquired as to the managers' work habits, ability to energize people, decisiveness on tough issues, ability to get things done through others, and their follow through. The probing questions asked of the local CEO were: How does she set priorities? What qualities is she known for? Does she include people in decision making? What is her work ethic and her energy level and enthusiasm for execution? Does she get excited by doing things, as opposed to talking about them? Is her life full of achievement and accomplishment? Generally lasting 14 hours these intensive reviews forced the local CEO's to identify their A, B, and C players. "A" players were considered the stars—future leaders in need of exposure to broader responsibilities. They were included in succession plans for all key jobs. In every potential leader, Welch looked for what he now calls "E to the fourth power." That was his term for people who have enormous personal energy, the ability to motivate and energize others. "E" stands for Edge, the GE code word for being instinctively competitive and having the skill to execute. The B players were sent to the Coffee Pot for further leadership training. The C players either improved performance or were moved out. No one with poor performance got to remain on the bottom for more than a year without action being taken. Welch says the key was getting the top tier of employees excited, giving them the self-confidence to reach and do more, rather than focusing on poor performers.

The Work out. The principles behind the idea of the Work-Out program was that, if you give people local autonomy and a reason to focus on improving quality, you can supercharge productivity. The idea was created after reflection on a teaching stint Jack Welch took at the Coffee Pot. He was expounding on his core value of openness when his managers told him that they didn't have enough voice in the direction of their unit or department. Jack came up with idea of the Work Out process, a session convened by a senior manager on challenges that need improvement. They simply had to say "let's do a Work Out on that." It was founded on three key principles: (a) all Work-Out sessions would involve cross functional and cross level groups (45–100 people each), (b) sessions would be led by a senior executive who had to take part in the discussions, but could use trained facilitators to help the group work through their problems, and (c) at the end of the day long process the leader had to say "yes" or "no and here's why" to every idea presented during the session. While the leader could ask for more information, they could not say they would "take it under advisement." The Work Out process is now a time tested method that placed a problem with the work to be done in the middle of people who know it best. It resulted in streamlining existing processes, eliminating nonproductive work, identifying and prioritizing new business initiatives, making speedier decisions and implementing them, creating clear lines of accountability, and encouraging ownership of organizational members in work and results improvement. Approved recommendations are tied to action plans that are implemented within 90 days. Welch said that Work Out meant just what the words implied: taking unnecessary work out of the system.

There are several lessons that can be extracted from the way Welch managed GE that can help us learn the secrets to building institutions. First, through the CEC and surprise visits, he gathered direct information from people at the top and people on the line. Through the Coffee Pot and the annual get-togethers, he was able to get his message, priorities and values directly to those who could implement them. The Session C Reviews enabled him to understand the level of talent in the company and how it was being developed and compensated. Finally, the informality he encouraged not only made the connection between leader and follower easier, it also meant he could violate the chain of command and communicate across organizational layers.

ASSURING HIGH PERFORMANCE

Strategic leaders understand that the best way to assure results is by engaging in performance and institutional building actions that create a cohesive high performance culture. Culture is the code name for the organization's mindset. It influences decision making, and the way events are interpreted. Schein (1992) says that culture helps organizational members know important (shared values), how things work (beliefs), and how to behave (norms).

These assumptions are either taught by formal and/or informal leaders or discovered by newly hired members. Once these norms, beliefs, and shared values are accepted they shape behavior and are used to discipline members. An established culture orients organizational members for action, and produces support, or becomes the biggest barrier to assuring results.[3] Once culture is established, all organizational members are expected to conform or face isolation or punishment. For example, a short-lived television sitcom, *The Boys*, was premised on the following story line:

Four late middle aged male friends who lived on the same street for over 20 years engaged in a weekly card game at one of their homes. Over the years the card game became an organizing event for their social lives and that of their families. A crisis of sorts occurred when one of the members, Gordon, suddenly died. His wife put the house up for sale and went to live with her children. The new occupants, John and Marilyn, were young, self assured, and not married. The Boys invited John to join them for their weekly card game. John, with some trepidation, decided that for the sake of harmony he would try to fit in. During the card game, John was prone to "bluff" or make bets that were beyond the norms of the group. Each time, one of the boys would say, "Gordon wouldn't have done that." Similarly, when Marilyn visited with the wives she found them to be just as uncompromising. For example, one day as they gathered over the back fence to discuss the events of the day, she invited them to come in for a drink. One of the girls rebuffed her by saying, "Helen wouldn't have done that."

The Boys illustrates how cultural structures protect the social unity of both the card game and those back fence discussions against the intrusion of new members and ideas. Culture inhibits actions that are foreign to it. *The Boys* also offers an important lesson for leaders. When they are first hired, they face a problem of first understanding the culture and then either accepting it, changing it, or being changed by it. Much of the research on organizational culture focuses on two dimensions—those related to issues of internal cohesiveness and those related to organizational fitness with environmental changes or as Schein (1992) says, the leaders two tasks are internal integration and external adaptation.

People are motivated by ideas but values bind them together. Organizations differ on the extent that culture is cohesive. In cohesive organizations a common culture is found organization wide. In fragmented cultures one may find either consistent work group cultures or many little cultural groups. United and focused people are a source of strength. A cohesive culture exists when there is a high level of agreement among organizational members about what is valued, coupled with a high level of commitment to these values. Strategic leaders focus followers on achieving organizational priorities. The more ownership they accept, the better they perform, and the less formal direction they need.

Cohesiveness alone may not lead to strong organizational performance. It can appear as either a manifestation of work group culture or corporate culture. Corporate culture consists of the values and goals espoused by top management. In a cohesive organization the corporate culture is found organization wide. Work group cultures are found in the everyday work life of groups who share similar tasks or interests and who adopt their own rituals, beliefs, and practices that may or may not be supportive of organizational values or priorities. Therefore, left unattended, strong workgroup or personal values provide reference points for organizational members and eventually cause the organization to fragment. It's these unattended sub cultures that facilitate or erect barriers to change.

Organizational fitness, however, requires that the organization possess the ability to adapt to changes in its environment based on its core competence and experience. This adaptation can occur through *coping* or *transformative learning*.

Coping can be accomplished through single-loop learning which Argyris and Schön (1978) emphasize that the core set of organizational norms does not change. In the single loop mode, learning is understood to be essentially problem solving; the assumptions of the current model are not questioned. The focus is on correction and meeting current goals. The emphasis is on techniques and making the organization more efficient (Usher & Bryant, 1989). Single loop learning is applied in organizations where members adapt to the external and internal environment by detecting errors and altering strategies within the existing organizational culture. Single loop learning facilitates frame sustaining change where leader and followers are interested in making the current organizational model sleeker and faster. It doesn't require a change in culture.

The key to culture change is found in the use of double loop learning tactics to induce transformative learning.[4] Double loop learning, which is deeper than single loop learning, is employed to determine if the organization's current mindset; its core set of principles, beliefs and norms must change. It is applied when simply *coping* does not maintain organizational fitness. Double loop learning, therefore, facilitates frame breaking change which changes the trajectory of the organization.

There are several lessons that can be extracted from the organizational culture studies. First, to overcome resistance requires a change in mindset and a culture of agility and learning that supports both the proactive frame breaking (innovative) and reactive frame sustaining (adaptive) nature of change. So the first question strategic leaders should address when executing the statement of strategic intent is whether the current culture helps or hinders its execution. When the answer to this question is negative, organizational effectiveness and change is not possible without cultural change. Unfortunately, culture change seldom occurs from the bottom up. Leader action is required.

The second lesson is to understand that culture boosts organizational performance when it is (a) intentionally shaped, (b) strategically relevant, (c) people centric, (d) cohesive, (e) agile, and (f) has a supportive social architecture. Culture becomes high performing when the shaping of culture is intentional. If left to chance, culture will develop within an organization. When proposed changes infringe on the basic assumptions on which the organization rests, followers resist. It is too important to leave to chance. Like Andy Grove, former chairman of Intel, strategic leaders understand that "culture eats strategy for lunch every day."[5]

Culture becomes strategically relevant when it reinforces the organization's strategic intent; it is internally integrated and externally adaptive. The strategic intent must be embedded into the daily routines of practitioners in order for it to be learned. It is achieved by creating a clear and elevating aspiration, a results driven structure, competent team members, unified commitment, an inquiry climate, and external support and recognition. By focusing on performance and culture, strategic leaders focus followers on the organization's aspiration and priorities, and establish a process of accountability, empowerment, and renewal.

Culture becomes people centric when leaders play a direct role in enabling others to handle tasks. They assure results by establishing a learning process that allows quick adjustments to be made so change sticks. They establish an organization populated with followers who support implementation of the strategic intent. They enable high-performance that emphasizes innovation and change. In such organizations *inspiring* and *influencing* are hallmarks of *articulating* and *aligning*.

Culture becomes cohesive when the anchoring tools include extensive communication and employees are involved in the culture development process. The leader's goal is to inspire commitment, not demand compliance. As Confucius noted in the *Analects*:

> lead the people by laws and regulate them by penalties, and the people will try to keep out of jail, but will have no sense of shame. Lead the people by virtue and restrain them by rules of decorum, and the people will have a sense of shame, and moreover will become good. (Cited in Little & Reed, 1989, p. 5)

Culture supports organizational agility when it emphasizes rapid and effective learning. An agile culture assures results by encouraging a bias toward activity and a focus on measurable results. It establishes an inquiry based mentality so quick adjustments can be made to stick. Agility is fostered when individuals are empowered and leaders refrain from giving answers and advice but ask questions to get people engaged. They then listen to and pay attention to the answers. It is not enough to simply delegate responsibility and decision making; the leader must play a direct role in enabling others to handle tasks.

Culture becomes high performing when the organization has a supportive social architecture[6] composed of its structure and processes (the hardware) and its norms and culture (the software). It is true that a social architecture that focuses just on structure and processes can result in high performance when demand for services can be anticipated. However, when demand for services is highly uncertain long term high performance is strengthened with an appropriate combination of human behavior, structure and culture. For long term high performance, the hardware and the software must be consistent and mutually reinforcing. From a hardware perspective, strategic leaders reduce hierarchy and distribute authority and responsibility throughout the organization to those committed to its intent. They encourage diversity of thought and informality rather than rigidity.

From a software perspective, strategic leaders create a culture that is both cohesive and adaptive. Such a culture has norms operating at three levels. Cooperating norms such as trust, reciprocity, and shared intent permeate the organization to reinforce cooperation, coordination and information sharing, rather than hierarchical norms. Leaders also create strong expectations for individual and work group performance. Performing norms such as going the extra mile, taking initiative, assuming responsibility and being honest provide the necessary reinforcements for a focus on performance. Innovating norms support participation and experimentation by focusing on the facts and believing that good ideas can come from anywhere. Cooperating, performing, and innovating norms pull the organization to high performance. Focusing on structure and processes pushes the organization toward high performance.

The third lesson is that the way in which strategic leaders shape culture has clearly been identified in research studies. Strategic leaders replace old science shaping tools—primarily—bureaucratic controls and pushing and pressuring the organization to perform—with new science levers. They:

- Make the change target concrete and clear.
- Track performance.
- Teach the organization's point of view.
- Achieve agility by making learning a priority.
- Put people at the center of things.
- Recruit and select for performance and culture fit
- Tie rewards to business results, individual growth, capability, and contribution

THE LEVERS TO DEVELOP HIGH PERFORMING ORGANIZATIONS

Strategic leaders find out quickly that they either manage culture or culture manages them. What this means is that culture forms organically in organizations, units, and groups. Left unattended it can impede or facilitate the productivity and efficiency of the organization. Fortunately culture can be adjusted. Table 7.1 describes seven key levers strategic leaders can use to create a high performing culture and organization.

Lever #1: Make the Change Target Concrete and Clear

A major difference between higher-performing and lower-performing organizations has been attributed to the clarity and logic of the organization's strategic direction by Collins and Porras (1994) and Vickers (2007). Higher-performing organizations are much more likely than lower-performing ones to have a clear, well-thought-out, flexible, and inspiring vision. Strategic leaders meet this criterion by their generative approach to establishing the statement of strategic intent which enables organization members to understand fully the expectations for performance.

Lever #2: Track Performance

Strategic leaders can create a high performing culture by putting a measurement system in place that provides feedback on whether a strategy is working. The single largest gap between high and low performing organizations is due to whether organization-wide performance measures

Table 7.1. The Levers Strategic Leaders Use to Create High Performing Organizations

#	*Levers*	*Tactics*
1	Make the change target concrete and clear	What leaders pay attention to, measure, and control Create Statement of Intent with mission, aspiration, guiding principles and initiatives
2	Track performance	Create short list of transparent metrics Report progress publically
3	Teach the organization's point of view	Intensive socialization and training Surface and challenge mental models Model organization values Teach, coach, and mentor through informal and formal training Embrace appropriate rites, rituals, symbols, and narratives
4	Make learning a priority	Foster inquiry Promote dialogue Balance inquiry and advocacy Create psychological safety Build community Learn continuously Foster strategic thinking skills at all levels
5	Empower	Identify members who will take initiative Remove barriers. Examine what encourages engagement. Establish high profile activity, everyone can rally around. Emphasize the development of follower self-management or self-direction.
6	Recruit and select for culture fit	Find people who think and act like owners. Develop culturally consistent selection criteria Emphasize person-culture fit in addition to person-job fit. Replace influential employees who hold outdated assumptions with those who embrace the more progressive assumptions.
7	Manage the reward system	Link individual performance with organizational performance.

matched the organization's strategy as stated in their strategic intent. In other words, the proper alignment between performance and strategy seems to make a big difference to organizational success.

There are many types of measurement systems. They can be as extensive as the *balanced scorecard*,[7] or as simple as a self determined, parsimonious dashboard of indicators. Each has advantages and challenges. Regardless of which you choose, it must be transparent, implemented throughout the organization, and reviewed periodically to keep the collective eye on the ball. It really is as simple as Schein (1999) declaration that "what gets measured gets done." The advice from these sources is to carefully select a few, but meaningful metrics, to monitor, and report progress at the beginning of the execution phase of your statement of strategic intent. Many times organizations fall into the trap of having a laundry list of metrics because they cannot get agreement on a smaller list. Avoid this trap at all costs because one reason change efforts is that they over rely on "data gathering and analysis, report writing and presentation" and as Kotter and Cohen (2002) suggest less on the leader relating, reaching, and persuading through the use of empowering actions which lead followers to *see* and *feel* the change.

Metrics are, however, a good focusing device but no single performance measure is sufficient to assure that the desired outcomes result. Soft and hard measures are necessary to create a snapshot that you can depend on to judge performance. A dozen key metrics will serve to measure three important areas of performance: (a) overall organizational performance such as profitability, market share, and growth rates, (b) progress on the initiatives found in the statement of intent, and (c) cultural cohesiveness and organizational fitness such as customer/client and employee satisfaction, and quality.

The final test for your shortlist of metrics is to ensure they are **S**pecific, **M**easurable, **A**ctionable, **R**elevant and **T**imely. Many strategic leaders assemble their SMART metrics in an easy to read *dashboard* that makes them transparent to all stakeholders. The clearer the metrics are to internal and external stakeholders, the easier it is for them monitor their performance and identify the specific actions they need to take to improve.

Lever #3: Teach the Organization's Point of View

Organizations are more fragile when their leaders fail to teach their members the organization's point of view. As Peter Senge (1990, p. 5) noted, much of the leverage leaders can actually exert lies in helping people achieve more accurate, more insightful, and more empowering views of reality. This view of the leader as teacher replaces or modifies the traditional view of leader as an expert … whose job it is to teach people the correct view of reality. In postmodern times the strategic leader's role is to help everyone in the organization, including themselves, to gain more insightful views of current reality, the challenges that are faced, and the opportunities that are presented to the organization.

Strategic leaders make sure that followers clearly understand the strategic direction of the organization and the key values and activities that underpin it. They provide superior follower training so they do their jobs and act upon the statement of intent's guiding principles. Often good leaders can become great leaders by teaching the organization's point of view and by using the following tactics:

- Offering followers mental models, to influence how they perceive problems and opportunities and make choices. As long as assumptions remain unexpressed there is little possibility of challenging their validity or forming an organization wide culture.

- Reshaping the way they talk. When strategic leaders make a request, they take a little extra time to put it into context and explain why they are making it. They communicate stories about important events and people that reinforce the culture

- Modeling an inclusive approach in the communication process: They acknowledge that others may have legitimate questions, misgivings, fears, doubts or other perspectives. They invite questions, reactions, and other feedback and they respond to feedback in ways that show people's concerns have been heard and taken seriously.

- Holding others and themselves accountable. Remember, making and meeting commitments is one of the best ways to build trust and get followers to accept responsibility. Strategic leaders treat commitments as promises.

- Creating psychological safety through maintaining some continuity with the past. Strategic leaders embrace appropriate rites, rituals, symbols, and narratives.

- Being genuine and honest in speaking about personal commitment and managing expectations.

- Managing culture through intensive selection, socialization and training of followers. New followers should be selected on the basis of having the "right" set of assumptions, beliefs, and values. It's not only important that new members acquire knowledge about the core values, abilities and expected behaviors but also that they create strong bonds with their colleagues so that they are accountable to one another for upholding those values. Strategic leaders, therefore, establish processes where new hires are trained, exposed to, and assume the organization's cultural assumptions and values.

- Stepping outside the normal means of organizational communication to create new points of contact. Strategic leaders send multiple messages about how they themselves are being held accountable, and what people can expect to see and experience differently. In some organizations, leaders have used a series of town meeting forums to meet with large groups in a setting that fosters personal contact and the modeling of an inclusive leadership style. Others have used video messages, telephone messages, letters, and e-mails.

Lever #4: Make Learning a Priority

Leaders and their organizations tend to fail not because they make mistakes, but because they fail to learn. The advantage gained from learning is that the organization becomes agile—able to quickly and effectively respond to opportunities and threats. Gohm (2003, p. 216) points out that a learning priority is not developed randomly but by the strategic leader's establishing the internal conditions for learning. Often good leaders can become great leaders by making learning a priority with such tactics as:

- Developing habits of learning, asking questions, giving feedback, and being tolerant of dissent and ready to hear new views. Particularly essential is the ability to ask open-ended questions, listen to the responses, and lead a productive discussion free from superficiality, rigidity, or miscommunication. Rather than providing answers let the answers emerge from the discussion.
- Encouraging colleagues to adopt the habits of learning such as openly discussing mistakes in order to learn from them, identifying the skills they need for future work tasks, and giving open and honest feedback to each other.
- Promoting and nurturing a learning culture based on sharing of experience, trust, honesty, and openness. A culture where people ask the question, "What can we do so this problem does not happen again?" A culture that insures removal of root causes as an explicit part of jobs and enough time is allocated for such efforts. A culture that provides frequent opportunities for communication of problems and allows potential solutions to occur between those who observe the problem and those with the authority to fix it. A culture which provides a safe environment for all of its members where communication is clear and authentic and people are exposed to multiple perspectives and culture that confirms the interweaving of learning and doing.
- Establishing structures or processes that encourage learning, such as an interdepartmental working group that has the assigned purpose of sharing acquired information to solve problems or develop

strategies related to core competencies and dedicating a person responsible for resolving problems that cross boundaries.

- Fostering a continuous improvement process where people constantly analyze the quality, cost of producing, and the introduction of new products and services. An improvement process that includes knowledge-sharing centered on intelligence gathering, interpretation, reflecting on experience, and experimentation. What information should we collect? What does the information mean? What cause-and-effect relationships are at work? How do we translate our findings into action?

- Providing continuous learning opportunities which acknowledge the importance of group process and community-building by creating experiences for others that are an example of the desired future.

- Initiating and convening conversations that shift people's experience through the way they are brought together and the nature of the questions used to engage them.

- Holding individuals and managers accountable for meeting development objectives and sharing the knowledge they gain with the organization.

Lever #5: Put People at the Center of Things—Empower

High performing organizations empower. Leaders and their organizations tend to fail not because they make mistakes, but because they fail to recognize that the work of organizations gets done through the actions of people, individually or collectively. Psychologists tell us that performance stems from ability multiplied by motivation. Empowerment provides the motivation to higher performance by emphasizing the development of follower self-management or self-direction. Self managed and self directed teams are based on different assumptions. Self managed teams work together toward a common goal which is defined outside of the team. The team does their own work scheduling, training, rewards and recognition. A self directed team is one which works together toward a common goal which they define.

Often good leaders can become great leaders by empowering organization members with such tactics as:

- Developing the habits of empowerment. "Voice your thanks and gratitude to others on every occasion. Praise them for every accomplishment. And pay close attention to them when they talk and want to interact with you"[8]

- Enabling colleagues at all levels of the organization to make decisions without referring them to someone else.

- Empowering colleagues at all levels so they feel that they own a piece of the organization, have input into decisions that affect their work, and that their work directly connects to the goals of the organization.[9]

- Encouraging more responsibility for work by removing barriers such as ineffective supervisors, inflexible systems and procedures, insufficient information, and outdated mental models.[10] Determine what existing policies and practices get in the way. Find out what skills, financial, and information systems resources need to be put into place to facilitate the execution of the statement of intent.

- Examining what encourages colleague engagement. Do you know what drives their productivity and motivation levels?

- Involving colleagues in improving the way work is accomplished and results are achieved.

- Foster collaboration by building trust, giving power away, offering support, communicating that participation is open and expecting ideas and initiatives from above and below.

- Replacing a culture of formality with a culture of familiarity.

- Reinforcing a sense of family that has long been an institutional value.

Lever #6: Recruit and Select For Performance and Culture Fit

In his 1992 book, *Organizational Culture and Leadership,* Schein identifies personnel actions as one of the most effective measures available to leaders who wish to shape the culture of the organization. Since performance is related to recruiting, socializing, training and empowerment, anticipate whether your organizational culture will be rewarding for potential recruits. Hire people who will fit the culture. People can learn new skills; establishing cultural fit is much harder. Often good leaders can become great leaders by recruiting and selecting people for performance and cultural fit with such tactics as:

- Determining if you have the right kind of people to execute the plan.

- Hiring for person/culture fit in addition to person/job fit.
- Developing culturally consistent selection criteria. For example, consider General Electric's description of desirable candidates, who "stimulate and relish change and are not frightened or paralyzed by it, see change as an opportunity, not a threat," and "have a passion for excellence, hating bureaucracy and all the nonsense that comes with it." These are qualities that differentiate between people who are, and are not, successful at GE.[11]
- Being mindful of recruiter characteristics because you will get more of them back.[12]
- Finding people who think and act like owners; who have high aspirations, who make decisions, and take prompt action.
- Replacing influential employees who hold outdated assumptions with those who embrace the assumptions of your strategic intent.

Lever #7: Tie Rewards to Results

Pressure for performance must be accompanied with a meaningful reward system that is properly designed to keep members focused on the execution of the organization's initiatives and their performance targets. The design of the system is where it gains power. For example, to establish your position as the low-cost provider, you must reward performances that help reduce costs. However, in deciding which incentives to use in such a system it is a good idea to identify a meaningful reward for your employees.

Good leaders can become great performance and institution builders by tying rewards to results with such tactics as:

- Identifying the drivers of organizational value and then relentlessly and consistently rewarding these outcomes. If you preach the importance of being a team player and of achieving quality standards, but you rank order employees based only on their individual quantitative results, you can't expect the compensation to support these goals or vice-a-versa.
- Creating rewards that support commitment including stock options or profit sharing.
- Using intangible rewards as well as monetary ones such as the chance to win a prime parking spot or recognition by management and peers. Flexible work schedules, advancement opportunities, and job customization are effective in all three areas, making each especially important to lower-performing companies.

- Customizing the reward program to capitalize on demographic preferences. What motivates depends on career stage, gender and generational factors. A good place to start is to ask followers "What should be rewarded to support our organization's business objectives?"
- Making rewards meaningful. Rewards have to be high. If they are only marginal then the power of rewards disintegrates because they do not provide enough motivation. Researchers in the field of compensation have long held that, for incentives to be truly effective, the actual reward must be significant, at least 15% to 20% of base._
- Making sure the effort or activity that's required in order to receive the reward is reasonable compared to the value of the reward.
- Making payouts immediate. Organizational members need to feel the impact of rewards for their efforts.
- Making the rewards visible. Be sure they are easy to understand and communicate and that members know what they have to do to earn them.
- Rewarding results not performance of assigned functions.
- Giving rewards according to contribution to the success of the organization. Tie rewards and recognition to organization and team performance and enhancement of skills, rather than placing too strong an emphasis on pay for individual performance.
- Choosing incentives and an approach that can be sustained

As powerful as these seven levers are to build a high performing organization there is no best approach that is right for all organizations and for all members.[13] For example, when Jack Welch identified GE's ability to tie rewards to performance many other CEOs tried to emulate him. However, many times when they replicated the compensation and reward tactics he used; they failed. What they didn't have was GE's culture or capabilities that had been honed over the 20 years of Jack's tenure. The final lesson is that there are many actions, tactics, and levers available to the strategic leader; they are only powerful when artistically applied.

CLIFF NOTES

Habit 6: Assuring Results

This chapter described how to drive the statement of intent throughout the organization by building a high performing culture of excellent performance and results. Assuring results requires consensus, learning and accommodation. Strategic leaders are proactive and rely on the principles of creative tension and a generative learning approach to close the gap between the statement of intent and the prevailing norms and processes within the organization. The takeaway is that strategic leaders assure by focusing, and getting their followers focused on the organization's aspirations, guiding principles and initiatives. They assure by being performance and institutional builders.

Performance builders influence performance directly. They focus on external adaptation priorities such as profits. They explore new markets in business contexts, make learning gains and develop new techniques in educational contexts. They value data based decision-making. They face the hard facts and they build a culture in which people are encouraged to tell the truth, even if it is unpleasant. They measure progress in a transparent way and encourage continuous progress.

Institution builders influence performance indirectly. Developing a cohesive, adaptive, learning culture is the focus of their work. They institutionalize the values and systematize the processes. They build a strong organizational culture and create consensus among employees on a set of values that enhance performance. They use learning as a way to positively impact performance. Strategic leaders use seven levers to create the internal cohesiveness and organizational fitness necessary for high performance. They:

- Make the change target concrete and clear.
- Track performance.
- Teach the organization's point of view.
- Make learning a priority.
- Put people at the center of things.
- Recruit and select for performance and culture fit
- Tie rewards to business results, individual growth, capability, and contribution.

Review the way Jack Welch ran GE. What Levers did he use to create a high performing culture?

NOTES

1. I used the following sources to piece together Mr. Ghosn's responses to the four questions; Fonda (2003, p. 78); Ghosn (2005); Greising (2002); Magee (2003, 2004, p. 72); Taylor, (2003); http://www.time.com/time/2001/influentials/ybghosn.html
http://www.businessweek.com/2001/01_02/b3714015.htm
and http://www.nissanusa.com/insideNissan/CorporateBiographies.

2. House and Howell (1992, p. 83) describe this leadership style as (a) based on egalitarian behavior, (b) service to collective interests; not driven by the self-interest of the leader and, (c) developing and empowering others.

3. The interdependence between culture and change is well-accepted and crucial to the success of planned change initiatives. Cameron and Quinn (1999) argue that as many as three quarters of change efforts have failed entirely or have created problems serious to the survival of the organization (p. 1) due to failure to consider the organization's culture as an important factor in the change process.

4. Also called adaptive and generative learning by Senge (1990), and single loop or double loop learning by Argyris and Schön (1996).

5. As quoted in Crupi and Paparone (2008)

6. Kotter (1978, p. 17), in providing a model of organizational dynamics, defined a "social system" as comprised of "culture" ("those organizationally relevant norms and values shared by most employees (or subgroups of employees") and "social structure" ("the relationships that exist among employees in terms of such variables as power, affiliation and trust"). See also Byrne (1998) on "How Jack Welch runs GE."

7. Created by Kaplan and Norton (1992) to put strategy and vision, rather than control, at the center of management. It also includes innovation and learning as one of the four key indicator groups of success; the others being financial measures, operational measures on customer satisfaction, and measures on internal processes. It looks at organizations from the perspective of the customer, the shareholder, and identifies what the organization excels at; while also analyzing whether it can continue to improve and create value.

8. Cited in http://www.1000ventures.com/business_guide/crosscuttings/employee_empowerment.html

9. G. Spreitzer (1995).

10. See Kotter and Cohen (2002), particularly "empowering action" (p. 103).

11. See Chatman (1991); Chatman and Cha (2003).

12. Connerly and Rynes (1997) offered the "similarity-attraction effect." We are attracted to people who are similar to ourselves.

13. For example, teaming is a popular organizational structure to increase productivity and raise employee commitment. It has been estimated that 80% of U.S. companies use teams (Gross & Safier, 1995). A fundamental dilemma is how to find ways to compensate teams and/or team members fairly, while at the same time providing incentives to enhance productivity and performance. Merit pay for individual accomplishment, for

instance, could conflict with pay for team accomplishment (Weinberger, 1998). Long-term collective incentives like gain-sharing and profit-sharing sometimes suffer from line-of-sight problems (Lawler, 1990). Differentiating pay among team members who are highly marketable versus those who are less marketable can introduce another source of conflict (Taylor, 1997).

CHAPTER 8

THE EPILOGUE

Frequently Asked Questions

This chapter is in a question and answer format. It reports the dialogue the author has had with colleagues, clients and students on the concept of strategic leadership.

1. What could you best say to describe your strategic leadership (SL) theory?

Response: The new story of leadership success is a saga of connecting organizations to the vital themes emanating from the environment, being agile enough to seize opportunities, and constantly balancing opposing interests, forces and tensions while always working toward the goals of the organization or constituency. It deals with the present and the future simultaneously. It is clear that leaders who can

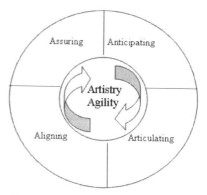

Figure 8.1.   The Leader's Wheel.

The Strategic Leader: New Tactics for A Globalizing World, pp. 183–192
Copyright © 2009 by Information Age Publishing
All rights of reproduction in any form reserved.

negotiate these tensions remain the most important ingredient for organizational success.

Leaders engaged in strategic leadership are involved in understanding their environment, determining ends, creating a coherent organization, establishing power networks, and crafting a responsible learning organization. Therefore, strategic leadership can be defined as the ability to make consequential decisions about ends in complex and ambiguous environments while aligning the organization to execute them.

While strategic leaders anticipate change, lead change, and foster a mindset of change, they do so with a clear understanding of the necessity for maintaining a level of stability in order for transformational change to be successful. This approach enables the leader to embed the organization within a strategic context, while balancing the ethical nature of the tasks, the political influences, and the organization's need for change and stability. Leadership that meets these twin challenges of leading for stability and change and for "what is possible" and "what is right" is referred to as "strategic leadership. To work in this fashion, leaders must be able to manage and managers must be able to lead. Strategic leaders and their colleagues accept the inevitability of change and the need to reexamine their internal beliefs, mental models, and understanding of changes impact on organizational life. They promote managerial change to maintain present success, making the machine run faster, more efficiently and more productively. They actually promote meaningful, momentous, transformational change as a way to provide long-term stability to their organization. In accomplishing these purposes, they act as moral stewards who interpret and understand the political realities they face. Strategic leaders ask: "how do I retain what we have and make it better?" and "when do we abandon what we have and move to something new?" However, they also promote balance between the ethical nature of the task and the political realities that exist so that they can lead their organization through the maze of modern complexities.

2.   What have you learned through your leadership journey?

Response: Of course much of what I have learned is in the book. But if I were to relate what I learned to playing golf, it would go something like this:

- First, leaders must act. Planning to act is not enough. As in the game of golf, reading provides a basic understanding of the rules of the game, and the thoughts of others on how to hit a golf ball straight and long. But you can't learn to play golf by reading a book or talking to others about it. You must take your clubs to the course, tee up the ball and hit it!

- Second, active initiation of change brings anxiety. Teeing up the ball for the first time produces anxiety. This anxiety is greater if others are watching. It's even greater if many others are watching. When any change of note in an activity occurs, people are anxious and need support. A few encouraging words from the golf pro or a friend help. Similarly, change must be nurtured in a supportive climate.

- Third, beliefs and practices must change. And, it's better if they change simultaneously. But if I could only have one change it would be behavior—culture follows. The golfer must believe that the effort expended to change a flaw in her swing is worthwhile to her score. Change must be approached from a values and practice point of view to foster lasting change.

- Fourth, ownership is not a precondition of change. Ownership grows as one changes. The golfer becomes more willing to continue to work on her swing as she becomes more skilled. Organizational members develop ownership of changes as they experience success. Change must be nurtured and even small successes should be celebrated to maintain the momentum of the change.

- Fifth, change does not necessarily create improvement. The golfer may try three or four swing adjustments before one seems to give him or her better results. The changes leaders seek to carry out should be carefully chosen and monitored and the results reported so their effect becomes visible and valuable. The golfer has it easier here than the leader. Every hole has a standard number of strokes allocated to par. Improvement is easily recognized. The lesson is that change must account for improved results and processes. A singular focus on one or the other is not sufficient.

- Sixth, first, and second level change must be identified and addressed. First level change addresses problems of process and program quality. It focuses on changes in the core competencies of the business. Continuing our golfing analogy, golfers must use a correct grip on the club. Second level change addresses organizational and governance structures and processes. For example, organizations reduce hierarchy and encourage self management. Golfers must have the correct length of clubs to strike the ball consistently. The changes needed must be matched with the right type of reform. Put first things first!

- Seventh, change can occur at the center of the organizational core in mainstream programs, or on the periphery in satellite programs.

Golfers can change their full swing to hit the ball straighter and longer. Or they can change their chipping and putting routines so they can score lower. Businesses can focus on their core competencies, they can develop spin-offs, or they can expand their product line in new ways. Schools can focus on the core subjects, or they can work with alternative schools which don't affect the mainstream "regular" programs of the school. Change must occur at the point it is needed. Changes in the wider system occur to accommodate these first order changes.

- These seven general guidelines are useful to focus a leader's change efforts. But the big question is, "What needs to change?" Just as golfers need to decide whether it is their full wood shots, short irons, or putting that need to be changed. The second big question is, "What changes should be attempted?"

3. What makes this theory so different from other leadership theories?

Response: In one way, my thoughts are different because they do not differentiate between leadership and management. Both leadership and management actions support change. In the case of management it is frame sustaining change. In the case of leadership it is frame breaking change. Yet, this dichotomy only exists in conceptual terms not on the playing field. In fact, what I believe is that managerial and transformational actions, and political and ethical actions, are all types of leadership. They can be used singularly but they are more powerful when the leader can integrate the four action sets. But these actions are not enough. One must also be able to establish direction and gain the emotional commitment of those who join in its quest.

This leads to a second difference. Scholars have created leadership brands which specify a limited set of behaviors and strategies. What I have found is that when the context changes the brand scholars were advocating for doesn't work as well. Strategic leaders need to be trained in a wider bandwidth of actions and tactics that enable them to remain successful when the context changes.

I have tried to provide leaders with a simple way to think about positioning their organization in a changing environment. From my perspective the first thing leaders do is ask "what has to happen here?" When the answer to that question comes forward, they then set direction by engaging those within their sphere of influence (colleagues) to assess where they have been, and where they need to go to be successful, then commit to doing something about it. Without this commitment, leaders are always fighting with one arm tied behind their back. Once the commitment is made, they need to flexibly apply the four action sets; managing, transforming, political, and ethical.

I tried to make the decision about when to apply the four actions a simple choice. The key challenge is to find out what is needed in the entity you are attempting to lead—stability or change? If your judgment is stability (order) then a managerial approach is the main thrust of your leadership. Political and ethical considerations are balancing arms that enable you to make the "machine" run faster, smoother, and more productively. Of course some of the transforming actions can also be supportive. If your choice is to foster change then transformational behaviors are the main thrust of your leadership and political and ethical considerations are balancing arms that enable you to bring about a new order. Of course some of the managing actions can also be supportive.

4. What are the challenges facing organizations facing today, and how does your leadership thinking address them?

Response: I think the major challenge that leaders face today is the need of followers for order, and the need of the organization for change. What I see happening is that the environment confronting most leaders today is complex, ambiguous and messy. These characteristics are created by the effects of globalization, multiculturalism, shifting populations, advanced information, and communication technologies and an increasing level of diversity. We simply are living in, and will continue to live in, a very complex, and at times, chaotic world which requires a degree of unity from leadership and organizations. There is a need for creativity, imagination, diversity and openness.

Leaders need be trained differently. They need agility of the mind and actions. Rather than a linear mindset they need to develop a strategic mindset. Rather than standing firm in a changing world they need to connect their organizations to the current major themes associated with success. Rather than assuming followers will follow they need to connect necessary changes into the minds and spirit of their followers and thereby benefit from empowerment and self-management. Rather than seeing their organizations as independent of others they need to recognize dependencies and connect with the significant forces on their critical path to success. Rather than relying on vertical skills of command and control behaviors they need to learn horizontal skills of coordination and collaboration. Rather than using a limited set of leadership actions to influence followers to join in a common cause they need to embrace a wider bandwidth of leader actions so they can be successful in many different situations.

5. Do you think that strategic leadership will fit into the Eastern world? Why?

Response: I believe the concepts I suggested earlier in this interview, and in my book, lend themselves to an Eastern way of viewing the world but not so much in application of leadership. I have found that there has been a greater shift in the way Western and Eastern traditions are interacting and in many cases blending.

The traditional, mutually exclusive dichotomy between paradigms has changed significantly over the past 50 years. Historically, increasing interest and contact between one and the other began in the mid-twentieth century, with the fascination principally with Zen, Hinduism, and Buddhism manifested by the countercultural literati of the beatniks and the hippies (Jack Kerouac, Allen Ginsberg, Alan Watts, Gary Snyder, and The Beatles) and religious philosophers like Thomas Merton. This coincided with the move to the West of spiritual masters such as Krishnamurti, Paramahansa Yogananda, the Maharishi Mahesh Yogi, and the exile from Tibet of the current Dalai Lama. This initial contact has evolved considerably, to involve practitioners and academics from both traditions interested in learning and assimilating the best of each, which has led to the building of a rich knowledge base that is greater than the sum of its parts. For example, this shift is increasing our understanding of the role and function of the more subtle aspects of human growth and development in attaining successful outcomes in personal and professional settings, aspects which the West has traditionally overlooked with some notable exceptions being Mary Parker Follett and Daniel Goleman.

The continued difference I see in some of the developing cultures is a reliance on command and control leadership behaviors. In these cultures hierarchy and the unassailable right, even duty, of leaders to be the decision makers and "bosses," are culturally sine qua non even though the transformational literature of Bass and Kouzes and Posner report the effectiveness of transformational behaviors over a wide area of the world. In the long-term changes are inevitable. I feel sure that over time the transition to more modern forms of leadership will occur as it is doing in the West.

6. What are the steps that strategic leaders take in order to change a chaotic environment/organization?

Response: The situation you describe is made to order for a strategic leader. They turn chaotic environments into complex but orderly ones by simply employing the six habits: artistry, agility, anticipating, articulating, aligning, and assuring. The ordering of these habits is not meant to convey linearity. The first two—artistry and agility, are internal to the leader.

The other four; anticipating, articulating, aligning, and assuring are part of the learning cycle organizations go through to respond to new stimuli. Even though one usually starts with anticipating one could as easily start with assuring. There are several keys for success. First colleagues must articulate the direction and basic values they will live by. It is the key to gaining cooperation and being able to build the team. The second key here is to understand that once the four interlocking habits are put into play, they are supported by the leader's artistic use of the four sets of actions: managerial, transformational, political and ethical leadership.

7. Using the strategic leadership perspective, what must a dean in a college do in order to bring changes to his/her organization?

Response: This question gets to the beauty of the strategic leadership model. It really doesn't make any difference if it's a dean, a congressman running for office, a school principal, a manager of a small business, or the head of a large corporation. The strategic leadership habits, actions, and tactics are useful to all. So my answer is that all leaders first apply the four interlocking strategic leadership habits to set direction with their followers and build the supportive culture, then artistically apply the actions and tactics from there.

I think there are a few differences that should be noted as to whether one practices Organizational Leadership, Political Leadership, or Public Leadership. The differences in these contexts are the ability of the leader to rely on the use of authority. Most university deans in the Western world work from a reduced authority base therefore they should focus on transformational behaviors rather than managerial behaviors to bring about change. From what I know deans in the Eastern world have more authority over faculty, therefore they could use more managerial behaviors. But I would bet that the more successful ones use transformational and ethical actions to a greater degree than managerial or political actions.

8. I am wondering about the scale of political versus ethical actions. In any given situation, it seems that a leader would use morals and ethics as the situation demanded to achieve his goals, and then would set them aside if not appropriate to the political pressures. Would this not be a bit limited given the fact that as organizations align themselves with the principles of justice in action, they will achieve more success in this postmodern world?

Response: It seems you are assuming that organizations align themselves with justice. Are there not some which align with just production? In any case, I don't think morals and ethics are set aside by most leaders; but they do come under great pressure from multiple constituencies and societal and political demands.

Doing what is possible is hopelessly embedded in doing what is right so long as you are doing what is possible in the service of your organization's goals and those goals are shared by the members of your team. The downside, however, is anyone capable of using political behaviors to further the goals of the organization might also be capable of using those behaviors to further their own goals. In this case—personal interest—such behaviors would be independent of justice.

There is an argument that being right is enough. My experience has led me to believe, however, that *being right is not enough*. My son, a former state senator, related to me (when I asked him what he learned from his first year in the senate), that *relationships trump ideas* in that context. I believe ideas may yield to politics in the short term but trump all in the long run.

9. How do you set direction when it has all ready been set externally?

Response: As I said in chapter 1, the use of strategic leadership at all levels will be challenged by those in management or supervisory roles who believe they do not have enough discretion to fully make strategic choices about ends. This perception is a relic of the legacy model of leadership. It is true that the greater the internal and external constraints—whether they stem from demography, ideology, or personality—the less discretion the leader enjoys. However, today's emphasis on flatter organizations and leaders pushing the authority to act down the chain of command, results in more leaders possessing more discretion. Lower level leaders may not perceive that they have discretion or they may not want the responsibilities that come with the ability to make strategic choices, until they make their own personal transition to the new conditions.

Whereas discretion increases the likelihood that leaders will seize opportunities and influence the direction of the organization, most leaders in lower echelon positions still have strategic choices to make regarding the ends they promote and the ways and means of implementation in their sphere of responsibility. What managers or team leaders do is treat the organization's direction as one of the important themes they must address but they also scan and anticipate others as they articulate the department or team intent. Rather than act as organizational functionaries, or worse still—insurgents, their approach should be thought of as counter insurgency—working to get the organization and higher echelon leaders to support what they know they need to do to build a high performing organization.

10. How can you make sure your organization not only keeps its edge over its competitors, but also seizes new opportunities?

Response: Organizations, like people, have a world view. Like strategic leaders they must practice agility in terms of thinking, processes, and structures. To stay on top it's important to maintain an open mind set in order to sense and exploit new opportunities in your environment. They must be agile and flexible.

The key to doing this is to have what Yves Doz refers to as *resource fluidity*—the ability to invest, redeploy, or divest resources quickly enough to exploit the emerging opportunities. You need some loose change, or people with slack, to try some new things and see if they work. You adjust means not ends. Doz also found that rather than being pulled by the centralization-decentralization tension (delegation to sub units on one hand and unity of command on the other) there must be leadership unity. These distributed models of leadership challenge leadership unity because when people are self directed they are reluctant to focus on the whole entity. We all like our own babies. The whole organization must be mentally agile and understand that in the present complexities the outside world rather than the inside takes prominence.

11. Is there any particular leader in American politics that you see most fits your strategic leadership characterization?

Response: I have mentioned several in the book—Abraham Lincoln, Franklin Roosevelt, Bill Clinton, Dwight Eisenhower, and the first George Bush come close to the characterization. Each of them practiced primarily as artists rather than scientists. They were leaders *and* managers, politicians, and moralists.

Barack Obama presents a most interesting model of strategic thinking and leadership. He relies on collaboration and coordination rather than just command and control. He proceeds deliberately in concert with allies rather than acting independently and quickly. In the 2008 democratic primary he used new science principles such as a generative approach, minimum specifications, and organizational fitness to win the nomination over Hillary Clinton. But he is a strategic leader poster child for other reasons. He has grasped the importance of relationships and internal and external alliance building to strengthen his power and persuasiveness, and he has incorporated these elements into his approach to governance.

THANK YOU FOR YOUR QUESTIONS—I HOPE YOU FIND THE HABITS AS USEFUL AS I HAVE FOR TURNING THE LEADERSHIP WHEEL!

APPENDIX A

Reflective Questions

CHAPTER 1: A FRESH LOOK

Reflective Questions

Before delving deeper into these thoughts in following chapters review Table 1.1 which provides an advanced organizer of the tasks, tactics, actions, and metaphors associated with strategic leadership that will be further discussed in the following chapters. Then reflect on these questions.

1. Review times of parenthesis diagram. What does this tell you about change?
2. Reflect on the vignettes of the leaders presented earlier in the chapter. What parts of the Leadership Wheel can you see in action?
3. Observe the way leaders operate in your organizations. What parts of the Leadership Wheel can you see in action? What has been the success of these leaders you have observed?
4. Reflect on the way you were taught to view leadership and the way you are led. Are there similarities between what you have been taught and observed and the notion of strategic leadership? What are the differences?

CHAPTER 2: ARTISTRY

Reflective Questions

Before exploring the other four strategic leader habits, reflect on the following questions to gain a deeper of the artistic actions strategic leaders employ

1. What lessons can you draw by comparing the artistry represented in the strategic leader's wheel and the artistic ideas of Leonardo Da Vinci?
2. Observe the way your boss operates. Compare their actions to those on Table 2.3. Can you distinguish among their use of managerial, transformational, political and ethical actions? Now think about their effectiveness. Do you see any relationship between the way they act and how effective they are? Compare your notes with associates. Is there a general pattern of strategic actions and leader effectiveness?
3. Do you think that leaders who use political and ethical action sets in combination with either managing or transforming actions are more successful than leaders who use them singularly?
4. In frame-sustaining situations, do you think that leaders who combine managerial, political, and ethical actions are more successful than leaders who do not?
5. In frame-breaking situations, do you think that leaders who combine transformational, political, and ethical actions are more successful than leaders who do not?
6. Reflect on the labyrinth? Did this illustration resonate with you? Which ones? Based on your reflections, what changes would you make in your approach to leadership?

CHAPTER 3: AGILITY

Reflective Questions

Before delving deeper into how strategic leaders use these actions and tactics, review the summarization found on Tables 3.1 and 3.2 to gain a more holistic understanding of the relationship of strategic leader's wheel and the principles and tactics suggested by the new science. Then reflect on these questions.

1. What do you think Dr. Wilson's principles mean? What do you think of the way Dr. Wilson developed his principles?

2. Consider the descriptions of the *old science* found in Table 3.1. How would you compare them to those offered by the *new science*?

3. Which worldview is dominant in your organization? Is the dominant view the right way to understand how your organization really works?

CHAPTER 4: ANTICIPATING

Reflective Questions

Before we move on to developing an understanding of how strategic leaders use social intelligence to mobilize their followers, review Table 4.2 in this chapter and the strategic leader's action sets (managing, transforming, political, and ethical) presented in chapter 2. Then reflect on these questions.

1. How would you lead an organization with a high number of subordinates?

2. How would you lead an organization composed of a high number of competitors?

3. How would you lead organizations composed of a high number of colleagues?

4. Apply the readiness to change tools (Figure 4.4a. & b, and Table 4.3) to your organization. Is it ready to change? What led you to your answer?

5. Reflect on your organization. Which of the four cultures dominates: group, development, hierarchical and rational? Would a strategic leader try to find innovations that would be supported by the current culture or ones that might require the culture to change?

CHAPTER 5: ARTICULATION

Reflective Questions

Before moving on to developing an understanding of how strategic leaders establish and maintain momentum, reflect on these questions to gain a more holistic understanding of the relationship of the strategy of articulating.

1. Think about a time in your personal or organizational life when a new direction was undertaken. Where did it come from—the senior leaders? The managers? The supervisors? The workforce? Or was it a combination of the four levels? Was the new direction anticipated and set out in advance in a strategic plan or did it emerge? What was the level of enthusiastic support given to the direction?

2. Review the aspirations of Southwest Airlines, John Kennedy's space program, and the University of Illinois provided in the text. Do they provide a sense of direction, and a sense of destiny?

3. Review the strategic view Andy Grove provides for Intel Corporation. How does Grove frame Intel's strategic problems? How does he structure his report? Was there something lacking in Grove's personal vision?

4. Consider Antonio's story. What tactics did Antonio use to connect his school to its strategic context?

5. Review your organizational mission statement and compare it to the outline of a statement of strategic intent found on Table 5.1.

CHAPTER 6: ALIGNING

Reflective Questions

Before we move on to developing an understanding of how strategic leaders assure results, reflect on these questions to gain a more holistic understanding of the tactics available to create cohesion, trusting relationships, and alliances.

1. Review the questions that followers ask themselves before they commit to the carrying out the organizations intent efficiently. Apply these questions to your work place. Now answer this question, is your workplace a trusting place to work.

2. Review the three vignettes about how Victor Joppolo led the people of Adano at the conclusion of World War II. Then review French and Raven's taxonomy of social power. What tactics did Joppolo use in Adano?

3. Review the Armand Hammer vignettes and then the Cialdini's principles of social influence. What tactics did Hammer use?

4. Review the levers strategic leaders have to motivate followers. What motivates you?

5. Can you give specific examples of the tactics of relating and persuading?

CHAPTER 7: ASSURING

Reflective Questions

A statement of intent is just a mirage unless it is executed and embedded deeply into the conscious and unconscious level of organizational members. Reflect on these questions to gain an in-depth understanding of the relationship of assuring and the development of high performing organizations.

1. Distinguish between those leaders who operate from a performance building role and those operating from a institution building role? Can you identify individuals from your experience that fit both roles. What are the advantages and disadvantages of operating from either role?

2. Review the questions that followers ask themselves before they commit to the carrying out the organizations intent efficiently. Apply these questions to your work place. Now answer this question, is your workplace a trusting place to work.

3. Seven key levers were identified in the chapter to assist the leader in embedding the strategic intent into the heart and minds of people in the organization? Which levers are used in your organization? How successful are leaders in using them? What outcomes can you attribute to the use of each lever? Are there circumstances where an identified lever is unacceptable to use in an organization?

4. What are the biggest mistakes leaders make in trying to build performance?

APPENDIX B

The Strategic Thinking Questionnaire (STQ©)

The STQ© is a reliable and valid assessment tool designed to provide an evaluation of the use of three cognitive skills important to strategic thinking. The STQ©:

- Measures the participant's capability to think strategically.
- Assesses the use of three mental processing skills: reflection, reframing and systems thinking revealing the test takers ability to think flexibly, conceptually and strategically.
- Provides participants with a deeper understanding of their own mental processing skills and its relationship to their effectiveness in managing and leading followers.
- Enables respondents to compare their performance to norms drawn from a baseline set of data.
- Identifies the best talent to hire, promote, and develop.
- Is useful in self-assessment for personal growth.
- Is useful to consultants in organizational development and seminars
- Has been translated into Spanish, Mandarin, Malay, and Turkish.

The studies undertaken to test the STQ include managers and executives from for-profit and not for-profit companies and organizations. In total around there have been 3,000 plus test takers.

The Instrument

The STQ© is built on three dimensions of strategic thinking—systems thinking—reframing—reflection. It is six pages long and consists of 48 Likert type questions and provides an assessment of the three skills of; *systems thinking, reflection,* and *reframing.* The STQ© asks respondents how often they use the skills when confronted with problems. It is only available in a self-format since only the test taker can describe how often they employ the skills. Typically, participants return the instrument directly to the researchers or seminar facilitator. The STQ© takes approximately 15 or 20 minutes to complete and is capable of being either self or electronically scored.

The STQ© was originally developed from an interpretation of the literature on strategic thinking as being composed of systems thinking, reframing and reflection. Using the definitions as guides, statements were written describing skills required to think in systems thinking, reframing, and reflection terms. A panel of five experts knowledgeable about strategic thinking reviewed the resulting 180 items. They sorted the statements into the three categories. In an iterative fashion, the statements were modified or discarded following lengthy discussions and repeated feedback sessions between the panel and researchers. Items on the STQ© are cast on a 5-point Likert scale. A higher value represents greater use of a cognitive skill, as noted below:

1. = Almost Never uses
2. = Rarely uses
3. = Sometimes uses
4. = Frequently uses
5. = Almost Always uses

Psychometric Properties

The STQ© in statistical evaluation has shown acceptable reliability scores and has demonstrated content, face, predictive and discriminate validity.

Reliability. Following each administration (four) of the STQ, the items were subject to empirical analyses followed by discussions conducted in an iterative fashion until the statements were representative of the strategic thinking construct. Ongoing analysis and refinements in the instrument continue, with a database of over 3,000 respondents. Table 10.1 presents

Table 10.1. Means, Standard Deviations and Reliability Coefficients of the Subscales of the Strategic Leadership Questionnaire: Version3, 2007 and Version4, 2008

Dimension	Version3					Version4				
	M	SD	N	Alpha	# Items	M	SD	N	Alpha	# Items
Systems thinking	3.55	.318	643	.713	12	3.67	.486	330	.870	17
Reframing	3.45	.286	643	.777	12	3.43	.433	330	.818	17
Reflecting	3.48	.281	643	.752	12	3.66	.416	330	.742	14
Strategic thinking	3.50	.247	643	.891	36	3.59	.411	330	.928	48

the means, standard deviations, and Cronbach Alpha's for the STQ© Version3 and Version4.

In STQ©v3, the rank order of skill usage is systems thinking (3.55), reframing (3.45), and reflecting (3.48). Based on the mean scores, it was expected that systems thinking would be the skill most frequently used, followed by reframing. Internal reliabilities of Version3 were assessed through the standardized Cronbach's alpha. A .70 value generally considered to indicate a sufficient reliability by classical psychometric authorities (Nunnally, 1978; Peterson, 1994). Reliability statistics for the STQv3 (based on approximately 643 ratings by a multisector sample of managers in business and education) were computed. Internal reliabilities ranged between .71 and .77 for the subscales and .89 for the total scale. Other studies have found similar reliabilities. For instance, Pisapia, Reyes-Guerra, and Coukos (2005) reported reliabilities ranging from .77–.83 on subscales and .91 for the scale.

As seen on Table 10.1, internal reliabilities (Cronbach alphas) on the STQ©v4 are higher than Version3 on all scales except reflecting. This may be explained by difference in number of items on the scale from v3 to v4. They range between .74 and .87 for the subscales and .93 for the scale meeting the .70 standard. Additionally, the rank order of the means on the subscales reveal that systems thinking is the cognitive skill most frequently used as expected from the version3 and earlier administrations. However, reflecting skills (3.66) surpassed reframing (3.43) as the second most used skill. Thus, the rank ordering of means among the v4 sub scales is exactly the same v3 subscales except that they were used more often by this sample.

Factor Structure. The STQ© was originally developed from an interpretation of the literature on strategic thinking as being composed of systems thinking, reframing and reflection. The literature portrayed reframing as part of reflection. The researchers believed that reframing was an important skill in its own right. Hence, it was originally extracted and tested as a unique variable from reflection in order to give it emphasis.

The STQ©v4 includes 17 items from systems thinking, 14 from reframing, and 14 reflection items. The STQ©v3, when subjected to factor analysis, produced one predictive factor—the overall strategic thinking score (Pisapia, Reyes-Guerra, & Yasin 2006). Revisions were made in the items and they were retested in version 4.

The STQ©v4 was subjected to a principle axis factoring method with iterative communality estimation and oblimin with Kaiser Normalization rotation. The two factors (systems thinking and reflection) with Eigenvalues greater than 1.0 reported in Table 10.2 accounted for 52% of the variance. Values less than the .10 threshold were suppressed and not reported on the table.

By factoring the 48 questions on the STQ©v4, two interpretable factors that are consistent with the definitions of systems thinking and reflection were obtained. This result is inconsistent with the hypothesized three subscales of the STQ© but consistent with the literature on the subject. The two factors (systems thinking and reflection) will guide continued research on relationships of strategic thinking and selected outcome criteria. For professional developers it is thought that in daily use, the three cognitive skills overlap considerably; but are best taught singularly.

Study Results

Several studies have been completed. Pisapia, Reyes-Guerra, and Yasin studied (2006) 138 for-profit and not-for-profit managers and executives. Pang and Pisapia (2007) conducted a study of 543 school principals in Hong Kong. Zsiga (2007) studied 540 YMCA directors in the United States. Pisapia, Pang, Hee, Ying, and Morris (2009) studied 328 students preparing for educational management roles in Hong Kong, Malaysia, Shanghai, and the United States.

Seven major impressions were left from statistical analyses presented in these studies. First, strategic thinking is strongly associated with self reported effectiveness. That supervisors and managers in our samples score lower than the executives as expected. However, the high performers (the top 20% on effectiveness scores) in each management category used these mental skills significantly more often than less successful managers. Second, there is a cumulative impact when the three capabilities which form the strategic thinking construct are used. Third, the strength of the relationship between strategic thinking and leader success increases

**Table 10.2. Factor Structure (Factor Loadings) for
the STQ©v4. (*n* = 328)**

Item #	Factors		Item
	Systems Thinking	Reflecting	Stem: *When facing difficult problems, How often do you:*
4	.738	.169	Ask those around you what they think is changing?
6	.594		Try to find a common goal when two or more parties are in conflict?
44	.544	−.167	Think about how different parts of the organization influence the way things are done?
24	.523		Try to identify external environmental forces which affect your work?
13	.429	−.138	Engage in discussions with those who hold a different world view?
47	.397	−.131	Define the entire problem before breaking it down into parts?
17	.370	−.242	Consider the results of past actions in similar situations?
3	.321	−.183	Try to extract patterns in the information available?
31		−.792	Frame the problems you face in ways that allow you to understand them?
29		−.667	Look at actions being taken to correct the discrepancy between what is desired and what exists?
20		−.642	Ask "WHY" questions to develop an understanding of problems?
33	.206	−.558	Use different points of view to map out different strategies?
26	.170	−.525	Try to understand how the people in the situation are connected to each other?
32	.244	−.501	Look for fundamental long-term corrective measures?

Extraction Method: Principal Axis Factoring. Rotation Method: Oblimin with Kaiser Normalization. Rotation converged in 17 iterations. Values less than the .10 threshold were suppressed.

as leaders use the three dimensions in tandem. Fourth, the use of these skills is similar in the United States and Malaysia. Fifth, there is a significant relationship between strategic thinking capabilities and self directed learning. Sixth, the use of these skills improves with age and experience —the younger you are the less you use these skills. Seventh, the STQ appears free of cultural and gender bias; but reveals an age bias. Our overall conclusion is that successful leaders use the three strategic thinking capabilities more often than less successful leaders.

We believe that the results are useful for the development and identification of executive talent. From an organizational point of view, the STQ$^©$ can provide another tool to use in considering who gets selected and placed on the fast-track. From the participant point of view, it provides him/her with the necessary feedback for their continuous development on an important and hereto untouched set of skills. We have worked in the following ways in using the instrument.

Executive development – we administer the test as a pretest and then provide training seminars in strategic thinking.

Executive identification – we administer the test in companies who use the results to identify their top managers and executives for succession training.

If you would like to take the STQ please send an e-mail to jpisapia@fau.edu

APPENDIX C

The Strategic
Leadership Questionnaire (SLQ©)

The Strategic Leadership Questionnaire (SLQ©) is a reliable and valid assessment tool designed to assess a leader's use of four strategic leader actions: Managing, Transforming, Political and Ethical. The SLQ©

- Measures the participant's capability to use a multifaceted set of leader actions.
- Assesses the use of four sets of leader actions: Managing, Transforming, Political, and Ethical.
- Informs the respondent of the relationship of their actions to their effectiveness in managing and leading followers
- Enables respondents to compare their performance to norms drawn from a baseline set of data
- Identifies the best talent to hire, promote, and develop
- Is useful as a self-assessment for personal growth. Is useful to consultants in organizational development and seminars
- Has been translated into Spanish, Turkish, and Malay

The Instrument

The SLQ©'s dimensions were extracted from John Pisapia's theoretical model of strategic leadership. It is three pages long and consists of 81 Likert type questions. The SLQ© provides an assessment of four sets of leader actions: managing, transforming, political and ethical.

The instrument is available in both self and other configurations. The self version asks leaders how often they use the actions. The other version asks subordinates, peers, and superiors how often they observe the leader use the actions. Hard copy and digital versions have been produced. Typically, participants return the instrument directly to the researchers or seminar facilitator. The SLQ© takes approximately 15 minutes to complete and is capable of being either self or electronically scored.

The literature surrounding each dimension was reviewed and definitions for each was crafted and submitted to a panel of five leadership experts for review and adjustments. Once definitions were agreed upon, we and others familiar with the model, wrote statements describing various leader actions within each of the four dimensions. The panel was then asked to sort the statements into one of the four dimensions. Then the panel evaluated the statements for clarity, duplication, and applicability. Four of five panel members had to be in agreement on placement and clarity of the item for it to be included in the first version of the instrument.

The statements were then subjected to two pilot tests. Between the two tests items were further culled and clarified in iterative stages until reliability was established. From the initial presentation of 189 items describing particular actions, the series of pilot tests produced the SLQ©v1 with a revised pool of 62 items used to assess leader activities. Based on empirical studies by Yasin (2006) and Urdegar (2008) and lengthy discussions and repeated feedback with respondents of SLQ©v1, 19 additional items were developed and submitted to the panel of experts to explore statistical identification of the four dimensions.

The SLQ©v2 is currently three pages long and consists of 81 items cast on a seven point Likert scale. The higher value represents greater use of the leader action as noted below:

1. Never
2. Almost Never
3. Rarely
4. Occasionally
5. Frequently

6.   Almost Always

7.   Always

Psychometric Properties

The STQ© in statistical evaluation has shown acceptable reliability scores and has demonstrated content, face, predictive, and discriminate validity.

Reliability. Following each administration of the SLQ, the items were subject to empirical analyses followed by discussions conducted in an iterative fashion until the statements were representative of the strategic Leadership construct and ongoing analysis and refinements in the instrument continue. Table 11.1 presents the means, standard deviations and Cronbach Alpha's for the SLQ Version1 and Version2.

Internal reliabilities were assessed through the standardized Cronbach's alpha. A .70 value generally considered to indicate a sufficient reliability by classical psychometric authorities (Nunnally, 1978; Peterson, 1994). Reliability statistics for the SLQv1 range between .71 and .77 for the subscales and .89 for the total scale. The SLQv2 yielded Cronbach Alpha scores of Transforming .958, Managerial .950, Political.939, and Ethical .949. The SLQ© appears free of cultural bias.

Factor Structure. The SLQv1 was not subjected to factor analyses due to low case numbers. Revisions were made in the items and they were retested in version 2. The SLQv2 was subjected to a principle axis factoring method with iterative communality estimation and oblimin with Kaiser Normalization rotation. By factoring the 77 questions on the SLQ©v2, four interpretable factors consistent with strategic leadership theory were obtained. The Kaiser-Meyer-Olkin measure of sampling adequacy was .946, and the four factors extracted explained 65.4% of the

Table 11.1.   Means, Standard Deviations and Reliability Coefficients of the Strategic Leadership Questionnaire: Version1, 2007 and Version2, 2008

Dimension	*Version1*					*Version2*				
	M	*SD*	*N*	*Alpha*	*# Items*	*M*	*SD*	*N*	*Alpha*	*# Items*
Transforming	3.79	.711	124	.944	15	5.93	.886	330	.870	17
Managing	3.86	.655	124	.934	15	4.69	1.11	330	.818	17
Political	3.19	.719	124	.689	15	6.08	.861	330	.742	14
Ethical	3.73	.741	124	.950	15	4.00	1.21	330	.928	48

variance. Values less than the .20 threshold were suppressed and not reported on Table 11.2.

The managing and transforming action sets yielded one factor which we are calling Man/Trans. SL theory identifies two independent action sets as an ideal type but in actual use proposes that leader's lead-manage-lead-manage in an iterative fashion. The *Lead/Man* factor indicates that for the population studied with SLQv2—school principals—the responsibilities are not sufficiently disparate to break into two independent factors. A study of upper echelon leaders needs to be undertaken to determine if in fact the factor remains as a combination of transforming and managing. The political action sets yielded two separate factors which we have called *reaching for power* and *bartering*. The ethical action set yielded one factor which we call *relating*. These results are consistent with SL theory and the further delineation of the political action set seen as an improvement.

Studies

Two studies have been completed with SLQ©v1. Yasin (2006) found that a multifaceted use of strategic leadership actions was strongly associated with self reported effectiveness as well as effectiveness reported by followers. Urdegar (2008) and Reyes-Guerra (2009) found components of the transforming, political and ethical dimensions were associated with more cohesive and supportive work cultures. The preliminary analysis indicates that the frequency of use of these action sets can also be used to define leadership styles.

If you would like to take the STQ please send an e-mail to jpisapia@fau.edu

Table 11.2. Factor Structure (Factor Loadings) for the STQv4 (n = 328)

#	Factors				Item
	Msn/ Trans	Reaches for Power	Relates	Barters	Stem: *How often does the person use the* **Actions**
72	.908		−.219		Holds us accountable for results.
71	.854				Evaluates individual performance.
44	.796				Sets time lines for our work.
55	.750				Helps us develop a shared vision.
38	.743				Provides structure for my work unit.
60	.731				Promotes conversation with us about the future and our ability to meet it.
15	.728				Makes professional learning a priority.
65	.712		.254		Works to create a shared vision.
50	.704				Specifies team goals.
68	.698		.235		Promotes our commitment to our organization's long-term goals.
23	.694		.203		Helps us to enhance our professional learning as a group.
17	.688				Specifies individual goals.
70	.688		.255		Aids us in shaping ideas.
51	.677		.234		Helps us to enhance our professional learning as individuals.
7	.636		.238		Helps us to visualize future possibilities.
37		.855			Develops alliances with people from outside of the organization.
73		.834			Maintains alliances with people of power and influence
35		.759			Strengthens his/her position by gaining the allegiance of others inside the organization

Table continues on next page.

Table 11.2. Factor Structure (Factor Loadings) for the STQv4 (n = 328)

#	Factors				Item
	Msn/ Trans	Reaches for Power	Relates	Barters	Stem: *How often does the person use the* <u>*Actions*</u>
56	.716				Develops alliances with people from inside the organization.
41	.693	-.229			Uses influence to advance his/her agenda.
47	.642				Has access to people who have influence over getting things done.
25	.611				Associates him/herself with individuals who have influence.
36	.454				Makes us question our beliefs about how things are working.
3	.382				Allocates resources to influence his/her purposes.
5			.917		Is honest with us.
13			.840		Does the right thing.
43			.820		Can be trusted to do the right thing.
16			.693		Makes decisions by following policy.
67			.602		Respects our privacy.
14			.579		Ensures that procedures are followed.
2			.485		Helps us try to keep promises.
27			.419		Stands firm on decisions based on principle.
45				.779	Gives something in exchange for help.
49				.762	Gives rewards when s/he is helped.
24				.623	Promises rewards to get what s/he wants
77				.622	Compromises to make deals.
11			.216	.468	Willing to barter to make deals.

Extraction Method: Principal Axis Factoring. Rotation Method: Oblimin with Kaiser Normalization. Rotation converged in 17 iterations. Values less than the .20 threshold were suppressed.

REFERENCES

Adams, J. (1988). Building Critical Mass for Change. *OD Practitioner, 20*(2), 7–10.

Adams, J. (2003). Successful change: Paying attention to the intangibles. *OD Practitioner, 35(4)*, 1–7.

Agor, W. (1988). Finding and developing intuitive managers. *Training and Development Journal, 42*(3), 68–70.

Anthony, W., Bennett, R., Maddox, N., & Wheatley, W. (1993). Picturing the future using mental imagery to enrich strategic environmental assessment. *Academy of Management Executive, 7*, 43–56.

Argyris, C., & Schön, D. (1978). *Organizational learning: A theory of action perspective.* Reading, MA: Addison Wesley.

Armstrong. M. (2006). *A handbook of human resource management practice.* London: Kogan Page.

Ashforth, B., & Mael, F. (1989). Social identity theory and the organization. *The Academy of Management Review, 14*(1), 20–39

Badaracco, J. (2002) *Leading quietly.* Boston: Harvard Business School Press.

Bailey, T. A. (1935). The sinking of the Lusitania. *The American Historical Review, 41*(1), 54–73.

Bak, P. (1996). *How nature works.* New York: Copernicus.

Barbuto, J. (2002). How is strategy formed in organizations? A multi-disciplinary taxonomy of strategy-making approaches. *The Journal of Behavioral and Applied Management, 3*(1), 64–72.

Barnard, C. (1938). *The functions of the executive.* Cambridge, MA: Harvard University Press.

Baron, J. (1994). Nonconsequentialist decisions. *Behavior and Brain Sciences, 17*(1), 1–10.

Bass, B. M. (1985). *Leadership and performance beyond expectations.* New York: The Free Press.

Bass, B. M. (1998). *Transformational leadership: Individual, military and educational impact*. Mahwah, NJ: Erlbaum.

Beer, M., & Nohria, N. (Eds.). (2000). *Whole-scale change: Unleashing the magic in organizations*. San Francisco: Berrett-Koehler.

Bennis, W., & Nanus, B. (1985). *Leaders: The strategies for taking charge*. New York: Harper & Row.

Bentham, J. (1988). *The principles of morals and legislation* Amherst, NY: Prometheus Books.

Berrio, A. A. (1999). Organizational culture and organizational learning in public, non-profit institutions: A profile of Ohio State University extension. *Dissertation Abstracts International, 60,* 11A

Best, S. & Kellner, D. (1997). *The post-modern turn*. New York: Guilford.

Black, J. A., & Boal, K. B. (1994). Strategic resources: Traits, configurations and paths to sustainable competitive advantage. *Strategic Management Journal, 15,* 131–148.

Bluedorn, A., Johnson, R., Cartwright, D., & Barringer, B. (1994). The interface and convergence of the strategic management and organization domains. *Journal of Management, 20(2),* 201–262.

Boal, K., & Hooijberg, R. (2001). Strategic Leadership research: Moving on. *The Leadership Quarterly, 11(4),* 515–549.

Bolman L., & Deal T. (2003) *Reframing organizations*. San Francisco: Wiley.

Bonn, I. (2001). Developing strategic thinking as a core competency. *Management Decision, 39(1),* 63–70.

Bonn, I., & Christodoulou, C. (1996). From strategic planning to strategic management. *Long Range Planning, 4(29),* 543–551.

Bourgeois, L. J., & Brodwin, D. (1984). Strategic implementation: Five approaches to an elusive phenomenon. *Strategic Management Journal, 5,* 241–264.

Bramly, S., & Reynolds, S. (1991). *Leonardo: Discovering the life of Leonardo da Vinci*. New York: HarperCollins.

Bress E., & Gruber Mackye, J. (2004). *The butterfly effect* (Motion Picture). United States: Alliance Films.

Buenger, V., Daft, R. L., Conlon, E. J., & Austin, J. (1996). Competing values in organizations: Contextual influences and structural consequences. *Organization Science, 7(5),* 557–576

Burns, J. M. (1978). *Leadership*. New York: Harper & Row.

Burns, R. (2002). *Pathfinder: First in, last out*. New York: Ballantine Books

Burt, R., & Knez, M. (1996). Trust and third-party gossip. In R. M. Kramer & T. R. Tyler (Eds.), *Trust in organizations: Frontiers of theory and research* (pp. 68–89). Thousand Oaks, CA: SAGE.

Byrne, J. (1999). *Chainsaw: The notorious career of Al Dunlap in the era of profit-at-any-price*. London: Harper Business Books.

Byrne, J. (1998, June 8). How Jack Welch runs GE. *Business Week*. Retrieved May 10, 2007, from http://www.businessweek.com/1998/23/b3581001.htm#Main%20Story

Cameron, K., & Quinn, R. (1999). *Diagnosing and changing organizational culture: Based on the competing values framework*. Reading, MA: Addison-Wesley.

Campbell, J. P., Dunnette, M. D., Lawler, E. E., III, & Weick, K. E., Jr. (1970). *Managerial behavior, performance, and effectiveness.* New York: McGraw-Hill

Cannella, A. A., Jr., & Monroe, M. J. (1997). Contrasting perspectives on strategic leaders: Toward a more realistic view of top managers. *Journal of Management, 23*(1), 213–238.

Capra, F. (2002). *The hidden connections.* New York: Doubleday

Casciaro, T. (1998). Seeing things clearly: Social structure, personality and accuracy in social network perception. *Social Networks, 20,* 331–351.

Castells, M. (1996). *The rise of the network society.* New York: Blackwell.

Chatman, J. (1991). Matching people and organisations: Selection and socialization in public accounting firms. *Administrative Science Quarterly, 36,* 459–484.

Chatman, J., & Cha, S. (2003). Leading by leveraging culture. *California Management Review, 45*(4), 20–34.

Chermack, T., & Kasshanna, H. (2007). The use and misuse of SWOT analysis and implications for HRD professionals. *Human Resource Development International. 10*(4), 383–399.

Chilcoat, R. (1995). *Strategic art: The new discipline for the 21st century.* Carlisle, PA: U.S. War College.

Cialdini, R. (2004). What lovers tell us about persuasion. *Harvard Management Update, 9,* 9.

Cialdini, R. B. (1998). *Influence: The psychology of persuasion.* San Francisco: Quill.

Ciulla, J. B. (1995) Leadership ethics: Mapping the territory. *Business Ethics Quarterly, 5,* 5–28.

Clements, K. A. (2004). Woodrow Wilson and World War I. *Presidential Studies Quarterly, 34*(1), 62.

Cohen, W., & Levinthal, D. (1990). Absorptive capacity: A new perspective on learning and innovation. *Administrative Science Quarterly, 35*(1), 128–152.

Cohen, M, Thompson, B, Adelman, L. Bresnick, T., Shastri, L., & Riedel, S. (2000). *Training critical thinking for the battlefield: Basis in cognitive theory and research.* Ft. Leavenworth, KS: U.S. Army Research Institute.

Coleman, J. (1988). Social capital in the creation of human capital. *American Journal of Sociology, 94,* 95–120.

Collins, J. (2001). *Good to great: Why some companies make the leap … and others don't.* New York: Harper Business.

Collins, J., & Porras, J. (1994). *Built to last: Successful habits of visionary companies.* New York: HarperCollins.

Conger, J. A., & Kanungo, R. N. (1987). Toward a behavioral theory of charismatic leadership in organizational settings. *Academy of Management Review, 12,* 637–674.

Conger, J., & Kanungo, R. N. (1988) *Charismatic leadership: The elusive factor in organizational effectiveness.* San Francisco: Jossey-Bass.

Connerly, M., & Rynes, S. (1997). The Influence of recruiter characteristics and organizational recruitment: support on perceived recruiter effectiveness: Views from applicants and recruiters. *Human Relations, 50,* 1563–1583.

Cooperrider, D. L., & Srivastva, S. (1987). Appreciative inquiry in organizational life. In R. Woodman & W. Pasmore (Eds.), *Research in Organizational Change and Development* (pp. 129–169). Greenwich, CT: JAI Press.

Cooperrider, D. L. (1986). Appreciative inquiry: Toward a methodology for understanding and enhancing organizational innovation. Case Western Reserve. Abstract in *Dissertation Abstracts International* 47/05-A (1986): 1805.

Covey, S. (1989). *The seven habits of highly effective people.* New York: Free Press.

Cross, R., Parker, A., & Borgatti, S. P. (2002). Making invisible work visible: Using social network analysis to support strategic collaboration. *California Management Review, 44*(2), 25–46

Crupi J., & Paparone, C. (2008) Key insights for the strategic leader. *Leadership.* Retrieved June 10, 2008, from http://www.dau.mil/pubs/dam/11_12_2005/cru_nd05.pdf

Cunningham, N. E. (1987). *In pursuit of reason: The life of Thomas Jefferson.* Baton Rouge: Louisiana State University Press.

de Bono, E. (1996). *Serious creativity.* London: HarperCollins Business.

De Pree, M. (1989). *Leadership is an art.* New York: Currency Doubleday.

Deal, T., & Peterson, K. (1994). *The leadership paradox: Balancing logic and artistry in schools.* San Francisco: Jossey-Bass.

Denison, D. R., & Spreitzer, G. M. (1991). Organizational culture and organizational development. In R. W. Woodman & W. A. Pasmore (Eds.), *Research in organizational change and development* (pp. 1–21). Greenwich, CT: JAI Press.

Dewey, J. (1933). *How we think.* Chicago: Henry Regnery.

Drucker, P. (1999). Managing oneself. *Harvard Business Review, 77*(2), 72.

Drucker, P. (2002). They are not employees, they are people. *Harvard Business Review, 80*(2), 70–77.

Dweck, C. S. (2006). *Mindset.* New York: Random House.

Eisenhardt, K. (1989). Making fast strategic decisions in high-velocity environments. *Academy of Management Journal, 32*(3), 543–576.

Ellis, J. J. (1995, July/August). Editing the Declaration. *Civilization,* 58–63; Drafting the Documents. Retrieved June 12, 2008, from http://www.loc.gov/exhibits/declara/

Engardio, P. (2007, August 2). The Last Rajah. *Business Week.* Retrieved November 14, 2008, from http://www.businessweek.com/globalbiz/content/aug2007/gb2007082_325502.htm

Fallesen, J. (1995). *Overview of practical thinking skills for battlefield command: Research report 1685.* Alexandria, VA: U.S. Army Research Institute.

Finkelstein, S., & Hambrick, D. (1996) *Strategic leadership: Top executives and their effects on organizations.* St Paul, MN: West Publishing.

Fonda, D. (2003, Dec.). He did so well, let's give him two CEO Jobs: Carlos Ghosn Renault. *Time,* p. 78.

French, J., & Raven, B. (1959). The basis of social power. In D. Cartwright (Ed.), *Studies in Social Power,* (pp. 150–165). Ann Arbor, MI: Institute for Social Research.

Gabarro, J. J. (1978). The development of trust, influence, and expectations. In A. G. Athos, & J. J. Gabarro (Eds.), *Interpersonal behavior: Communication and understanding in relationships* (pp. 290–303). Englewood Cliffs, NJ: Prentice Hall.

Gamble, T., & Gamble, M. (1994). *Public speaking in an age of diversity.* Boston: Allyn Bacon.

Gardner, H. (1995). *Leading minds: An anatomy of leadership*. New York: Harper Collins.

Gardner, J. W. (1989). *On leadership*. New York: Free Press.

Gerstner, L. V. (2002). *Who says elephants can't dance?* New York: HarperCollins.

Ghosn, C. (2001). Nissan CEO. *Time*. Retrieved March 10, 2007, from http://www.time.com/time/2001/influentials/ybghosn.html

Ghosn, C. (2001). Nissan Motors. *BusinessWeek*. Retrieved March 10, 2007, from http://www.businessweek.com/2001/01_02/b3714015.htm

Ghosn, C. (2005). *Shift: Inside Nissan's historic revival*. New York: Doubleday.

Gladwell, M. (2000). *The tipping point. How little things can make a big difference*. Boston: Little, Brown

Gohm S. (2003). Improving organizational learning capability: Lessons from two case studies. *The Learning Organization, 10*(4), 216–227.

Goleman, D. (1998). *Working with emotional intelligence*. New York: Bantam

Goodman, E. A., Zammuto, R. F., & Gifford, B. D. (2001). The competing values framework: Understanding the impact of organizational culture on the quality of work life. *Organization Development Journal, 19*(3), 58–68.

Goodwyn, W. (2002). Southwest Airlines soars above industry's turbulence. *National Public Radio*. Retrieved January 4, 2006, from http://www.npr.org (Colleen Barrett interview).

Greising, D. (2002, October 25). Nissan CEO Carlos Ghosn: Lets team drive turnaround. *Chicago Tribune*, p. 1.

Gretzky, W., & Riley, R. (1990). *Gretzky: An autobiography*. New York: HarperCollins.

Grimmett, P., & MacKinnon, A. (1992). Craft knowledge and the education of teachers. *Review of Research in Education, 18*, 385–456.

Gross, S. E., & Safier, S. (1995). Unleash the power of teams with tailored pay. *Journal of Compensation and Benefits, 11*(1), 27–32.

Grove, A. (1996). *Only the paranoid survive: How to exploit the crisis points that challenge every company*. New York: Doubleday.

Halpren, D. (1996). *Thought & knowledge: An introduction to critical thinking*. Mahwah, NJ: Erlbaum.

Hambrick, D. C. (1989). Guest editors' introduction: Putting top managers back in the strategy picture. *Strategic Management Journal, 10*(1), 515.

Hamel, G., & Prahalad C. (1989). Strategic intent. *Harvard Business School Review, 67*, 63–76

Hamel, G., & Prahalad, C. (1994). *Competing for the future*. Boston: Harvard Business School

Hammer, A., & Lyndon, N. (1987). *Hammer*. New York: G. P. Putnam & Sons.

Handy, C. (1994). *The age of paradox*. London: Penguin.

Harvard Business Review. (2000). Driving change: An interview with Ford Motor Company's Jacques Nasser. In *Harvard Business Review Interviews with CEOs*, (pp. 1–33). Cambridge, MA: Harvard Business Review Paper Back Series.

Heath, C., & Heath, D. (2007). Talking strategy: Three straightforward ways to make your strategy stick. *Change This, 31*(5), 1–25. Retrieved March 3, 2007, from http://www.changethis.com/archives

Heifetz, R. A. (1994). *Leadership without easy answers*. Cambridge, MA: The Belknap Press.

Hersey, J. (1988). *A bell for Adano*. New York: Random House.

Hertzfeld, A. (2004). *Revolution in the valley*. Cambridge, MA: O'Reilly Books.

Herzberg, F. (1987). One more time: How do you motivate employees? *Harvard Business Review, 65*(5), 107–120.

Herzberg, F., Mausner, B., & Snyderman, B. (1959). *The motivation to work*. New York: Wiley.

Hinkin, T. R., & Schriesheim, C. A. (1989). Development and application of new scales to measure the French and Raven (1959) bases of social power. *Journal of Applied Psychology, 74*, 561–567.

Holland, J. H. (1995). *Hidden order*. Reading, MA: Addison-Wesley.

Hollander, E. P., & Offermann, L. R. (1990). Power and leadership in organizations: Relationships in transition. *American Psychologist, 45*, 179–189

Hooijberg, R., Hunt, J. G., & Dodge, G. E. (1997). Leadership complexity and development of the leaderplex model. *Journal of Management, 23*(3), 375–408.

Hooijberg, R., & Petrock, F. (1993). On cultural change: Using the competing values frame-work to help leaders execute a transformational strategy. *Human Resource Management, 32*(1), 29–51.

House, R. J. (1977). A 1976 theory of charismatic leadership. In J. G. Hunt & L. L. Larson (Eds.), *Leadership: The cutting edge* (pp. 189–207), Carbondale, IL: Southern Illinois University Press.

House, R., & Aditya, R. (1997). The social scientific study of leadership: Quo Vadis? *Journal of Management, 23*(3), 409–473.

House, R., & Howell, J. (1992). Personality and charismatic leadership. *Leadership Quarterly, 3*, 81–108.

Hunt, J. (1991). *Leadership: A new synthesis*. Thousand Oaks, CA: SAGE.

Ireland, R., & Hitt, M. (1999). Achieving and maintaining strategic competitiveness in the 21st century: The role of strategic leadership. *Academy of Management Executive, 13*(1), 43–57.

Ireland, R., Hitt, M., & Vaidyanath, D. (2002). Alliance management as a source of competitive advantage. *Journal of Management, 28*(3), 413–446

Isenberg, D. (1984). How senior managers think. *Harvard Business Review, 62*(6), 80–90.

Isenberg, D. (1987). The tactics of strategic opportunism. *Harvard Business Review, 65*(2), 92–97.

Jameson, F. (1991). *Postmodernism, or, the cultural logic of late capitalism*. London: Verso.

Kalliath, T., Bluedorn, A., & Gillespie, D. (1999). A confirmatory factor analysis of the competing values instrument. *Educational and Psychological Measurement, 59*(1), 143–158.

Kaplan, R., & Norton, D. (1992, January-February). The balanced scorecard—Measures that drive performance. *Harvard Business Review*, 71–79.

Karnani, A. (2006). *Essence of strategy: Controversial choices* (Working Paper Series, 1032). Ross School of Business: University of Michigan.

Katz, E. (1987). Communications research since Lazarsfeld. *Public Opinion Quarterly, 51*(50th Anniversary Issue), S25–S45.

Katz, E., & Lazarsfeld, P. (1955), *Personal influence; the part played by people in the flow of mass communications*, Glencoe, IL: Free Press.

Kauffman, S. (1995). *At Home in the universe: The search for the laws of self-organization and complexity.* New York: Oxford University Press.

Kelley, R. (1992). *The power of followership.* New York: Doubleday.

Kendall, A. (1990). *The creative leader: Concepts for Air Force leadership.* Maxwell AL: Air University.

Kets de Vries, M. (2001). *The leadership mystique: A user's manual for the human enterprise.* New York: Prentice Hall.

Kotter, J. (1978). *Organizational dynamics.* Reading, MA: Addison-Wesley.

Kotter, J. (1988). *The leadership factor.* New York: The Free Press.

Kotter, J. (1996). *Leading change.* Boston: Harvard Business School Press.

Kotter, J. (1998). Leading change: Why transformation efforts fail. In *Harvard Business Review on Change* (pp. 1–20). Boston: Harvard Business Paper Backs.

Kotter, J. (1999). *On what leaders really do.* Boston: Harvard Business School Press.

Kotter, J., & Cohen, D. (2002). *The heart of change: Real life stories of how people change their organizations.* Boston: Harvard Business Books.

Kouzes, J., & Posner, B. (2003). *The Leadership Challenge* (3rd ed.). San Francisco: Jossey-Bass.

Krackhardt, D. (1987). Cognitive social structures. *Social Networks, 9,* 109–134.

Krackhardt, D. (1990). Assessing the political landscape: Structure, cognition, and power in organizations. *Administrative Science Quarterly, 35,* 342–369.

Krackhardt, D., & Hanson, J. (1993). Informal networks: The company behind the chart. *Harvard Business Review, 71,* 104–111.

Kramer, R., & Tyler T. (Eds.). (1996). *Trust in organizations: Frontiers of theory and research.* Thousand Oaks, CA: SAGE.

Lala, R. M. (2006). *The creation of wealth: The Tatas from the 19th to the 21st century.* New Delhi: The Eastern Book Corp.

Larkin, L., & Larkin, S. (1996, May–June)). Reaching and changing frontline employees. *Harvard Business Review, 74,* 95–104.

Lawler, E. E., III. (1990). *Strategic pay: Aligning organizational strategies and pay systems.* San Francisco: Jossey-Bass.

Leithwood, K., & Steinbach, R. (1992). Improving the problem-solving expertise of school administrators. *Education and Urban Society, 24*(3), 317–345.

Lewicki, R., & Bunker, B. (1996). Developing and maintaining trust in work relationships. In R. M. Kramer & T. R. Tyler (Eds.), *Trust in organizations: Frontiers of theory and research* (pp. 114–139). Thousand Oaks, CA: SAGE.

Lindblom, C. (1959). The science of muddling through. *Public Administration Review, 19,* 79–88.

Lindblom, C. (1979). Still muddling, not yet through. *Public Administration Review, 39,* 517–526.

Locke, E. (1968). Toward a theory of task motivation and incentives. *Organizational Behavior and Human Performance, 3,* 157–189.

Locke, E. (1991). Goal theory vs. control theory: Contrasting approaches to understanding work motivation. *Motivation and Emotion, 15*(1), 9–28.

Locke, E., & Latham, G. P. (1990). *A theory of goal setting and task performance.* Englewood Cliffs, NJ: Prentice-Hall.

Lombardi, V., & Heinz, W. C. (1963). *Run to daylight.* Englewood Cliffs, NJ: Prentice-Hall.

Lorenz, E. (1963). Deterministic nonperiodic flow. *Journal of Atmospheric Sciences, 20*, 130–141.

Lyotard, J. (1984). *The postmodern condition.* Minneapolis: University of Minnesota Press.

Magee, D. (2003). *Turnaround: How Carlos Ghosn rescued Nissan.* New York: Harper-Collins.

Magee, R., & Somervell, B. (1998). *Strategic leadership primer.* Carlisle Barracks, PA: U.S. Army War College.

Malan, L., & Kriger, M. (1998). Making sense of managerial wisdom. *Journal of Management Inquiry, 7*(3), 242–251.

March, J., & Simon, H. (1958). *Organizations.* New York: Wiley.

Maslow, A. (1954). *Motivation and personality.* New York: Harper & Row.

McClelland, D. (1975). *Power: The inner experience.* New York: Irvington.

McClelland, D., & Burnham, D. (1976). Power is the great motivator. *Harvard Business Review, 54*(2), 100–110.

McClelland, D. (1955). *Studies in motivation.* New York: Appleton.

Metcalf, H., & Urwick, L. (Eds.). (1941). *Dynamic administration: The collected papers of Mary Parker Follett.* New York: Harper & Brothers.

Mezirow, J., & Associates. (1990) *Fostering critical reflection in adulthood.* San Francisco: Jossey-Bass.

Mintzberg, H. (1994a). *The rise and fall of strategic planning: Reconceiving roles for planning, plans, and planners.* New York: The Free Press.

Mintzberg, H. (1994b, January-February). The fall and rise of strategic planning. *Harvard Business Review,* 107–114.

Mintzberg, H. (1995). Strategic thinking as "seeing." In B. Garratt (Ed.), *Developing strategic thought: Rediscovering the art of direction-giving* (pp. 79–83). London: HarperCollins.

Morgan, G. (1986). *Images of organization.* Beverly Hills, CA: SAGE.

Newell, A., & Rosenbloom, P. (1981). Mechanisms of skill acquisition and the law of practice. In J. R. Anderson (Ed.), *Cognitive skills and their acquisition* (pp. 1–55). Hillsdale, NJ: Erlbaum.

Nunnally, J. C. (1978). *Psychometric theory* (2nd ed.). New York: McGraw-Hill.

Nutt, P., & Backoff, R. (1993). Transforming public sector organizations with strategic management and strategic leadership. *Journal of Management, 19*(2), 299–347.

Nutt, P., & Backoff, R. (1995). Strategy for public and third sector organizations. *Journal of Public Administration Research and Theory, 5*(2), 189–211.

Pang, S., & Pisapia, J. (2007). *The strategic thinking capabilities of school leaders in Hong Kong.* Presented at the Annual Conference of the American Education Research Association, Chicago.

Pisapia, J., Pang, N. S. K., Hee, T., Ying, L., & Morris, J. D. (2009). A comparison of the use of strategic thinking skills of aspiring school leaders in Hong Kong, Malaysia, Shanghai, and the United States: An exploratory study. *International Journal of Educational Studies, 2*(2), 48–58.

Perkins, D. N. (1995). *Outsmarting IQ: The emerging science of learnable intelligence.* New York: Free Press.

Peters, T. J., & Waterman, R. H. (1982). *In search of excellence*. New York: Harper-Collins.

Peterson, R. A. (1994). Cronbach's Alpha Coefficient: A meta-analysis. *Journal of Consumer Research, 21,* 381–391.

Pfeffer, J. (1981). *Power in organizations*, Marshfield, MA: Pittman.

Pfeffer, J. (1992). *Managing with power: Politics and influence in organizations*. Boston: Harvard Business School Press;

Pinzur, M. (2004, May 18). New schools chief is inspiring, tough. *The Miami Herald,* Section 1B.

Pisapia, J. (2006a). Mastering change in a globalized world. In P. Singh, J. Bhatnagar, & A. Bhandarker (Eds.), *Future of work: Mastering change* (pp. 303–327). New Delhi: Excel Books.

Pisapia, J. (2006b). *New direction for leadership* (Education Policy Studies Series No. 61). Hong Kong: The Faculty of Education and the Hong Kong Institute of Educational Research. (Monograph)

Pisapia, J. (2006c, November). *Strategic thinking capabilities and leader success.* Presented at the Biannual Meeting of the National HRD Network. New Delhi, India.

Pisapia, J., & Reyes-Guerra, D. (2007, November). *Leadership assessment tools: The strategic thinking questionnaire.* Presented at the Annual Conference of the International Leadership Association, Vancouver, CD.

Pisapia, J., & Reyes-Guerra, D. (2008). *The Strategic Leadership Questionnaire.* Boca Raton: Florida Atlantic University.

Pisapia, J., Reyes-Guerra, D., & Coukos, E. (2005). Developing the leader's strategic mindset: Establishing the measures. *The Leadership Review, 5(1),* 41–68.

Pisapia, J., Reyes-Guerra, D., & Yasin, M. (2006, July). *Strategic thinking and leader success.* Paper presented at the Annual Meeting of the International Conference on Advances in Management, Lisbon Portugal.

Pisapia, J., Coukos-Semmel, E., & Reyes-Guerra, D. (2004). Assessing the cognitive processes of leaders: Do effective leaders think differently than less effective leaders? In A. Lazaridou (Ed.), *Contemporary Issues on Educational Administartion and Policy* (pp 147–170). Athens, Greece: Athens Institute for Education and Research.

Pisapia, J., Reyes-Guerra, D., & Coukos-Semmel, E. (2005). Developing a Strategic Mindset: Constructing the Measures. *Leadership Review, 5,* 41–68. http://www.leadershipreview.org/2005spring/article2_spring_2005.asp

Pisapia, J., Pang, N. S. K., Hee, T., Ying, L., & Morris, J. D. (2009). A comparison of the use of strategic thinking skills of aspiring school leaders in Hong Kong, Malaysia, Shanghai, and the United States: An exploratory study. *International Journal of Educational Studies, 2(2),* 48–58.

Podsakoff, P. M., Niehoff, B. P., Moorman, R. H., & Fetter, R. (1990) Transformational leader behaviors and their effects on followers' trust in leader, satisfaction, and organizational citizen behaviors. *Leadership Quarterly, 1,* 107–142.

Porter, M. (1996, Nov/Dec). What is strategy? *Harvard Business Review,* 62–79.

Porter, M. E. (1979). How competitive forces shape strategy. *Harvard Business Review, 57(2),* 135–145.

Powaski, R. (1991). *Toward an entangling alliance: American isolationism, and Europe.* Westport, CT: Greenwood Press.

Priem, R., Lyon, D., & Dess, G. (1999). Inherent limitations of demographic proxies in top management team heterogeneity research. *Journal of Management, 25*(6), 935–953.

Quinn, R. E. (1988). *Beyond rational management: Mastering the paradoxes and competing demands of high performance.* San Francisco, CA: Jossey-Bass.

Quinn, R., & McGrath, M. (1985). The transformation of organizational cultures: A competing values perspective. In P. J. Frost, L. F. Moore, M. R. Louis, C. C. Lundberg, & J. Martin (Eds.), *Organizational culture.* Beverly Hills, CA: SAGE.

Quinn, R., & Spreitzer. G. (1991). The psychometrics of the competing values culture instrument and an analysis of the impact of organizational culture on quality of life. *Organizational Change and Development, 5,* 115–142.

Quinn, R., & Kimberly, J. (1984). Paradox, planning and perseverance: Guidelines for managerial practice. In J. R. Kimberly & R. E. Quinn (Eds.), *Managing organizational transitions.* Homewood, IL: Dow Jones-Irwin.

Quinn, R., & Rohrbaugh, J. (1981). A competing values approach to organizational effectiveness. *Public Productivity Review, 5,* 122–140.

Quinn, R., & Rohrbaugh, J. (1983). A spatial model of effectiveness criteria: Towards a competing values approach to organizational analysis. *Management Science, 29,* 363–377.

Raven, B. H. (1992). A power-interaction model of interpersonal influence: French and Raven thirty years later. *Journal of Social Behavior and Personality, 7,* 217–244

Raven, B. H., Freeman, H.E., & Haley, R.W. (1982), Social science perspectives in hospital infection control. In A. W., Johnson, O., Grusky, B. H. Raven (Eds.), *Contemporary health services: Social science perspectives* (pp. 139–176). Boston: Auburn House.

Reyes-Guerra, D. (2009). *The relationship of leadership actions and business and social justice cultures.* (Doctoral dissertation, Florida Atlantic University, Boca Raton, FL).

Riedel, S., Morath, R., & McGonigle, T. (2000). *ARI Workshop Proceedings.* Ft. Leavenworth, KS. US Army Research Institute

Ritz-Carlton employee promise. (2007). Retrieved March 7, 2007, from http://corporate.ritzcarlton.com/About/GoldStandards.htm

Rogers, E. M. (2003). *Diffusion of innovations* (5th ed.). New York: Free Press

Roosevelt, E. (1961). *The autobiography of Eleanor Roosevelt.* New York: Harper & Brothers.

Sashkin, M., & Rosenbach, W. (2001) *Contemporary issues in leadership: A new vision in leadership.* Boulder, CO: Westview Press.

Schein, E. (1985). *Organizational culture and leadership: A dynamic view.* San Francisco: Jossey-Bass.

Schein, E. (1991). What is culture? In P. J. Frost, L. F. Moore, M. R. Louis, C. C. Lundberg, & J. Martin (Eds.), *Reframing Organizational Culture* (pp. 243–253). Newbury Park, CA: SAGE.

Schein E. (1992). *Organizational culture and leadership.* San Francisco: Jossey-Bass.

Schön, D. A. (1983). *The reflective practitioner: How professionals think in action.* New York: Basic Books.

Selznick, P. (1984). *Leadership in administration: A sociological interpretation.* Berkeley: University of California Press. (original work published 1957)

Sendelbach, N. B. (1993). The competing values framework for management training and development: A tool for understanding complex issues and tasks. *Human Resource Management, 32*(1), 75–99.

Senge, P. (1990). *The fifth discipline.* New York: Doubleday.

Shamir, B. (1991). Meaning, self and motivation in organizations. *Organizational Studies, 12,* 405–424.

Shinbrot, T. (1995). Perspectives on the control of chaos, *Advances of Physics, 44,* 73–111.

Simon, H. A. (1947). *Administrative behavior* (1st ed.). New York: Harper & Row.

Simon, H. A. (1955). A behavioral model of rational choice, *Quarterly Journal of Economics, 59,* 99–118.

Southwest Airlines Mission Statement. (2006). Retrieved January 7, 2006, from http://www.southwest.com

Spreitzer, G. (1995). Psychological empowerment in the workplace: dimensions, measurement and validation. *Academy of Management Journal, 38,* 1442–1456.

Stacey, R., & Parker, D. (1994). *Chaos, management and economics: The implications of non-linear thinking.* IEA. Hobart Paper.

Stacey, R. (1996). *Strategic management and organizational dynamics* (2nd ed.). London: Pitman.

Stacey, R., & Parker, D. (1994). *Chaos, management and economics: The implications of non-linear thinking.* Paris: IEA.

Stanwick, P. (1996). Mental imagery: An alternative to top management team replacement for declining organizations. *Journal of Organizational Change Management, 9*(2), 47–65.

Sternberg, R. (2005). The WCIS model of giftedness. In R. Sternberg & J. Davidson (Eds.), *Conceptions of giftedness* (pp. 327–342). London: Cambridge University Press.

Taylor, T. (1997). How to pay and reward multidiscipline work teams. *Journal of Compensation and Benefits, 12*(6), 30–33.

Taylor, A. (2003, July 21). Nissan shifts into higher gear: Carlos Ghosn has revved up profits at the Japanese automaker. Now he wants to go faster. *Fortune,* 98.

Tedlow, R. (2006). *Andy Grove: The life and times of an American.* London: Penguin Books.

Thompson, L. (Ed.), (2003). *The social psychology of organizational behavior: Key readings.* Philadelphia: Psychology Press.

Thompson, L. (2005). *The mind and heart of the negotiator.* (3rd ed.). Upper Saddle River, NJ: Pearson Prentice Hall.

Thompson, L., & Hrebec, D. (1996). Lose-lose Agreements in Interdependent Decision Making. *Psychological Bulletin, 120*(3), 396–409.

Tichy, N. M., & Devanna, M. A. (1990). *The Transformational Leader* (2nd ed.). New York: John Wiley.

Tumulty, K. (2008, June 16). How Obama did it. *Time,* 4–5.

Urdegar, S. (2008). *Beyond fidelity: Relating educational practices and their determinants to student learning gains.* Doctoral dissertation, Florida Atlantic University, Boca Raton, FL.

Usher, R., & Bryant, I. (1989) *Adult education as theory, practice and research.* London: Routledge.

van Riel, C. B. M., Berens, G., & Dijkstra, M., (2007). *Stimulating strategically aligned behavior among employees.* ERIM Report Series Research in Management. Rotterdam, The Netherlands.

Vickers, M. (2007). The essentials of high performance organizations. *The Leader's Edge, 2*(8). Retrieved September 30, 2008, from http://www.amanet.org/LeadersEdge/editorial.cfm?Ed=575

Vroom, V. H. (1964). *Work and motivation.* New York: Wiley.

Weber, M. (2002). *The protestant ethic and the spirit of capitalism* (Peter Baehr and Gordon Wells, Trans.). New York: Penguin Books.

Weick, K. (1995). *Sensemaking in organizations.* Thousand Oaks, CA: SAGE.

Weinberger, T. E. (1998). A method for determining the equitable allocation of team-based Pay: Rewarding members of a cross-functional account team. *Compensation & Benefits Management, 14*(4), 18–26.

Weir, P. (Director). (1989). *Dead poets society.* Burbank, CA: Touchtone Pictures.

Welch, J. (2001). *Jack: Straight from the gut.* New York: Time Warner

Yasin, M. (2006). *The use of strategic leadership actions by Deans in Malaysian and American public universities.* Doctoral dissertation, Florida Atlantic University, Boca Raton, FL.

Yukl, G. A. (1998). *Leadership in organizations* (3rd ed.). Englewood Cliffs, NJ: Prentice-Hall.

Zaccaro, S., Gilbert, J., Thor, K., & Mumford, M. (1991). Leadership and social intelligence: Linking social perceptiveness and behavioral flexibility to leader effectiveness. *Leadership Quarterly, 2*(4), 317–347.

Zaccaro, S. (1996). *Models and theories of leadership.* Alexandria, VA: U.S. Army Research Institute for the Behavioral and Social Sciences.

Zaleznik, A. (1977). Managers and leaders: Are they different? *Harvard Business Review, 55*(3), 67–78.

Zsiga, P. (2008). Leader effectiveness from self-directed learning and strategic thinking. *International Journal of Human Resources Development and Management, 8*(4), 306–317.

ABOUT THE AUTHOR

 John Pisapia is a Professor of Leadership and Policy at Florida Atlantic University in Boca Raton, Florida. Prior to this post, he held tenured faculty positions at West Virginia University and Virginia Commonwealth University. Dr. Pisapia brings 23 years of management experience, and over 150 publications to his consultancies and his academic podium.

His research interests are leading organizations and people in a global perspective. He has been called the "global professor," having consulted with leaders in education and business, and taught in Argentina, Chile, Macau and Hong Kong China, Malaysia, South Africa, and Europe as well as in the United States. His book, *The Strategic Leader*, promises a new direction for leading in a globalizing society.

His work with strategic thinking has received national and international attention through papers presented to the American Association of Educational Research, the International Conference in Advances in Management, the International Leadership Association, the National Human Resources Network of India, and the International Leadership Academy of James MacGregor Burns, The University of Malaya, and the Chinese University at Hong Kong. His Strategic Thinking Questionnaire (STQ) measures the leader's use of systems thinking, reframing and reflection. His Strategic Leadership Questionnaire (SLQ) measures the leader's use of four sets of action in leading their organizations: managerial, transformational, political and ethical.

He has received many significant honors. John has been recognized as the first National Professor of the Year by the American Association of School Administrator's (AASA), honored as a Fulbright Scholar, and as recipient of the International Schools Association's Distinguished Service Award, and named Glenville State College's Alumnus of the Year. Cited for Outstanding Leadership in Education by Phi Delta Kappa, Significant Leadership in Public and Higher Education by West Virginia University, NCATE Recognition for exemplary work in founding the Metropolitan Educational Research Consortium (MERC), He received his doctorate from West Virginia University, United States.

Made in the USA
Lexington, KY
28 June 2015